ALMA MATER

ALMA MATER

Unusual stories
and little-known
facts from
America's
college
campuses

Don Betterton

Peterson's Guides
Princeton, New Jersey

To Finn, for all her help,
and to the children.

Library of Congress Cataloging-in-Publication Data

Betterton, Don M., 1938–
    Alma mater : unusual stories and little-known
facts from America's college campuses / Don
Betterton.
        p.   cm.
    Includes index.
    ISBN 0-87866-579-X
    1. Universities and colleges—United States—
Anecdotes. I. Title.
LA227.3.B49 1988
378.73—dc19   88-25263

Design by Virginia Jamalalldeen and C. J. Koop
Illustration by Doug Reinke
Cover photographs by (front, top to bottom) Focus on
Sports, Inc., Gerhard E. Gscheidle, and UPI/Bettmann
Newsphotos (2); (rear, top to bottom) UPI/Bettmann
Newsphotos and the Bettmann Archive, Inc.

Printed in the United States of America

10 9 8 7 6 5 4 3 2 1

CONTENTS

INTRODUCTION

In the fall of 1986, Casey Hegener, the editor in chief at Peterson's Guides, asked me if I would be interested in writing a book about college trivia. Nearly two years later, after filling half a room with college viewbooks, histories, and catalogs, making countless phone calls to college public information offices, and taking numerous trips to the Princeton library, *Alma Mater: Unusual Stories and Little-known Facts from America's College Campuses* was ready to go to press.

As you will see in the chapters that follow, *Alma Mater* turned out to be much more than a collection of college trivia. It is, as indicated by some of the possible titles we sorted through (*College Trivia, Fact, and Folklore; The College Almanac;* and *Colleges from A to Y*), a book with a multiple personality. For fans of esoterica, there is ample trivia, for example, the college with the shortest name or the southernmost location. Parts of the book resemble a collegiate version of the *Guinness Book of World Records* with categories such as the oldest, largest, first, and most unusual found on the nation's college campuses. For

readers who are interested in lists, there are dozens of rankings from NCAA sports champions to colleges with the biggest endowments. But *Alma Mater* is more than a collection of trivia, records, and lists. At its heart lie four centuries of wonderful stories about the rich history and exciting modern-day life of American colleges—from Harvard's founding in 1636 as the "College at Cambridg" to the 1987 breakthrough in superconductivity by researchers at the University of Houston.

Giving proper credit for a college's claims to distinctiveness turned out to be more complicated than it seemed at first glance. Take, for example, the question of which college had the first student newspaper. Although the *Dartmouth Gazette* first appeared in 1799, it was more of a town paper than a student publication. Miami of Ohio had two early claims as the first college to put out a student newspaper—the *Literary Focus* (1826) and the *Miami Student* (1867). The former was mainly a faculty literary journal with almost no student involvement, while the latter soon was limited to a monthly printing schedule.

Although the *Yale News* didn't come out until 1878, its continuous daily publication by students supports Yale's assertion that it is home to the oldest college newspaper.

After cross-checking with other colleges, I usually accepted an institution's claim that its building is the oldest, its professor the youngest, or its foreign study program the first. For example, I don't know for sure that Indiana's student center is the largest but they make a compelling case, and I did not run across a college that made a similar assertion. In trying to make sure that this record-book aspect of *Alma Mater* is accurate, I would welcome correspondence from readers who can provide supporting or contrary evidence to the claims made by the colleges themselves.

Alma Mater is an ambitious undertaking. It is intended to serve as a compilation of varied college achievements as well as an anthology of traditions and anecdotes. Yet I am well aware that I've only scratched the surface of a rich vein of college fact and folklore. I hope that the information in *Alma Mater* will spark the imagination and interest of readers to contribute a college tale or two of their own to what I have offered here. Certainly there is much more to add, and I would be pleased to hear from you. In encouraging readers to get involved with the book, I also realize that mistakes

may have occurred. Although every effort has been taken to make *Alma Mater* as accurate as possible, inevitably errors make their way into a manuscript. Here, too, readers should write me in care of Peterson's with their comments.

It would not have been possible to write *Alma Mater* without the assistance of the hundreds of college public information officers who provided catalogs, histories, press clippings, admissions brochures, and numerous descriptions of special events and notable achievements. In addition to the typical material, I received unusual items like a T-shirt, Christmas card, cassette tape, scratch 'n' sniff poem, and a book on etiquette—just about anything a public information officer thought told a story about his or her college. Often the involvement of the public information officer went beyond a one-time response when I made a follow-up phone call that necessitated further research. On some campuses it was not uncommon for three or four individuals to be involved in gathering material for *Alma Mater*. And nearly all of the numerous photographs in this book were provided by the colleges themselves and are reproduced with their permission.

Beyond the help provided by colleges, many other organizations sent material. To name a few: the National

Interfraternity Conference, the
Miss America Foundation, the
Council for the Advancement
and Support of Education, the
National Observatory, the
Association of Marshall Scholars,
the American Association of
State Colleges and Universities,
the Nobel Foundation, the
Association of Research
Libraries, and the National
Collegiate Athletic Association.
Finally, the section on college
nicknames was helped
immensely by the information in
Ray Franks's book, *What's in a
Nickname?*

Alma Mater is intended to
present a lively tour of America's
college campuses, both past and
present. Along the way the tour
makes stops at classrooms,
libraries, research labs, activity
centers, and playing fields
before making a final visit to the
alumni office for a look at the
contributions of well-known
graduates. I invite you along on
the campus tour. Enjoy your
journey.

A CAMPUS TOUR

COLLEGE PRESIDENTS, HONORARY DEGREES, COLORS, CAMPUS STORIES, DISASTERS, FAMOUS EVENTS, TRIVIA

The chapters that follow are filled with facts and stories about American colleges. Before turning to more defined aspects of the college scene like student life, faculty, and athletics, here's a tour of the nation's campuses that gives compelling evidence of the variety and vitality of American higher education, past and present.

College Presidents

TERM OF OFFICE

The college president who served the longest time was Eliphalet Nott of Union College. President Nott was Union's first president when the college was founded in 1804 and he stayed on for sixty-two years until his retirement in 1866.

Until his retirement during the summer of 1987 the president of a four-year college

Union's Nott.

with the longest term in office was Reverend Theodore Hesburgh, who headed Notre Dame for thirty-five years. Owing to a combination of

Father Hesburgh's length of tenure and the large increase in enrollment while he was president, about 80 percent of Notre Dame's 80,000 alumni have Hesburgh's signature on their diplomas. With Hesburgh's departure, the current record holder is W. Burkette Raper of Mount Olive College in Mount Olive, North Carolina, who assumed the presidency in 1954.

The shortest tenure as the head of a university system was that of Jack Freeman of the University of Maine, who resigned after less than two weeks on the job because of a public outcry over his $114,000 salary.

YOUNGEST

The youngest college president was Leon Botstein, who became the head of Franconia College in New Hampshire in 1970, when he was 23 years old. Five years later he was chosen to lead Bard. Botstein is now 41, with eighteen years of experience as a college president.

Notre Dame's Hesburgh.

Chicago's Gray.

WOMEN PRESIDENTS

The first woman president of a college was Julia Sears of Mankato State in 1872.

Hanna Gray became the first female president of a major university when she was selected to head the University of Chicago in 1978.

The youngest woman president was Ellen Futter, who

took over at Barnard in May 1981, at age 31. She was five months pregnant when she was appointed and gave birth to a baby girl on her thirty-second birthday, September 21, the same day the fall semester opened.

PRESIDENTIAL DROPOUT

President Jack Coleman of Haverford took a year's leave of absence in 1973 to see what life was like as a blue-collar worker. President Coleman worked on a dairy farm, spent time as a garbage collector, and was a cook in a seafood restaurant. He later wrote about his experiences in a book titled *Blue Collar Journal*.

GOOD SPORT

The presidential sense of humor award goes to the chancellor of the University of California at Santa Cruz, Bob Sinsheimer. For a number of years the Santa Cruz students unsuccessfully petitioned Sinsheimer to allow them to adopt the mascot of their choice—the banana slug, a bright yellow gastropod that is a familiar sight on the Santa Cruz campus following a rainfall.

Finally, in May 1986, the chancellor affirmed a 1,441 to 296 vote in favor of the banana slug with the words, "Although I would prefer a mascot with more spirit and vigor, the students are entitled to a mascot with which they can empathize. Therefore I

The banana slug became the official mascot of Santa Cruz in a runaway election.

hereby designate the banana slug as the official UCSC mascot, until such time as the students might wish to hold another election."

As it turned out, Chancellor Sinsheimer was far from a sore loser. With his decision made, he too caught the banana slug fever that swept the campus. His official Christmas card for 1986 depicted a slug with the words, "Chancellor Bob and Karen Sinsheimer wish you the very best of holiday seasons in 1986 (the Year of the Slug) and a peaceful, prosperous New Year to come."

HIGHEST PAID

Among presidents and chancellors who head public university systems (more than one campus) the highest paid is David Gardner of the University of California, which has nine campuses and 144,000 students: President Gardner's 1986–87 salary was $189,100. This figure does not include payments of approximately $43,000 per year for housing expenses or money paid by foundations to cover travel and entertainment expenses.

Along with Gardner, highly compensated chief executive officers of higher education systems are:

David Gardner	California	$189,100
Hans Mark	Texas	154,500
Thomas Bartlett	Alabama	125,000
John Ryan*	Indiana	125,000
Kenneth Keller*	Minnesota	125,000
Edward Jennings	Ohio State	119,260

*Left his position during the 1987–88 year

For presidents and chancellors of a single public campus, the highest paid are:

Frank Vandiver	Texas A&M	$141,250
William Cunningham	Texas	130,000
William Gerberding	Washington	128,200
William Lavery	Virginia Tech	121,000
Ira Heyman	U Cal Berkeley	120,000
Charles Young	UCLA	120,000

Although Frank Vandiver is the highest-paid president of a single-campus public university, he receives less than his football coach, Jackie Sherrill, who signed a $1.6-million six-year contract in 1982. It is unlikely that Jackie Sherrill has his eye on President Vandiver's job, but if he does, it wouldn't be the first time such a move took place. Walter Riggs, the founder of Clemson football and the Tigers' coach from 1910 to 1924, became Clemson's president after he retired from the sidelines.

continued

In only one state does the governor earn more than the president of the main public university. In 1986 New York Governor Mario Cuomo earned $100,000, compared to Vincent Leary's $95,700 at Albany State.

College presidents normally receive generous benefits in addition to their salaries. The usual perquisites are a home, a car, and an expense account. But for college presidents who have business connections, a seat on a corporate board is the most lucrative fringe benefit of all. The typical pay of a board member runs from $10,000 to $15,000, although some corporations pay as much as $30,000. Many college presidents sit on more than one board. For example, while president of Michigan, Harold Shapiro was a trustee of Unisys Corporation, the Kellogg Company, and the Dow Chemical Company, and he held a seat on a number of nonprofit boards.

The salaries of presidents of private colleges are confidential and are rarely divulged. However, based on the information that is available, John Silber of Boston University is believed to be the highest paid with a salary of $288,000. Trailing President Silber, with yearly incomes of about $250,000, are James Zumberge of USC, Edward Foote of Miami (Florida), and Hanna Gray of Chicago.

HOW TO GET A HEAD

While the salaries of many public college presidents are set by law, it is not uncommon for a newly appointed president to negotiate for extra benefits. An early example of a hard bargainer was James Burrill Angell, who was asked to head the University of Michigan when it moved to Ann Arbor in 1839. Before he would take the job he insisted that indoor plumbing be installed in his house. Angell's request was approved, and the President's House, which stands today as a historic landmark, was the first house in Ann Arbor to have a flush toilet.

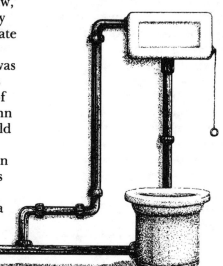

PRESIDENTIAL LEADERSHIP

In 1856 there were troubled relations between the University of South Carolina students and the town marshals of Columbia. There had already been one fight between the students and the police; then there was another outbreak. A major battle seemed imminent as 100 students faced a dozen police officers, both groups armed with guns and clubs. Actual firing was avoided when someone had the presence of mind to summon college president James Thornwell. Thornwell assured the students he would investigate the situation, and if they were right and no peaceful solution were possible, he personally would lead them in a fight against the police. Thornwell then marched toward the campus shouting, "College!" and the group of students followed. A week later the faculty found a number of students guilty of endangering the peace, and they were expelled. Since other students had pledged to share the fate of their classmates, South Carolina closed temporarily because of the withdrawals. Two weeks later the college reopened and the students were readmitted.

IS A PRESIDENT REALLY NECESSARY?

The University of Virginia did not have a president from its founding in 1819 until 1904. For nearly a century the chairman of the faculty also served as Virginia's chief administrative officer.

DON'T LOOK A GIFT HORSE IN THE MOUTH

In 1865, after the Civil War had ended, University of North Carolina President David Swain angered many of the state's inhabitants when he accepted a horse as a gift from Union General William Tecumseh Sherman. The spirited horse gave Swain problems from the start, escaping on three separate occasions. In the summer of 1868, while Swain was on a ride in the country, the horse ran wild, overturned the carriage, and fatally injured Swain. Many North Carolinians believed that justice had been served. Incidentally, General Sherman began his career in the South as president of a military college that later became Louisiana State University.

PAJAMA PARTY

In the year before the American Revolution, student patriotism at Columbia was running high. The leading spokesman was Alexander Hamilton, who had entered Columbia in 1773. The opposition was represented by Columbia's president, Myles Cooper, a noted Tory. The antagonism between the two factions continued to build until, on a May night in 1775, a mob advanced on Cooper's house shouting, "Hang him, hang him!" Hamilton, wanting no part of a lynching, distracted the crowd long enough for Cooper to escape out his back door. Cooper fled wearing only pajamas, leaving his cloak and wig behind. After spending the night in hiding near the Hudson River, he made his way to the waterfront, boarded a British frigate, and sailed safely to London.

LONGEST-WINDED PRESIDENT

Easily surpassing the 958-word sentence of Marcel Proust in his novel *Cities of the Plain,* Columbia President Nicholas Murray Butler included a 4,284-word sentence in the "Report of the President of Columbia University for 1942–43." The sentence contained all the important events of the year, beginning with the Conference on Wartime Problems and ending with a mention of the twenty-seven Columbia employees who were retiring.

CARRY A BIG STICK

Harvard's first president (then called headmaster), Nathaniel Eaton, was removed from office in 1639, after one year of service, for beating unruly students. He might have been able to survive the corporal punishment charge, but unfortunately he was also responsible for serving rotten, worm-infested food in the dining hall.

BAD LUCK

For the first thirty-seven years of its existence, Toledo didn't have a president. Based on the bad luck it had when it finally hired one, perhaps Toledo should have waited even longer. The average term of Toledo's first eight presidents was 4½ years. Jerome Raymond, Toledo's first president, resigned after eleven months. The second president, a 28-year-old faculty member, quit after 3½ years. The next president lasted for eleven years before being fired. Presidents four, five, and six didn't fare as well. One died after fourteen months, the second after nine days, and the third after four years. The next died after fourteen years, and the last of Toledo's first eight presidents passed away after two years. In the twenty-five-year period from 1925 to 1950, five consecutive Toledo presidents died in office.

Honorary Degrees

The practice of awarding honorary degrees dates back to 1692 when Harvard bestowed a doctorate on Increase Mather. By giving him this more distinguished title, Harvard tried to ensure that Mather would be more successful than a mere professor would when he was sent to England to raise money for the college.

Only a handful of honorary degrees were given before 1776, two of them master's degrees received by Ben Franklin. After the War of Independence, the honorary degree business picked up, and by 1800 hundreds had been awarded.

For many years, Herbert Hoover was the leading recipient of honorary degrees with 52. Easily breaking Hoover's record, Father Theodore Hesburgh, the former president of Notre Dame, is the current leader with an impressive 112 at last count.

Abraham Lincoln received three honorary degrees, one each from Princeton, Columbia, and Knox. The first two were fairly straightforward, but tiny Knox College of Galesburg, Illinois, was concerned whether the backwoods-bred Lincoln was worthy of its academic recognition. Because of this uncertainty, Knox's diploma was accompanied by a letter advising Lincoln to "be a scholar as well as a gentleman and deport yourself accordingly."

One of the most controversial honorary degrees was the one Bowdoin bestowed on Jefferson Davis in 1858 when he was a United States senator from Mississippi. The award attracted little attention at the time, but when Davis became president of the Confederacy, Bowdoin came under considerable pressure to rescind the degree. Bowdoin,

however, held fast to its decision and refused to yield. After the Civil War ended, Davis was subjected to a number of hardships including loss of citizenship and imprisonment. Throughout these troubled times, the one bright light for Jefferson Davis was the fact that Bowdoin did not take back its recognition of his honorable service as a senator.

The only instance of a U.S. president and his wife receiving simultaneous honorary degrees was when Lyndon and Lady Bird Johnson were awarded them from the University of Texas on May 30, 1964. The Doctor of Laws given to Lyndon and the Doctor of Letters awarded to Lady Bird were the last honorary degrees given by Texas.

MIT has never awarded an honorary doctorate. The closest it came was an honorary lectureship bestowed on Winston Churchill in 1949.

Gustavus Adolphus College of St. Peter, Minnesota, awards an honorary degree to every American Nobel Prize winner who speaks at its annual conference. In 1963, when Gustavus Adolphus dedicated its Nobel Hall of Science, twenty-seven American Nobel winners were in attendance, the third-largest gathering of laureates ever assembled. During Gustavus Adolphus's twenty-second annual Nobel Conference in October 1986, Dr. James Tobin, a Yale economist, became the sixty-fifth Nobel laureate to receive an honorary degree from the college.

Honorary degrees generally go to smart people, not dummies. An exception to the rule was made by Northwestern's School of Speech when it awarded an unofficial honorary degree on August 28, 1938, to Charlie McCarthy, the wooden friend of ventriloquist Edgar Bergen. The degree was "Master of Innuendo and Snappy Comeback." Edgar Bergen himself received an earned master's degree from Northwestern in 1941.

The honorary degree Harvard awarded to Andrew Jackson in 1833 proved to be unpopular with a Harvard graduate from the class of 1787. Upon hearing of the recognition given to his bitter rival, John Quincy Adams wrote to Harvard President Quincy that he "would not be present to witness [Harvard's] . . . disgrace in conferring her

highest literary honors upon a barbarian."

To show its ecumenical spirit, Carroll College of Waukesha, Wisconsin, a Presbyterian school with an enrollment of mostly Lutherans and Catholics, in 1979 gave an honorary degree to a Buddhist, His Holiness the XIV Dalai Lama, Tenzin Gyato.

Honorary-degree holders Bergen and McCarthy.

AWARDS

Columbia University holds the record for giving out the most prizes and awards. Columbia bestows the Pulitzer Prizes in journalism, letters, drama, and music; the Bancroft Prize in history; the Alexander Hamilton Medal; the Brevoort-Eikemeyer Award in art; the National Magazine Awards; the Chandler Medal in Chemistry; and twenty-five others.

College Colors

One of the sidelights of the boom in college athletics that occurred during the late 1800s was a scramble for team colors. Every college wanted distinctive colors for its players' uniforms. Harvard took crimson, Yale blue, Cornell red, and Princeton orange; Dartmouth claimed green just before City College of New York. CCNY then settled on lavender, only to have its choice protested by Wesleyan, which had staked a prior claim. In a compromise, CCNY added black and adopted lavender and black as its colors.

West Point's colors are black, gray, and gold. These are the colors of the components of gunpowder—charcoal, potassium nitrate, and sulphur.

When it was founded in 1866, the University of Kansas's colors were maize and sky blue like those of the University of

West Point's black, gray, and gold colors represent the components of gunpowder.

Michigan. In 1890 a Harvard graduate, John McCook, donated money for the Kansas football field. To honor McCook, the football team voted to adopt Harvard's crimson as their color. When Yale alumni on the faculty heard of the football team's action, they insisted that Yale blue be included. Kansas's colors have been crimson and blue since 1896.

Georgetown's colors are blue and gray, not to honor Yale and potassium nitrate, but in recognition of the colors of the opposing sides in the Civil War. The War Between the States was particularly divisive for Georgetown. Its student body was split down the middle, some joining the Union army and others enlisting with the Confederate forces. At the end of the war Georgetown adopted the colors of blue and gray to signify the union of the North and South.

In the late 1890s, when the Texas baseball team was leaving to play a game against Southwestern, students at a pep rally found there were no school colors. Two students rushed to a nearby store and bought orange and white ribbons, the only colors in stock. For the next ten years other color combinations were tried but none of them caught on. Eventually a campuswide vote was taken and orange and white were designated Texas's official colors on May 15, 1900.

Syracuse's original colors, adopted in 1872, were rose pink and pea green. A short time later pea green was replaced by blue, but pink remained. By 1889 Syracuse students had had their fill of the sarcastic comments opposing spectators shouted at the Syracuse teams about their pink uniforms and asked the Alumni Association to change the colors. The next year the association made orange the official and lone Syracuse color.

In 1906 it was proposed that the colors of Occidental College in Los Angeles be red, yellow, and green to represent the area's principal products—wine, oranges, and olives. But Occidental's president at the time, John M. McPherron, was a teetotaler and would not allow the color red. Instead, Occidental copied Princeton's orange and black and, while they were at it, adopted the tiger mascot as well.

Because of its religious affiliation, Catholic University in Washington, D.C., has two sets of colors. Since it is the only U.S. college with a papal charter, Catholic adopted for its official school colors those of the Pope, gold and white. Catholic's athletic teams, however, use red and black. The baseball team originally tried the papal colors, but switched to red and black when they discovered how dirty their gold and white uniforms looked after playing a game on a muddy field.

When Union College was invited to the intercollegiate crew championship in 1875, it pointed out to Harvard that Union had used magenta as its color since 1860 and requested that Harvard change from magenta to a different color. Harvard, outraged by the effrontery of the small college from upstate New York, firmly refused. As a result of the "Magenta War" of 1875, each college retained its original color, but Harvard began to call its magenta crimson, while Union labeled its magenta garnet.

Vassar's colors of rose and gray were selected for their symbolic value related to Vassar's pioneering role in advancing higher education for women. Vassar chose rose to represent the breaking of the dawn—the chance for women to receive the same college education as men—through the gray sky, the indication of the previous absence of such an opportunity.

Campus Stories
TOWN AND GOWN

New Mexico State scheduled its first graduation ceremony for March 10, 1893. It was canceled because the only senior, Sam Steele, was shot and killed the night before. A local cowboy, who had been drinking heavily, attempted to rob Steele; finding Steele had no money, the cowboy became enraged and killed him on the spot.

While New Mexico State had trouble with cowboys, another college had a problem with Indians. The University of Georgia held its first commencement in 1801. On the day of the exercises, there were reports of Indian hostilities in the area. To protect the graduation party, the local sheriff marched ahead of the procession with his sword drawn.

Over the years the participation of the sheriff in Georgia's commencement parade has become a tradition. Today, dressed in period costume and with his sword still held high, the sheriff of Clarke County leads the graduation party to the commencement site.

Georgia students may walk to graduation, but the women at Wells College in Aurora, New York, ride. Seniors travel to commencement in the splendor of an antique Wells Fargo stagecoach that has been restored to its original condition. The stagecoach tradition was started in 1868 by Henry Wells, the organizer of the Wells Fargo

Graduation ceremonies at Wells College.

and American Express companies. After founding the college, Wells was concerned that the students, who came to Lake Cayuga Village by barge, had no way to get to Aurora, some 10 miles away. Wells solved the problem by arranging for a company coach to meet the young women. Now, more than a century later, modern-day coeds are given the opportunity to relive the stagecoach experience of their pioneering sisters.

SPEAKING CAN BE HAZARDOUS TO YOUR HEALTH

MIT's founder and first president, William Rogers, died at the age of 77 while giving his university's 1882 commencement address. Rogers's last words were "bituminous coal."

Alben Barkley, Harry Truman's vice president, also met his fate while speaking at a college. Delivering the keynote address at Washington and Lee's Mock Democratic Convention on April 30, 1956, Barkley said, "I would rather be a servant in the house of the Lord than to sit in the seats of the mighty," and promptly died of a heart attack. The mock convention continued and nominated Adlai Stevenson as the Democratic candidate, three months before he was selected at his party's national convention.

FINDING A HOME

It is not uncommon for a college to start in one place and move to a more suitable location some time later. Since sailors have a reputation for going from port to port, perhaps it is not surprising that the U.S. Coast Guard Academy took a while to find a place to settle down. The academy was founded in 1877 as the U.S. Revenue Cutter School in New Bedford, Massachusetts. In 1889, by executive order of President Benjamin Harrison, the academy was closed. The school was restored in 1894, but its home was at sea aboard the USS *Chase*. In 1900 the Revenue School came ashore at Arundel Cove, Maryland. Next, in 1910, was a move to Fort Trumbull, Connecticut. During World War I, the Revenue Cutter Service was combined with the Life Saving Service to form the U.S. Coast Guard. Finally, in 1931, the academy was established at its present location in New London, Connecticut. After fifty-four years of wandering, the Coast Guard Academy had finally found a permanent home.

The U.S. Air Force Academy has had only one location, its beautiful campus in Colorado Springs. But no other college went through as complicated a process to determine where it would be located. After the creation of the academy was authorized in 1954, a commission traveled 21,000

The campus of the U.S. Air Force Academy in Colorado Springs, Colorado.

miles to visit 580 proposed sites in forty-five states. Perhaps influenced by an offer from the state of Colorado to contribute $1-million toward the purchase of property, the secretary of the Air Force selected the Colorado Springs location from among the final three possible sites.

MOST MODEST

Texas Woman's University was founded in 1901, but it wasn't until 1977 that the college permitted reporters to come on campus or had its name listed in the telephone directory. A college started to teach manners and culture to young ladies (called Tessies), TWU later emerged as the nation's largest university for women. Today TWU is a blend of past and present. While it boasts of the country's largest cookbook collection and enrollment in home economics, it also has its

own ROTC unit and a dormitory for single parents. TWU is one of two women's colleges supported by public funds.

TREES

I think that I shall never see
A poem lovely as a tree.
A tree whose hungry mouth is pressed
Against the earth's sweet flowing breast;

A tree that looks at God all day
And lifts her leafy arms to pray;

A tree that may in summer wear
A nest of robins in her hair;

Upon whose bosom snow has
   lain;
Who intimately lives with rain.

Poems are made by fools like me,
But only God can make a tree.

This famous poem, *Trees,* was written by Joyce Kilmer about a white oak that stood on the Rutgers campus in New Brunswick, New Jersey. When he wrote the poem, Kilmer was a student at Rutgers, which he attended for two years before graduating from Columbia in 1908. Kilmer was killed during World War I at the Battle of the Marne when he was 32 years old.

The white oak at Rutgers that inspired Joyce Kilmer.

MORE TREES

In the middle of the front lawn on the St. John's (Maryland) campus stands the Liberty Tree, which is now more than 350 years old. Shaded by its leaves, the Sons of Liberty met to hear patriot-orators in the spring of 1776. The tree was taking on its fall colors when French troops marched past it to join General Washington at Yorktown. Francis Scott Key graduated from St. John's in 1796 in a commencement ceremony held under the tree's branches.

The Liberty Tree, a tulip poplar, refuses to die. Experts thought it would die in 1840 when youngsters exploded two pounds of gunpowder in its trunk, but the next year the tree took on new growth. The Liberty Tree is now growing faster than it is decaying and should live into the twenty-first century, perhaps long enough to be part of St. John's 300th birthday celebration in 2014.

WORST WRITING

Professor Scott Rice of San Jose State sponsors the Bulwer-Lytton Fiction Contest for writing the worst opening line of a novel. The international contest is named after Edward Bulwer-Lytton, who began his novel, *Paul Clifford,* with the memorable words, "It was a dark and stormy night. . . ."

Lines that have been runners-up in the contest include:

"It was raining cats and dogs and I stepped on a poodle."
"Colonel Winterbottom was a cold, stern man."
"Call me Ishmael, anytime."

But the recent winner was: "Like an expensive sports car, fine-tuned and well-built, Portia was sleek, shapely and gorgeous, her red jumpsuit moulding her body, which was as warm as the seatcovers in July, her hair as dark as new tires, her eyes flashing like bright hubcaps, and her lips dewy as the beads of fresh rain on the hood; she was a woman driven—fueled by a single accelerant—and she needed a man, a man who wouldn't shift from his views, a man to steer her along the right road: a man like Alf Romeo."

CALIFORNIA

California colleges do not always look at tradition in the same way as their Eastern counterparts.

Cal State Fullerton is proud to have not the oldest, but the youngest accredited business and music departments. Fullerton describes its location not in relation to towns or historic landmarks, but by its proximity to Route 57, the Orange Freeway.

With some pride, the University of California at Irvine claims it has the first recreational-vehicle park on a college campus.

For those who prefer two-wheeled transportation, the

University of California at Santa Barbara has the most bicycles of any college campus. At last count UCSB had 11,000 bikes rolling over 7 miles of special paths.

In spite of California's fascination with the automobile, a college in another state wins "Drive-in U" honors. The University of Florida has 14,500 parking spaces on campus, gives out 32,000 parking permits, and has as many as 25,000 cars on its grounds during any given day.

SONGS AND YELLS

The tune for Cornell's alma mater, "Far Above Cayuga's Waters," is the most copied college song. It is used by LSU, Kansas, and at least forty other colleges.

For a football fight song, the "Washington and Lee Swing" has been counterfeited most often, by an estimated two dozen colleges.

One of the most famous college songs is the University of Texas's "The Eyes of Texas," to the tune of "I've Been Working on the Railroad." It was composed in 1903 by a student, John Lang Sinclair, on a piece of scrap paper as he sat at a benefit show for Texas athletic teams. The song has been translated into ten foreign languages. A silk-screened copy was taken to the moon in 1969 by astronaut Alan Bean, a Texas alumnus.

Georgia Tech's "The Ramblin' Wreck" was sung by Richard Nixon and Nikita

Khrushchev in 1959 when Nixon made a visit to Moscow. Ex-Beatle Paul McCartney bought rights to the Tech fight song in 1979.

A college yell that is unlikely to be copied is Albion's "Io Triumphe!" which goes:

Io Triumphe! Io Triumphe!
Haben swaben rebecca le
    animor
Whoop te whoop te sheller de-
    vere
Deboom de-ral de-i de-pa
Hooneka henaka whack a
    whack
A-hob dob balde bora bolde
    bara
Con slomade hob dob Rah!
Albion Rah!

THE IMPORTANCE OF THE JANITOR

In the 1880s at NYU the janitor was no mere emptier of wastepaper baskets, but a major force in the day-to-day operations of the university. He was the confidant of students, collected various fees, rented extra rooms, and signaled the break between classes by ringing a bell. NYU recognized the importance of the janitor's role by having him march at the head of the procession of faculty and students at commencement.

The supremacy of the janitor in the late nineteenth century extended beyond New York. One of the most powerful men at the University of West Virginia was its janitor, Doc Danser. In 1893 the Board of Regents asked

Danser to deliver an order requesting the resignation of the president and the faculty. Once, after his complaint that faculty meetings were too long was ignored, Danser locked the professors in their meeting room. When Danser died in 1902 after twenty-eight years of service, his funeral was held in Commencement Hall; he remains the only West Virginia employee ever to receive such an honor.

KIDS OF FAMOUS PARENTS

Offspring of famous parents can be found on nearly every college campus. But recently one university, Brown, seems to suit the "lifestyles of the rich and famous" more than most colleges. At the opening of the 1985–86 school year, for example, Providence, Rhode Island, was home to Amy Carter (Jimmy), Laura Zaccaro (Geraldine Ferraro), Bill Mondale (Walter), Vanessa Vadim (Jane Fonda and Roger Vadim), and Cosima Von Bulow (Klaus). Recent graduates have included John F. Kennedy Jr., Kerry Kennedy (Robert F.), Kate Burton (Richard), Matthew Scott (George C.), Casey Cole (Nat King), and Polly Segal (George).

THE MERGER THAT NEVER HAPPENED

In 1904, MIT president Henry Pritchett and Harvard president Charles Eliot, with the support of their boards of trustees, decided to merge MIT and Harvard. MIT, whose campus was in Boston at the time, was struggling, and Harvard wanted to add science and engineering to its traditional strength in liberal arts. For the agreement to become final, MIT had to provide money from the sale of its Boston campus. But the merger plan died when the Massachusetts Supreme Court ruled that MIT didn't have the authority to sell land it received under the Morrill Act. In response to this serious threat to MIT's existence, an alumni organization was formed to raise money. An anonymous gift of $2.5-million (later identified as coming from George Eastman, the founder of Eastman Kodak) allowed MIT to create the landfill in the Charles River basin on which its present campus was constructed.

MOVIES SET ON COLLEGE CAMPUSES

Winter Carnival (1939), starring Richard Carlson and Sonja Henie, at Dartmouth.

Love Story (1970), with Ryan O'Neal and Ali MacGraw, at Harvard.

The Exorcist (1973), with Ellen Burstyn and Linda Blair, at Georgetown.

The Way We Were (1973), with Robert Redford and Barbra Streisand, at Union.

Love Story at Harvard University.

Animal House (1978), with John Belushi, at Eberhard Faber University, a fictitious name for the University of Oregon.

Breaking Away (1979), starring Dennis Christopher, at Indiana University.

North Dallas Forty (1979), with Nick Nolte and Mac Davis, and *Breathless* (1983), featuring Richard Gere, at UCLA.

Ordinary People (1980), starring Donald Sutherland and Mary Tyler Moore, at Lake Forest.

So Fine (1981), with Jack Warden and Ryan O'Neal, at Drew.

Back to School (1986), with Rodney Dangerfield, at the University of Wisconsin.

With its Eastern-style campus, the University of the Pacific is a popular site for Hollywood movie producers looking for an Ivy League setting closer to home. The opening sequence from *Raiders of the Lost Ark* (1981), with Harrison Ford and Karen Allen, was filmed at Pacific.

The Four Seasons (1980), with Alan Alda and Carol Burnett, was shot at Agnes Scott College in Decatur, Georgia. Although it was springtime in Georgia, the script called for fall colors. Director Alda overcame the problem by having leaves glued to the flowering pink and white dogwoods, which were then spray-painted red and yellow to simulate autumn foliage.

Portions of at least twenty-five feature films have taken place at Occidental in California. Two of the most notable are *Horsefeathers*

The Four Seasons *at Agnes Scott College.*

(1932), with the Marx Brothers, and *Star Trek III* (1984), featuring William Shatner and Leonard Nimoy. In *Star Trek III,* when a craft from the starship *Enterprise* lands on an alien planet, it actually sets down at the futuristic fountain in the center of the Occidental campus.

One of the most successful movies of modern times was the 1967 film *The Graduate,* with Dustin Hoffman and Anne Bancroft. The novel on which the movie was based was set at U Cal Berkeley. When director Mike Nichols asked for permission to shoot the film on campus, he was turned down because the administration thought parts of the movie were in bad taste. Instead Nichols took his crew to USC where *The Graduate* was filmed. Before beginning production in Los Angeles, Nichols took a few unauthorized shots of Sproul Plaza to give the impression that the film was set at Berkeley. Other movies that have taken place at USC were the original *Hunchback of Notre Dame* (1939), with Charles Laughton and Maureen O'Hara, and *The Paper Chase* (1973), starring John Houseman and Timothy Bottoms.

TELEVISION

In the last few years the highest-rated television program has been *The Cosby Show,* a show whose success led to the creation of a spin-off called *A Different World.* "Hillman College," where

Cosby's daughter Denise, played by Lisa Bonet, goes to school, is actually Spelman in Atlanta.

Disasters

DARKNESS AT NOON

The eruption of the Mount Saint Helen's volcano on May 18, 1980, dumped half an inch of ash on the Washington State campus in Pullman. The fallout problem was so severe that the college closed for four days while students remained in their dormitories, worried about the lung damage that might result if they breathed the volcanic dust. Driving was extremely hazardous because the fine ground-glass-like ash created slippery conditions and poor visibility. By the time Washington State reopened, many of its students had gone home. Toward the end of the semester, classes were sparsely attended, athletic events were canceled, and fewer than one third of the seniors showed up for graduation.

SAN FRANCISCO EARTHQUAKE

The University of San Francisco (then called Saint Ignatius Academy) opened in 1855 in what was at the time a small gold-rush boomtown with a population of a few thousand. By the turn of the century the University of San Francisco was a thriving college with beautiful classical-style buildings and a large student body. But on the morning of April 18, 1906, the college's buildings came crashing down. What the San Francisco earthquake left standing, the fire that followed soon leveled. The college reopened a week later in a nearby shirt factory, which served as the University of San Francisco's home until 1927 when the college moved to its present campus near Golden Gate Park.

Stanford, which opened in 1891, was located 30 miles south of the earthquake's center and received less of a shock than the one that hit the University of San Francisco. Nevertheless, Stanford's clock tower tumbled and fell on the campus church. A library, gymnasium, museum, and large arch were damaged beyond repair, and classes were suspended for the rest of the year. The class of 1906's graduation was delayed until September and it was known thereafter as the "Earthquake Class."

HURRICANE

On September 17, 1926, when the University of Miami was scheduled to begin its first classes, one of the most devastating hurricanes ever to hit Florida struck the university head-on and leveled its main building. After delaying classes for a month, Miami opened in the abandoned Anastasia Hotel, which had hurriedly been converted to classrooms. The pasteboard partitions used to divide the classes gave Miami its first nickname, "Cardboard College." In spite of the devastation caused by the hurricane, the need for everyone to pitch in, help out, and work hard united the students and faculty. Over the next fifty years Miami would be completely rebuilt and grow to become the largest private research university in the Southeast.

YELLOW FEVER

The oldest educational institution in Texas is Austin College in Sherman. Established in 1849 at Huntsville, Austin moved to its present home in 1876. The primary reason for the change of location was a series of three yellow fever epidemics that struck the population of Huntsville. The financial problems caused by the spread of yellow fever, along with the difficult economic conditions of the post–Civil War period, made it necessary for the college to move to Sherman. Austin thrived in its new home and by the middle of the twentieth century it had developed into an excellent small liberal arts college.

CYCLONE

In June 1882 a cyclone passed through the Grinnell (Iowa) campus, destroying the college's two buildings and killing three students. The death toll could have been considerably higher, but luckily most of the student body was off campus at a baseball game when the cyclone struck.

TORNADO

The tornado grabbed the books from my hands and took a scarf off my head and knocked me down. By this time tree limbs and debris and who knows what were all flying through the air. Somehow we made it [to the east wall of the campus center] and sat with our backs to the wall—holding on to each other . . . and saying, "Oh, God, dear God" over and over.

Tornado damage at Hanover College.

This is a student's account of the tornado that hit Hanover College of Hanover, Indiana, on April 3, 1974. The violent storm damaged thirty-two of thirty-three campus buildings, completely demolishing six of them. Only the chapel sustained no damage. Fifty-five campus homes and an estimated 500 trees were destroyed. Oddly, when the water tower crashed onto the maintenance building, its thousands of gallons of water had mysteriously vanished, apparently carried away by the funnel of the tornado.

In the weeks after the tornado struck, the Hanover community rallied together to clean up the damage. Repairs to buildings and new construction were begun. Neighboring colleges Earlham and Wabash donated hundreds of trees. Classes started again at the end of spring break, only nineteen days after the tornado had caused $10-million worth of damage and threatened Hanover's ability to survive.

Buildings

EARLY STRUCTURES

The oldest academic building still in use is the Sir Christopher Wren Building (formerly called College Building) at William and Mary, which opened in 1697. It was gutted by fire in 1705 but the external walls remained standing. The building was reconstructed between 1705 and 1716. In 1859 the College Building burned and was rebuilt again. In 1862 it was set on fire by Union soldiers. The structure was rebuilt yet again on its original foundation in 1869. The restoration of Colonial Williamsburg in 1933 returned the building to its 1716 form. Today the Christopher Wren Building houses the president's

> *Replicas of Princeton's Nassau Hall can be found at Rutgers, South Carolina, Williams, Wesleyan, and Brown.*

office and other administrative departments.

After William and Mary, the University of North Carolina has the oldest state university buildings—Old East (1795) and Person Hall (1797).

Harvard's Massachusetts Hall, providing both dormitory space and laboratories (then called "scientific apparatus chambers"), was built between 1718 and 1720. Massachusetts Hall still stands at the entrance to Harvard Yard.

In terms of both architecture and historical significance, Princeton's Nassau Hall is one of the most important college buildings in the United States. Built in 1753 and in use today, Nassau Hall originally contained all the college's facilities— dormitory, chapel, dining hall, and classrooms. In 1783, during the Revolutionary War, the building temporarily served as the nation's capital when the Continental Congress met in the second-floor library. It was here that Congress received the news that a peace treaty with Great Britain had been signed. Since Nassau Hall was judged by many to be the ideal college building, it was copied dozens of times. Replicas include Old Queen's College at Rutgers, Rutledge

Hall at South Carolina, Griffin Hall at Williams, the Academy building at Wesleyan, and University Hall at Brown.

The importance of campus architecture during the Colonial period was shown by the size of the buildings. When they were constructed, the main college buildings at Harvard (1638), William and Mary (1697), and Princeton (1753) were the largest structures in the colonies.

Old West at Dickinson College in Carlisle, Pennsylvania, designed by Benjamin Latrobe, the architect of the Capitol in Washington, D.C., was completed in 1804. At that time Old West contained a chapel, a dining hall, and rooms for forty students. Today it houses administrative offices and is used in Dickinson's graduation ceremony: as a reminder of Dickinson's rich educational history, each senior is given a diploma upon descending Old West's stone steps.

Randolph Hall at the College of Charleston, constructed in 1829, is one of the oldest campus buildings in continuous use.

Hampden-Sydney has the oldest four-story brick dorm, Cushing Hall, built in 1855.

TALLEST

The University of Pittsburgh's Cathedral of Learning is forty-two stories, or 535 feet, tall. It contains 1,200 rooms with 328,340 square feet of usable space. The only higher college structure in the world is the main building at the University of Moscow.

LARGEST ACADEMIC BUILDING

Surpassing Pitt's Cathedral of Learning by about 50,000 square feet, Cal Berkeley's Life Sciences Building is the largest academic building in the United States. Its 376,000 square feet house thirteen separate academic departments with room left over for 500 laboratories. Built in 1930 at a cost of $1,836,000, it is to be refurbished in 1988 at a projected cost of $60-million.

DORMITORIES

The largest college dormitory is Bancroft Hall at the Naval Academy. All 4,600 midshipmen sleep in one building. It contains 1,873 rooms, nearly 5 miles of corridors, and 33 acres of floor space. Besides providing sleeping quarters, Bancroft also serves as a giant student center, with a bookstore, a cobbler shop, three barber shops (along with a recently added beauty shop), a travel agency, a laundry, a computer store, and a uniform shop.

Michigan State, with twenty dormitories, has the largest residential system on a college campus. The halls house a total of 17,280 students—16,400 undergraduates and 880 graduate students.

The 500 students at Wisconsin's Silver Lake College have to draw lots for 20 beds.

Other colleges that have rooms for more than 10,000 undergraduates are Purdue, Tennessee, Penn State, U Mass, Indiana, and Iowa State. The two-year college offering the most dormitory space is Vincennes University in Indiana, which has a capacity of 2,800.

Of all the four-year colleges that provide dormitory space for their students, Silver Lake College in Manitowoc, Wisconsin, has the fewest rooms. Silver Lake's 500 undergraduates have to draw lots for only twenty beds.

DORMS ON WHEELS

In 1986 West Oregon State College eased its student housing crunch by purchasing nineteen mobile homes. Spacious by trailer standards, each unit has seven bedrooms and two baths and holds fourteen students. The homes formerly were owned by the Oregon commune organized by cult leader Bhagwan Shree Rajneesh.

DINING HALLS

The biggest dining halls are at the service academies—West Point, Air Force, and Annapolis. Each is designed to feed its entire cadet corps, approximately 4,600, at one sitting.

An example of a massive college dining operation is the Air Force Academy's eating area, which covers more than 1½ acres. Each year its kitchen produces about 4.5 million meals. More than 360,000 gallons of milk, 90,000 gallons of juice, 2 million eggs, 1 million pounds of beef, and 12 miles of frankfurters are consumed annually. After the cadets take their seats, they are served family-style and finish the meal in 25 minutes. To ensure quality as well as speed there are 28 managers, 166 waiters, 59 mess attendants, 63 cooks, 15 bakers, 13 meat cutters, 17 supply clerks, and 44 advance preparation personnel.

The biggest college eating facility as measured by the total number of meals served daily is the Brody Complex at Michigan State, with fifteen separate dining halls. Brody, the largest residence-hall food service facility in the world, serves as many as 66,000 meals a day and a total of 13 million during the year.

STUDENT CENTERS

Indiana University's Memorial Union is the world's largest student center. Its floor area is equivalent to eight football fields and includes a 200-room hotel, a bookstore, personal computer stations, a photocopy center, a barbershop, a beauty parlor, a bowling alley, a camping equipment rental store, five restaurants, and assorted meeting, game, and TV rooms.

BELL TOWERS

The chimes in Cornell's McGraw Tower were played on the university's opening day in 1868. They were the first chimes to ring out over an American campus.

Michigan's Charles Baird Carillon is the heaviest musical instrument in the United States and the third largest in the world. The biggest of its fifty-three bells weighs 12 tons.

The organ in the Cadet Chapel at West Point is the world's largest church organ. Its more than 18,000 pipes are capable of reproducing the sound of thunder, military drums, bugles, musical instruments, and chimes.

The Development of College Architecture

Harvard, William and Mary, and Yale were all built along the lines of a typical English quadrangle, but they are more spacious and open. Princeton extended William and Mary's idea of a rural campus with its center-piece, Nassau Hall, set well back from the street and fronted by a large lawn. In fact, the term campus (Latin for field) originated at Princeton; it wanted to distinguish its grounds from the Harvard Yard.

The term 'campus' originated at Princeton, which wanted to distinguish its own grounds from Harvard's 'yard.'

The next significant step in college design occurred in 1813 at Union College in New York. Union was one of the first colleges to educate not only the privileged, but also the sons of merchants and farmers. Like the education it offered, Union's campus was designed to be open to all. Joseph Ramée, a French architect, grouped various neoclassical buildings around a central focus. The ends were anchored by North and South Colleges, and a series of paths and gardens led to a curved colonnade in the middle of which stood the president's house. The campus was oriented to the west to symbolize the direction in which the new nation would fulfull its destiny.

The most famous work of campus architecture is Thomas Jefferson's design for the University of Virginia. As the American colonies had rebelled against the mother country, Jefferson's vision of an academic village broke with the tradition of the English college quadrangle. His building plan for Virginia was brick-and-mortar evidence of democracy in a college setting. Believing that the ideal education depended on a personal relationship between teachers and students, Jefferson linked faculty houses (with classrooms on the first floor) and student rooms around a spacious mall. The mall was enclosed on one side by the Rotunda, which contained the library. The buildings were designed in Greek revival style to suggest the Athenian principles of democracy and wisdom.

Following Jefferson's lead, Greco-Roman buildings were built at other colleges until about 1850. Outstanding examples were the halls that housed the literary and debating societies at Davidson and Emory, along with groups of buildings at Charleston, Tulane, Georgia, and Washington and Lee.

In the middle decades of the nineteenth century the Gothic style found favor with architects, especially the designers of the Kenyon, Knox, Bowdoin, CCNY, Lehigh, and Worcester Tech campuses.

After the passage of the Morrill Act in 1862, college design moved toward a variety of styles and practical simplicity. The leading practitioner of the new trend was park planner Frederick Law Olmsted. Colleges like Michigan State, Iowa State, and Kansas State were laid out with informal clusters of buildings in parklike settings. This was the arrangement Olmsted and Charles Coolidge planned for Stanford until Leland Stanford took personal control and changed the open scheme to one of enclosed quadrangles accessible through a large memorial arch. The success of Stanford's more formal layout led to similar plans for Washington (St. Louis), Rochester, Chicago, Columbia, and NYU.

The early twentieth century saw the revival of the English classical quadrangles like those at Oxford and Cambridge. This style was incorporated into plans for the original campuses at Trinity (Connecticut) and Reed and affected the design of new buildings at many other colleges.

Collegiate Gothic reappeared with Ralph Cram's work at West Point, Duke, and Princeton. Outstanding examples of the Gothic revival are two soaring structures, the Cathedral of Learning at Pittsburgh and Harkness Tower at Yale.

In the 1930s modernism came on the scene, strikingly exemplified by Mies van der Rohe's famous 1938 design for the Illinois Institute of Technology in Chicago. The buildings were arranged symmetrically and constructed of glass and exposed steel frames. Frank Lloyd Wright further advanced the modernist cause when he built a new-style campus at Florida Southern.

Modernism, variety in design, and the effective use of land contours marked the post–World War II period. These trends can be seen in urban campuses like Illinois at Chicago and Cleveland State; in two-year rural colleges like Foothill and Cypress in California; and in the crown jewel of post-1960 construction, the University of California at Santa Cruz. With the purchase of the 2,000-acre Cowell Ranch, surrounded by redwood forests and grasslands and within view of the Pacific Ocean, Santa Cruz took

advantage of an unparalleled opportunity to build a new campus in a beautiful location. An outstanding example of modern college architecture, Santa Cruz successfully integrates its academic and residential structures into its dramatic natural landscape.

ARCHITECTURAL AWARDS

The American Institute of Architects annually gives an honor award to colleges for excellence in planning or building design.

Since the awards started in 1954, Yale has been honored most often, with recognition in five separate years, as well as a special twenty-five-year award in 1979. Among Yale's award-winning buildings are the Bienecke Library, the Center for British Art, and Stiles and Morse colleges.

The AIA award for overall campus design has gone to four California colleges: Santa Monica City College, Foothill, Santa Cruz, and De Anza. The AIA's highest award, the Gold Medal, went to the University of Virginia in 1976 for Jefferson's beautiful design of the campus in Charlottesville.

In 1987 the AIA gave its honor award to five college buildings: U Cal Irvine's Information and Computer Science/Engineering Research Facility (designed by Frank Gehry), Princeton's Lewis Thomas Laboratory (designed by Payette and Brown), Emory's Museum of Art and Archeology (renovated by Michael Graves), the Hood Museum of Art at Dartmouth (designed by Charles Moore and Chad Floyd), and Columbia's Computer Science Building (designed by R. M. Kliment and Frances Halsband).

ARCHITECTURAL HIGHLIGHTS

From the pen of a writer on college architecture comes this list of personal favorites:

Most Influential Architects
    Thomas Jefferson
    Charles Follen McKim
    Henry Hornbostel
    John Galen Howard
    Henry Hobson Richardson

Ralph Adams Cram
Ludwig Mies van der Rohe
Michael Graves

Especially Pleasant Campuses

Virginia
Stanford
Charleston
Santa Cruz
Pomona
Princeton

Notable Buildings

Cathedral of Learning, Pittsburgh
College of Fine Arts, Carnegie Mellon
Michael C. Carlos Hall, Emory
Nott Memorial, Union
Eumanean and Philanthropic halls, Davidson
Hearst Women's Gym, U Cal Berkeley
Kresge College, U Cal Santa Cruz

OTHER ARCHITECTURAL BITS AND PIECES

— Best Stairway: Sackler Museum, Harvard.
— Best Faculty Club: U Cal Berkeley.
— Most Impressive Library Room: Pratt Library at Johns Hopkins's Peabody Conservatory of Music.
— Best Use of a Train Station: Construction of studios for Maryland Institute, College of Art.
— Most Notable Gateway: Stanford's memorial arch,

which collapsed in the 1906 earthquake.
— Most Insensitive Architecture: McKim, Mead, and White's closing of the Lawn at the University of Virginia with three buildings.
— Best Use of a Former State Capitol: The Old Capitol building at the University of Iowa.
— Best Disguised Smokestacks: The clock tower at Detroit and Hamerschlag Hall at Carnegie Mellon.
— Most Unusual Library: U Cal San Diego.
— Most Pleasant Group of Buildings: Dartmouth Row.
— Oddest Conversion of a Chapel: Rensselaer Polytechnic Institute's Voorhees Computing Center.
— College Designed Along the Lines of a Factory: Clark (Mass.).
— Most Spectacular Chapel: U.S. Air Force Academy.
— Best Duplicate of Philadelphia's Independence Hall: Stetson's Elizabeth Hall.
— Most Playful Stonework: The masonry on the buildings at Rice University. The buildings include caricatures of philosophers, scientists, students, faculty members, squirrels, and owls. The top of one carved column shows a student being devoured by a dragon whose smiling face is that of Rice's first chemistry professor, Harry Weisel.
— Best New Use for Old Buildings: Restoring two

early-twentieth-century buildings and connecting them with a glass-enclosed atrium to form a new student center at Case Western Reserve; similarly the Science Center at Wellesley.

— Best Restoration Following a Fire: The new campus of Clarke College in Iowa.

— Best Campus Design Taken from a Magazine: In 1916 Texas El Paso decided to build a new campus on the rocky

An example of the architecture at the University of Texas at El Paso.

western slope of Mount Franklin. The wife of the dean noticed that the landscape resembled the rugged terrain shown in a *National Geographic* article, "Castles in the Air: Experiences and Journeys in Unknown Bhutan." Photographs featured several "dzongs," fortresslike buildings the Bhutanese used

as monasteries and art museums. The decision was made to construct the new campus in Bhutanese-style architecture— light brown stucco buildings with high inset windows, inwardly slanting walls trimmed with red brick bands, and overhanging tile roofs. The university museum and the student union have large sculptures of Buddhist prayer wheels flanking their entrances. Even the guard booths that house the campus police resemble miniature Bhutanese temples.

Famous Events That Took Place at Colleges

THE LINCOLN-DOUGLAS DEBATES

In 1858 Stephen Douglas and Abraham Lincoln, running for a Senate seat in Illinois, agreed to a series of seven debates. In the early going Douglas was the clear favorite, but by the fifth debate in Galesburg, Lincoln had improved his style and delivery greatly. The debate took place on October 7 on a platform set against the east wall of Old Main, the central building at Knox College. Lincoln was never more eloquent about his opposition to slavery, insisting that the Supreme Court was wrong in its Dred Scott ruling that Congress did not have the power to exclude slavery from federal territories. Lincoln clearly won the Knox debate and seized the momentum from Douglas. Within weeks Douglas's campaign started to unravel, and Lincoln went on to win the November election. Although Lincoln never attended college, when he entered the speaker's platform by stepping through a window in Old Main, he remarked, "Now I've gone through Knox College."

BATTLE OF GETTYSBURG

At Gettysburg, Pennsylvania, on July 1–3, 1863, the Confederate forces invaded Northern territory for the second and last time in the Civil War. Much of the July 1 battle between the Union army and the Confederates occurred on the campus of Gettysburg, then called Pennsylvania College. (On June 29 fifty-seven Gettysburg students, calling themselves Company A, had a brief skirmish with an advance party of Confederate soldiers. When Company A learned that the Confederate forces numbered 5,000, they beat a quick retreat.) At the outset of the battle, positions were established to the west and north of the campus. A strong Confederate attack broke the Union lines to the north, and the troops retreated through the campus, using Pennsylvania Hall, one of the three college buildings at the time, as a hospital. Later, the Confederates gained control of the grounds and also used Pennsylvania Hall to treat their wounded. During the next two days the Battle of Gettysburg moved a short distance south of the college, where the Confederates, unable to break through the Union lines, were forced to retreat. The North's decisive victory at Gettysburg, coupled with the Union's capture of Vicksburg on the same day, were the turning points of the Civil War. From July 1863 onward, the North began to see victory ahead while the South could only hope to prolong the war and wait for an improvement in their fortunes.

MARSHALL PLAN

General George C. Marshall received an honorary degree at Harvard's 1947 commencement. In his acceptance speech, the general announced his intention to introduce the European Economic Recovery Act—the Marshall Plan.

"IRON CURTAIN" SPEECH

The gymnasium at Westminster College in Fulton, Missouri, was the scene of one of the most important occurrences of the post–World War II period, Winston Churchill's "Iron Curtain" speech. In his remarks following the receipt of an honorary degree from Westminster, Churchill accused Russia of violating the democratic principles for which

World War II was fought, with the words:

> . . . it is my duty to place before you certain facts about the present position in Europe. From Stettin in the Baltic to Trieste in the Adriatic, an iron curtain has descended across the continent. Behind that line lie all the capitals of the ancient states of central and eastern Europe . . . in what I might call the Soviet sphere, and all subject, in one form or another, not only to Soviet influence but to a very high and in some cases increasing measure of control from Moscow.

The Peace Corps was modeled after Grinnell's In-Service Scholarship program that supported students working in underdeveloped countries.

PEACE CORPS

President Kennedy outlined his idea for the Peace Corps on October 14, 1960, during a campaign speech at the student union at the University of Michigan. The model for Kennedy's plan was Grinnell's In-Service Scholarship program, which supported students working in underdeveloped countries.

RACIAL INTEGRATION

A significant milestone in breaking down the barriers of racial segregation in the United States was reached at the University of Mississippi. On September 10, 1962, the Supreme Court ordered Mississippi to admit James Meredith, holding that his application was rejected solely because he was black. To overcome the resistance of Governor Ross Barnett (who appointed himself registrar so he could bar Meredith from enrolling), Robert Kennedy, the Attorney General, called out 3,000 federal troops and 400 United States marshals to protect Meredith from violence as he attended classes. In spite of the numerous obstacles, Meredith persisted, graduated from Mississippi in 1963, and went on to Columbia Law School.

CAMPUS PROTEST

The first major student protest, the U Cal Berkeley student revolt, started on September 14, 1964, and continued throughout the fall semester. The point of contention was the dean of students' prohibition against soliciting funds for off-campus political action groups.

U.S.-RUSSIAN SUMMIT

The subjects of the U.S.–U.S.S.R. summit conference were problems in the Middle East, efforts to halt the proliferation of nuclear weapons, and the status of U.S.–Soviet relations. The time was not 1988 but twenty-one years earlier. The meeting between President Lyndon Johnson and Soviet Premier Aleksey Kosygin took place on June 23 and 25, 1967, at the home of the president of Glassboro State College in Glassboro, New Jersey. Although no formal agreements were reached after ten hours of discussion, the cordial feelings that developed between the two world leaders gave rise to the "spirit of Glassboro," a temporary relaxation of the Cold War tension between the two superpowers.

ASSASSINATION ATTEMPT

President Reagan was rushed to the George Washington University Medical Center on March 30, 1981, after he was shot in the chest by William Hinckley Jr. Surgery to remove a bullet lodged in Reagan's lung was performed by Dr. Benjamin Aaron and Dr. Joseph Giordano of the George Washington hospital staff.

Trivia

A book about colleges would be incomplete without noting some of the largely insignificant characteristics of the nation's 3,100 colleges.

HIGHEST AND LOWEST

The college campus situated at the highest elevation is Colorado Mountain College, Timberline Campus, a two-year institution in Leadville, elevation 10,000 feet.

The highest four-year college is Western State in

GEOGRAPHIC LOCATION

Colleges that mark the boundaries of the United States are:

	4-Year	2-Year
Northern	U of Alaska at Fairbanks, 65 degrees N. (Continental U.S.: Western Washington at Bellingham, 49 degrees N.)	Chukchi College, Kotzebue, Alaska, 66 degrees N. (Continental U.S.: North Dakota State at Bottineau, 49 degrees N.)
Western	U of Hawaii–West Oahu College in Pearl City, 158 degrees W. (Continental U.S.: Humboldt State in Arcata, California, 124 degrees W.)	Northwest Community College, Nome, Alaska, 164 degrees W. (Continental U.S.: College of the Redwoods, Eureka, California, 124 degrees W.)
Southern	U of Hawaii at Hilo, 20 degrees N. (Continental U.S.: U of Miami at Coral Gables, 26 degrees N.)	U of Hawaii at Maui, 21 degrees N. (Continental U.S.: Florida Keys, Key West, 24 degrees N.)
Eastern	U of Maine at Presque Isle, 68 degrees W.	Northern Maine Vocational Technical at Presque Isle, 68 degrees W.

Western State's "W."

Gunnison, Colorado, 7,734 feet above sea level. Western State also has another entry in the superlative hall of fame. The "W" on a nearby mountain, constructed of rock and painted white, is the largest college symbol, measuring 320 feet by 420 feet.

Two colleges share the honor of being lower than all others. Tulane and Loyola, located within blocks of each other on St. Charles Street in New Orleans, have an average altitude of 4 feet below sea level. The construction of levees in that section of New Orleans makes it possible to build on land that is lower than the surface of the nearby Gulf of Mexico.

CAMPUS SIZE

The largest college is Berry College in Mount Berry, Georgia. Berry is a four-year private coed college with an enrollment of 1,400 and a campus that covers 28,000 acres. Although Berry's main grounds consist of only 4,000 acres, the remaining 24,000 acres are connected lands used for Berry's agriculture and forestry operations. Other colleges with large campuses are the Air Force Academy (18,000 acres), West Point (16,000), and Paul Smith's College (15,000).

Even with its modest enrollment and extensive lands, Berry College does not hold the record for acres per student.

Deep Spring, a two-year college in California, has a 10,000-acre campus, but only twenty students.

Deep Springs in California is a two-year college set on 10,000 acres, ample elbow room of 500 acres for each of its twenty students.

In contrast, there are four urban colleges with campuses that occupy less than an acre: Marymount Manhattan in New York, Mundelein in Chicago, Southeastern in Washington, D.C., and Woodbury in Los Angeles.

OLDEST

The oldest four-year college is Harvard, founded in 1636.

The oldest two-year colleges are Becker Junior College in Leicester, Massachusetts (1784),

Louisburg in Louisburg, North Carolina (1787), and Vincennes University in Vincennes, Indiana (1801).

OLD IS NEW

Old College, a private coed institution in Reno, Nevada, is one of the newer colleges in the country, founded in 1980. Unfortunately, Old may not be around long enough to age gracefully; the college is scheduled to close after the 1987–88 academic year.

LONGEST NAME

The college with the most letters in its title is the State University of New York College of Environmental Science and Forestry at the Syracuse University Campus.

In second place is the School for Lifelong Learning of the University System of New Hampshire.

SHORTEST NAME

At first it appears to be a five-way tie among Bee (Texas), Coe (Iowa), Lee (Tennessee and Texas), New (California and Florida), and Old (Nevada). But the college with the shortest name is DQ University of Davis, California. The "D" represents an Iroquoian Indian prophet and the "Q" stands for an Aztec Indian prophet. The college does not write out its full name because the prophets' names are considered sacred and can be used only in religious ceremonies. One of DQ's school holidays is June 25, the anniversary of the Little Big Horn.

FROM A TO Y

As convenient as it would be to say that colleges run from A to Z, in fact, they don't. Alphabetically, colleges start with Abilene Christian in Abilene, Texas, and end with Yuba College in Marysville, California. Even the lonely letter X has two Xaviers (Ohio and Louisiana), and the letter Q is represented by three Queens and a Queensborough, two

MOST COMMON NAME

Concordia College is the winner, with one 2-year and seven 4-year institutions. Concordia Colleges are located in:

River Forest, Illinois
Ann Arbor, Michigan
Moorhead, Minnesota
St. Paul, Minnesota

Bronxville, New York
Portland, Oregon
Mequon, Wisconsin
Selma, Alabama (two-year)

These eight Concordias do not include Concordia Lutheran in Austin, Texas, or Concordia Teachers in Seward, Nebraska.

The runners-up for the most common college name are St. Joseph's (6), Columbia (5), and Bethel (4).

Quincys, a Quinnipiac, a Quinebaug, and a Quinsigamond.

FAMILY NAMES

Often colleges are named after individuals; some use both first and last names like Agnes Scott (Georgia), Mary Baldwin (Virginia), and Roger Williams (Rhode Island). Now and then there is a touch of informality like Bob Jones of South Carolina, Sue Bennett of Kentucky, or Ed Reid of Alabama. Some founders feel more possessive about their institutions and add an apostrophe, like Paul Smith's College in New York.

MOST MISSPELLED COLLEGE NAME

There is John Brown University, John Carroll University, and the John Jay School of Criminal Justice. Then there is Johns Hopkins. Johns is not a possessive without an apostrophe but a first name that was a last name. Johns Hopkins, the founder of the college, was given the last name of his great-grandmother, Margaret Johns, as his first name.

DOWN AND ACROSS

Among crossword puzzle fans, at least four colleges are well known. Most often seen in crosswords because their names are short and vowel filled are Elon (North Carolina), Orono (Maine), Iona (New York), and UCLA.

MOST PREPPY?

Based on the percentage of freshmen coming from nonreligious private schools, the preppiest colleges are Bennington, Sarah Lawrence, Middlebury, Pine Manor, Rollins, and Hampden-Sydney. Using a different standard—an informal count of BMWs on campus and the prevalence of designer labels—SMU, Tulane, and Sweet Briar should be added to the list.

NAMES

For animal lovers, a college directory shows Beaver (Pennsylvania), Drake (Iowa), Antelope (California), Bee

(Texas), Turtle (North Dakota), Manatee (Florida), and Fox Valley (Wisconsin).

In a cafeteria line can be found Berry (Georgia), Catawba

COLLEGES WITH ODD NAMES

Isothermal	Ouachita Baptist
Sinte Gleska	Flaming Rainbow
Transylvania	Tougaloo
Ursinus	Oglala Lakota
Tunxis	Harvey Mudd
Slippery Rock	Wor-Wic Tech

NAME CHANGES

Original Name	*Present Name*
Liberty Hall Academy	Washington and Lee
Blount College	Tennessee
American Western	Ohio University
Central College	Virginia
Western University of Pennsylvania	Pittsburgh
Newark College	Delaware
Bacon College	Kentucky
University of Louisiana	Tulane
Normal College	Duke
New York Free Academy	CUNY
Ashmun Institute	Lincoln
Catholepistemiad of Michigania	Michigan
Farmer's High School	Penn State
The University of the Church of Jesus Christ of the Latter-day Saints	Brigham Young

(North Carolina), Curry (Massachusetts), Rice (Texas), Citrus (California), Lima (Ohio), Mount Olive (North Carolina), and Pepperdine (California).

Royalty is well represented with King (Tennessee), Duke (North Carolina), Queens (New York), Lord Fairfax (Virginia), Princeton (New Jersey), and Earlham (Indiana).

Some likely and not-so-likely partners:

Hope (Michigan) and Mercy (New York)

Paine (Georgia) and Cape Fear (North Carolina)

Walker (Alabama) and Rider (New Jersey)

Peace (North Carolina) and Defiance (Ohio)

Snow (Utah) and Frostburg (Maryland)

Athens (Alabama) and Troy (Alabama)

Madonna (Michigan) and Penn

WATCH YOUR SPELLING

Allegany (Maryland) and Allegheny (Pennsylvania)

Lasell (Massachusetts) and La Salle (Pennsylvania)

Capital (Ohio) and Capitol (Maryland)

Clark (Washington) and Clarke (Mississippi)

Seton Hall (New Jersey) and Seton Hill (Pennsylvania)

GEOGRAPHY LESSON

— Indiana University and California University are in Pennsylvania.
— The University of Georgia is in Athens.
— Manhattan is the home of Kansas State.
— Miami University is in Oxford, Ohio. The University of Miami is in Coral Gables, Florida.
— Boston College is in Chestnut Hill, about 10 miles from Boston.
— Northern Michigan is in Marquette. Marquette is in Milwaukee.
— Cornell College is in Mount Vernon, Iowa. Mount Vernon is in Washington, D.C.
— Southwestern is in Georgetown, not in the District of Columbia, but in Texas.
— Deep Springs is in California, but its mailing address is Dyer, Nevada.

MOST NAME CHANGES

As Michigan State tried to decide what it would be called, it changed its stationery at least five times.

1855 Agricultural College of the State of Michigan
1861 State Agricultural College
1909 Michigan Agricultural College
1925 Michigan State College of Agriculture and Applied Science

NAMES OF INDIVIDUALS IN HIGHER EDUCATION

Emory Walker, former director of admissions at Pomona, collects odd names as a hobby. Included in his college file are:

Sidney Aftergut	Medical student
Tom Economy	College accountant
Chet Runner	Track coach
William Shakespeare	English major
Ford Grant	College treasurer
Ben Stringsaver	College treasurer
Don Fee	College treasurer
Milton French	German professor
Professor Fish	Ichthyologist
Claude Grim	Dean of mortuary science
Deejay Notafraid	Football player
Judy Yellin	Cheerleader
Peter Gay	Lecturer in sexuality
Dan Drown	Swimmer
Jeff Float	Swimmer
Stanford Schwimer	Swimmer at Stanford
Solomon Gemmorrah	Lecturer on social reform
Emmett Bashful	Dean of students
Steve Smear	Football player
Jesse Bones	Professor of veterinary medicine

continued

Steve Pond	Professor of oceanography
Cyrus Field	Professor of geology
Garvin Crabtree	Professor of horticulture
Dean William Lawless	Law school dean

MORE NAMES

Here are more odd names, which appear in the book *Names,* by Paul Dickson.

Hiram Bird	Professor of poultry science
Bob Bugg	Professor of entomology
D. C. Curent	Lecturer in electrical science
Seville Flowers	Professor of botany
Bob Lucid	English professor

1955 Michigan State University of Agriculture and Applied Science
1964 Michigan State University

FIRST IN WAR, FIRST IN PEACE

Along with a gift of 50 guineas, George gave permission in writing for Washington College in Chestertown, Maryland, to use his name; it was the first college to do so.

The original name of Trinity in Hartford, Connecticut, was Washington College.

Washington University of St. Louis took the name because it was incorporated on February 22, 1853, George's birthday. The trustees wanted to name the institution Eliot College after the University's founder, William Greenleaf Eliot (T.S.'s grandfather), but he refused to accept the honor.

Two notable colleges pair Washington's name with those of other distinguished Americans—Washington and Jefferson in Pennsylvania and Washington and Lee in Virginia.

Even George's mother gets into the act with Mary Washington College in Fredericksburg, Virginia.

2

THE GROWTH OF AMERICAN COLLEGES

THE COLONIAL PERIOD, REVOLUTION TO CIVIL WAR, CIVIL WAR TO WORLD WAR I, WORLD WAR I TO THE PRESENT, DEVELOPMENT OF AN AMERICAN UNIVERSITY, STUDENT LIFE IN THE EARLY DAYS, EDUCATION OF WOMEN, EDUCATION OF BLACKS, HOW SOME COLLEGES BEGAN

The Colonial Period, 1636–1776: Starters and Survivors

"After God had carried us safe to New England, and we had builded our houses, provided necessaries for our livelihood, reared convenient places for God's worship, and settled the civil government, one of the next things we longed for and looked after was to advance learning and perpetuate it to posterity."

New England's First Fruits, 1643

American higher education began a mere sixteen years after the Pilgrims landed on Cape Cod, when, in 1636, the Court of Massachusetts voted to establish a "colledge at Cambridg."

In 1638 the school opened with a class of twelve students, a headmaster, and two tutors. Later that year the Reverend John Harvard died and in his will left 400 books and £800 to the struggling college, whose name was changed to honor his memory.

Nearly sixty years later and hundreds of miles to the south, in Williamsburg, Virginia, "Their Majesties Royal College of William and Mary" was granted a charter by the Privy Council on February 8, 1693. The college was named after the reigning monarchs, King William III and Queen Mary II of England.

In 1619, seventeen years before Harvard's founding, the Virginia Company of London set aside land for a college in Henrico on the James River. George Thorpe was put in charge of the project and workmen were hired to start construction. In 1622 Thorpe was killed in an Indian massacre that destroyed Henrico. The college plans were abandoned.

Harvard and William and Mary struggled along through the 1600s, encountering both financial and political obstacles. But they survived, slowly added students and faculty, and served as the northern and southern educational outposts of the colonies. Gradually, other colleges were begun—Yale, Princeton, Columbia, Penn, Brown, Rutgers, and Dartmouth.

By the time the Declaration of Independence was signed on July 4, 1776, there were nine colleges in the colonies, each a small and struggling school with an average enrollment of forty students. These Colonial colleges were originally funded by religious denominations and intended primarily to educate clergymen. Penn was an exception, the only one of the original nine that wasn't started by a church, although it later came under Episcopal control. Even with their strong emphasis on religion, however, the Colonial colleges were not seminaries. There never was a religious test for entrance, and from the beginning the colleges educated future public officials and other professionals as well as clergymen. While two thirds of the early graduates became ministers, by the early 1800s the number had dropped to one in four.

Entrance was based on passing a test in Greek and Latin. The curriculum consisted of Latin, Greek, Hebrew, logic, rhetoric, natural philosophy, and math. There was no choice of subjects. All students in the same class took the same courses. Toward the end of the Colonial period, Penn, based on Ben Franklin's ideas, began to move away from the classical curriculum by introducing courses in science, history, and English.

In the classroom, tutors read the lessons (books were very scarce) and students were called on to recite their assignments from memory. The days were long and difficult. They began with morning prayers as soon as there was enough light for the president to read from the Bible. A full day of classes was followed by evening prayers and time set aside for study.

While some of the students were wealthy, the colleges themselves were poor. Church donations and tuition payments were insufficient to keep the colleges going, so they asked their state legislatures for support. Lotteries were the most common way to raise money, but there were other means as well. Harvard received the profit from the Charlestown ferry, William and Mary income from a tobacco tax, and Yale proceeds from the sale of a captured French privateer. The Colonial institutions were not private colleges; they were controlled by both church and state.

The presidents of the Colonial colleges were clergymen who taught, administered discipline, kept student records, raised money, and preached in the chapel. The faculty consisted of a handful of tutors who helped the president teach. The tutors were barely paid a living wage, and opportunities for pay increases were so rare that many were forced to remain single. Some colleges allowed their faculty to collect additional fees from students, a sort of commission for good teaching.

Built on the English model, colleges were residential. Student behavior was controlled by strict moral discipline. The religious ethic was pervasive, dominating life both inside and outside the classroom. The atmosphere was more like that of a boys' boarding school than a college.

Students were not representative of the population, coming almost entirely from the middle and upper classes. Among the colonists, college attendance was uncommon. By 1776 only 1 person in 1,000 had attended college; there were a mere 3,000 graduates in a population of 3 million.

On the eve of the American Revolution a handful of small church-related colleges were teaching the classics to a small number of students, most of whom were headed toward the ministry. After 1776, the combination of the democratic feeling that swept the country and the growth of science that accompanied the Industrial Revolution would bring great changes to American higher education.

1636–1776

1636	Colledge at Cambridg (Harvard) established. Entrance is based on knowledge of Greek and Latin language and literature.	Roger Williams founds Rhode Island with emphasis on religious tolerance.

continued

1638	First library at Harvard opens with 400 books.	Peter Minuit, after delivering colonists to the New World, dies when his ship sinks on its return trip to Sweden.
1692	Increase Mather, sixth president of Harvard, receives the first honorary degree, a Doctor of Divinity.	Last execution for witchcraft takes place in Massachusetts.
1693	William and Mary is founded in Williamsburg by William Blair.	William Penn buys Pennsylvania lands from the Delaware Indians.
1701	Collegiate School in Connecticut (Yale) opens with an enrollment of one student.	Captain William Kidd, an American pirate, is hanged in England.
1717	Reverend Hugh Jones of William and Mary assumes first professorship in philosophy and mathematics.	American merchants are allowed to participate in the lucrative rum trade.
1718	Elihu Yale donates £562 to have the Connecticut Collegiate School named after him.	The French city of New Orleans is founded by immigrants from Canada and France.
1721	French missionaries establish short-lived Jesuit College in the Illinois territory at Kaskaskia.	The English Crown proclaims South Carolina a colony.
1729	William and Mary establishes college-level departments with a president and six professors.	Ben Franklin publishes the *Pennsylvania Gazette,* the first newspaper in the colonies.
1738	John Winthrop becomes chairman of the mathematics department at Harvard. He will give the first laboratory demonstrations of electricity and magnetism.	The colony of New Jersey receives permission to have its own governor rather than sharing one with New York.
1746	College of New Jersey (Princeton) opens in Elizabethtown.	The Ohio Company is organized to open the Western Territories for settlement.
1749	Ben Franklin helps found the Philadelphia Academy, the forerunner of the University of Pennsylvania.	The first American repertory acting company is established; its first production is *Richard III.*

continued

1750	The Flat Hat Club, the first student secret society, is formed at William and Mary. Thomas Jefferson is a member.	The Conestoga wagon makes it first appearance.
1754	King's College is founded. After suspending classes during the Revolution, it will reopen as Columbia.	The French and Indian War begins.
1755	College of Philadelphia (Penn) admits students.	British forces capture Quebec.
1764	College of Rhode Island (Brown) opens.	The Sugar Act imposes duties on rum and molasses.
1765	The College of Philadelphia is renamed the University of Pennsylvania when John Morgan starts the first medical school.	Declaration of Rights opposes taxation without representation.
1766	Queen's (Rutgers) begins operations in New Brunswick, New Jersey.	The Stamp Act is repealed.
1769	Dartmouth is founded to educate Indians.	Franciscan friar Junípero Serra establishes the first permanent Spanish settlement on the West Coast, the San Diego mission.
1773	Harvard ends its practice of listing students in its catalog in order of social prominence.	Boston Tea Party. Sons of Liberty throw 342 chests of tea overboard.
1776	Phi Beta Kappa founded at William and Mary.	Declaration of Independence adopted by Congress on July 4.

WHICH CAME FIRST?

While there is general agreement about the first nine colleges, other schools trace their origins back far enough to make competing claims. Based on the founding dates published by the institutions themselves, a list of the Colonial colleges looks like this:

Harvard	1636
William and Mary	1693
St. John's (Maryland)	1696
Yale	1701
Penn	1740
Moravian	1742
Delaware	1743
Princeton	1746
Washington and Lee	1749
Columbia	1754
Brown	1764
Rutgers	1766
Dartmouth	1769
Charleston	1770
Salem	1772
Dickinson	1773
Hampden-Sydney	1776

For colleges on this list, the connection between the original school (which may not have been a degree-granting college) and the present-day institution may be tenuous. For example, St. John's, in citing 1696 as its founding date, traces its beginning to King William's School, a precollege boys' academy. Before King William's School went out of business, part of it split off; it eventually became St. John's in 1784.

Revolution to Civil War, 1777– 1860: A Land of Colleges

After the Revolution, the spirit of the times caused the new Americans begin to want higher education to serve society as a whole rather than focus narrowly on classical studies for the privileged. This was an expansive time, not only in the growing number of institutions but also in the variety of courses offered. Liberal arts colleges added science schools and practical subjects like geography and commerce.

Special-purpose institutions such as West Point and Rensselaer Polytechnic opened their doors. North Carolina, Georgia, Tennessee, and South Carolina, the first state universities, enrolled students from a variety of economic backgrounds and offered some courses geared toward professional training. Private colleges like Williams, Bowdoin, and Union (New York) were founded to reach beyond the upper classes and admit the sons of farmers and merchants.

The first half of the nineteenth century was a time of national ambition and growth. Religious denominations used colleges as missions to ensure that Christian virtues went west with the people. Easterners re-created their small religion-oriented colleges on the frontier. A visitor to Oberlin, Carleton, Grinnell, or Beloit could very well think he was in a New England college town. The South gave rise to the first state universities. North Carolina opened in 1795, followed by Georgia, Tennessee, and, in 1825, Thomas Jefferson's University of Virginia, the nation's first college structured along the lines of a university. Public institutions also opened in the Midwest. The Northwest Ordinance of 1787 set aside land to be used for education. Ohio University and Indiana, among other colleges, were founded as a result.

The United States became a land of colleges. In the 1830s,

By the 1830s there were thirty-seven colleges in Ohio alone.

---

while England had only four universities and a population of

23 million, Ohio alone could count thirty-seven colleges and a population of 3 million. Although as many as 500 of the new country's colleges did not last, the survivors numbered about 200 by the time of the Civil War.

But providing higher education meant more than merely building colleges. The courses had to be of value to students. The early 1800s saw the beginnings of change in the traditional curriculum. College education started to become more practical. This meant that a focus on the past—classical languages and history—now combined with a study of the present—science, English, commerce, and geography. Union College and New York University were pioneers in offering students a choice between the old and the new. Union was the first liberal arts college to offer a scientific course. NYU gave its students a choice between enrolling full-time for a classical curriculum or taking career-related subjects part-time. Michigan State gave instruction in agriculture and mechanical arts, providing the model for the land-grant colleges created by Justin Morrill in 1862. Letter grades ranging from A to F replaced less formal evaluations. The eighteenth-century practice of weighing academic performance and moral character equally in assigning grades all but disappeared.

Change, however, came slowly to American higher education. The practical curriculum often was viewed as less prestigious, and many students preferred the status conferred by enrollment in traditional courses. Although the first steps in creating a modern curriculum were taken early in the century, real change would not occur until after the Civil War.

The faculty continued to struggle over its economic status. In the trade-off between keeping tuition low and raising professors' salaries, the faculty lost. Tuition had to be kept low because students were scarce. The college president who had been a jack-of-all-trades in the 1700s began to distance himself from the faculty and became more a representative of the college's governing board.

College libraries started to build their collections and for the first time contained more books than student literary societies had. For example, it wasn't until 1850 that Bowdoin's library holdings surpassed the 5,000 volumes held by the college's debating clubs.

The students of this period attempted to free themselves from the strict moral and religious discipline that was typical of the Colonial colleges. They began to rebel against the 3 hours a day of chapel services. By 1850, evening prayers and the second Sunday service were on the way out, and there was talk of making morning prayers voluntary.

The literary societies of the Colonial period began to give way to Greek-letter fraternities.

Greek-letter fraternities originated at Union College in 1825.

The first three fraternities were started at Union College, beginning in 1825. After an initially cool reception, the Greek societies took root and spread to other colleges. Fraternities offered an escape from the dreariness of college life. In spite of the accusations made by their detractors, fraternities did not cause gambling, drinking, and dating; they merely brought them together in one place.

With their elders concentrating on the soul, students wanted to exercise their bodies. Gymnastics came over from Germany in the 1850s. The first intercollegiate sports—boat races and baseball—began during this era. Departments of physical education, responsible for the health of all undergraduates, made their first appearance.

Some of the earliest campus rebellions protested the quality of the meals served in the dining halls. Some complaints, for example those about rotten butter or worms in the biscuits, were justified. Others, like an outburst over the lack of tea service, were ill-tempered. Either way, the quality of the food gradually improved. But as long as students take their meals in college dining halls, what they eat will remain an issue.

It was now possible to distinguish between state and church colleges. States started to direct their spending toward public universities, causing denominational colleges to turn to individual donors. Union College (New York) was very successful at fund-raising and by the time of the Civil War had acquired the largest endowment of any college.

1777–1860

1779	William and Mary establishes the first honor system.	John Paul Jones, on the sinking *Bonhomme Richard,* replies to the British, "Sir, I have not yet begun to fight."
1780	Transylvania, the first college west of the Alleghenies, opens.	Benedict Arnold offers to exchange West Point for money and a commission in the British army.

continued

1781	William and Mary starts the first law school.	The siege of Yorktown ends with the surrender of British General Cornwallis.
1783	The Continental Congress meets at Nassau Hall, the main academic building at Princeton.	Noah Webster publishes *The American Spelling Book.*
1785	A charter is granted to the University of Georgia as the first state institution.	Ben Franklin invents bifocals.
1787	The Northwest Ordinance sets aside land for colleges.	The Constitutional Convention opens in Philadelphia.
1789	Georgetown, in Washington, D.C., opens as the first Catholic college.	George Washington moves into the presidential home in New York City.
1795	North Carolina, the first public college, opens.	Daniel Boone creates the Wilderness Road.
1802	West Point is the first college to offer specialized training.	The first hotel in America, the Union in Saratoga, New York, opens.
1804	Ohio University in Athens is founded with a federal land grant.	Alexander Hamilton is killed in a duel with Aaron Burr.
1816	Architect Benjamin Latrobe lays out a plan for a National University to be located in the District of Columbia on the present site of the Washington Monument.	The federal government's debt totals $127-million, about $15 per person.
1818	Saint Louis University is the first college west of the Mississippi.	Illinois is admitted as the twenty-first state.
1819	Thomas Jefferson founds the University of Virginia. With eight separate colleges, UVA is the first to be structured along university lines.	Spain cedes Florida to the United States for $5-million.
1824	Rensselaer Polytechnic Institute opens as the first technical school.	Mexico designates Texas as one of its provinces.
1825	The first fraternity, Kappa Alpha, starts at Union (New York).	The Erie Canal opens.
1826	The first black college graduate is Edward Jones from Amherst.	Both Thomas Jefferson and John Adams die on July 4, 2 hours apart.

continued

1833	Oberlin opens. In 1837 it will become the first college to admit women.	Samuel Colt invents the six-shooter.
1836	Wesleyan Female College of Georgia becomes the first women's college in name.	General Santa Ana storms the Alamo, killing 182 Texans.
1842	Willamette of Salem, Oregon, becomes the first college organized on the West Coast.	Connecticut establishes the first public secondary school system.
1847	City College of New York opens as a free municipal university. Students will pay no charges until 1947.	The U.S. Post Office issues its first stamp.
1851	Cooper Union in New York City is the first college to have a charter prohibiting discrimination because of race, religion, or color.	The *New York Times* begins publication, selling for 1 cent a copy.
1852	The first intercollegiate sports event: a crew race between Harvard and Yale.	*Uncle Tom's Cabin* by Harriet Beecher Stowe is published.
1854	Ashmun Institute (later Lincoln) in Chester, Pennsylvania, is chartered as the first college for blacks.	Commodore Matthew Perry opens Japan to the West.
1855	Elmira College for Women is subject to the same New York State Regents' review as the men's colleges. Michigan State is founded as the first agricultural college.	"Bleeding Kansas." Pro- and anti-slavery forces fight over the territory.
1856	Iowa State is the first public college to admit women.	Representative Brooks of South Carolina nearly beats Senator Sumner of Massachusetts to death on the Senate floor.
1857	President Henry Tappan of Michigan proposes the first graduate degree program. His board of regents is not supportive, and he is dismissed.	First baseball convention sets the length of the game at nine innings.

Civil War to World War I, 1861–1916: Growth and Diversity

The half century between the Civil War and World War I was the most important period in the history of American higher education. The number of colleges increased tenfold, the Morrill Act democratized college education, the American university was born, intercollegiate athletics and extracurricular activities took hold, higher education for women made great strides, philanthropists gave millions to colleges, and religious influence waned.

The nation had 9 colleges prior to the Revolution and nearly 200 entering the Civil War. By 1917 there were about 2,000. The only part of the country that didn't produce a great many new institutions or elevate the status of older colleges was the South. After taking an early leadership role in organizing public colleges, it was dealt a crushing blow by the Civil War. It would be well into the twentieth century before the South would rise again educationally.

In the more than 200 years between Harvard's founding in 1636 and the mid-1800s, the nation's colleges had taken a few hesitant steps toward offering education on a more democratic basis. Then came the Morrill Act of 1862, the most significant piece of legislation in the history

---

The Morrill Act of 1862 was the most significant piece of legislation in the history of American higher education.

---

of American higher education, which opened college doors to the common man. The seventy-two land-grant colleges that were created under its provisions became the backbone of the nation's college system. The focus of the curriculum shifted from the ancient past to the relevant present. Cornell, with its special characteristics—coeducation, the absence of church control, and the merging of classics and humanities with agriculture and mechanical arts—was considered the model land-grant college. The Morrill Act was the culminating step in the broadening of college opportunity that started in the 1750s, moved forward after the Revolution, and gained acceptance under Jacksonian democracy.

Besides reaching out to educate more people, colleges reached upward to add a new level of education. This period saw the real beginning of the American university. While liberal arts colleges concentrated on teaching, universities, with their graduate schools, added research to instruction. Johns

Johns Hopkins and Chicago were the nation's first true universities.

Hopkins, modeled after the German university, and Chicago, overflowing with new ideas nurtured by John D. Rockefeller's financial support, were the nation's first true universities.

Jefferson's original idea for the University of Virginia, an American state university, came to pass at major public institutions like Michigan, Wisconsin, and Minnesota, which had both centralized structure and commitment to the educational needs of an entire state. Because most parts of the country lacked public schools, the land-grant colleges initially offered both secondary and higher education. For example, in 1861, when the University of Washington opened, only one of its first thirty students took college-level courses. By the mid-1880s, high schools had advanced to the point where colleges could, finally, become institutions of higher education.

This was also the period that saw the growth of big-time athletics. After Princeton and Rutgers played the first game in 1869, football in particular caught the public's fancy. By World War I, large and enthusiastic crowds were common, and the presidents of colleges like Wisconsin, Chicago, and Stanford spoke about how important the success of their football teams was to the reputation of their universities.

All kinds of publications appeared on campuses—literary journals, newspapers, and humor magazines. By the twentieth century the student newspaper had assumed the ascendant position. Clubs that catered to every possible interest—singing, drama, debate, and many others—were formed. Fraternities entered a period of growth, and in the late 1800s the first sororities were established. As time went on, fraternities and sororities began to provide rooms for their members, fundamentally changing the nature of residential colleges.

Religious dominance continued to lessen. While virtually every pre–Civil War college had mandatory chapel attendance, by 1913 only half of all colleges had such a requirement.

Vassar, Smith, and Wellesley led the way in establishing women's colleges of high quality.

The idea of coeducation was born prior to 1861, when girls' academies added college-level courses. But real change in women's education came after the Civil War. By 1917, except for a few hundred all-male colleges, women had gained equal rights of access. But acquiring equal educational rights was a different matter. Women were channeled into academic fields like teaching and social work that were judged appropriate for their gender. Vassar, in 1865, followed by Smith and Wellesley a decade later, led in establishing women's colleges of high quality. Cornell provided the model for coed colleges.

Educational opportunities for blacks improved even more slowly than those for women. Two notable black colleges, Howard and Fisk, were founded, and the second Morrill Act provided for black land-grant institutions. Black colleges, following the ideas of Booker T. Washington, concentrated on vocational and agrarian education. As the twentieth century opened, relatively few black students were pursuing liberal arts or scientific courses at either black or predominantly white colleges.

It was after the Civil War that Harvard, under the leadership of President Charles Eliot, introduced the elective system. Academic departments were organized and with them major fields of study. The revolution in science continued. Land-grant colleges taught science and engineering in their divisions of mechanical arts. Scientific institutes like Massachusetts Institute of Technology, Caltech, and Carnegie Tech and the Mellon Institute (later to become Carnegie Mellon) were founded. Liberal arts colleges developed

scientific schools so their students could take technical courses as well.

The status and economic position of faculty members improved. Colleges began to compete for outstanding teachers. As a result, salaries and working conditions improved, and academic tenure was introduced. Research universities like Chicago and Johns Hopkins made faculty quality their number one priority.

Both public and private colleges moved toward a more secure financial base. The proceeds from the sale of federal lands and state appropriations provided capital for land-grant colleges. Private colleges asked their alumni for support and courted the wealthy and famous. The University of Chicago received $35-million from John Rockefeller. In recognition of their sizable contributions, philanthropists like Ezra Cornell, William Marsh Rice, and Leland Stanford had colleges named in their honor.

As America moved into the twentieth century, colleges no longer were places that merely taught classical subjects and polished social graces for future clergymen and public servants. By 1910, only one third of all undergraduates were enrolled in liberal arts courses; the other two thirds were taking subjects geared to vocations. Students devoted considerable energy to extracurricular activities. They pledged fraternities and sororities, wrote for newspapers and magazines, joined clubs, and participated in athletics.

By World War I, the basic structure of the American college system had been established. While the next seventy years would see some additional innovation, it would be a period devoted primarily to the strengthening of the higher education fabric that had already been created.

1861–1916

1861	Brewer Matthew Vassar gives $1-million to found a women's college. Yale establishes the first earned doctoral degree.	Confederates fire on Union forces at Fort Sumter, South Carolina.
1862	Congressman Justin Morrill's proposal for land-grant colleges is signed into law by Abraham Lincoln.	Two armored warships, the *Monitor* and the *Merrimack*, fight to a draw off Hampton Roads, Virginia.
1868	Cornell opens as both a public and a private college. In its breadth of programs and service role, it is a model for the American state university.	The Senate fails by one vote to remove President Andrew Johnson from office.
1869	Harvard permits its students to elect courses from among a number of options.	The transcontinental railroad is completed at Promontory, Utah. Chewing gum is invented.
1870	Michigan State admits graduates of public high schools.	DNA (then called nuclein) is discovered. John D. Rockefeller founds the Standard Oil Company.
1876	Johns Hopkins opens. Primarily a center for graduate research and advanced study leading to a doctorate, it later will offer undergraduate programs and become the model research university.	Mark Twain's *The Adventures of Tom Sawyer* is published.
1878	Alcorn A&M becomes the first land-grant college for blacks.	The District of Columbia receives a constitution, but its residents are not permitted to vote in national elections.

continued

1881	The Wharton School, the nation's first business school, starts at Penn.	President Garfield is shot by Charles Guiteau, a disgruntled office seeker.
1884	Mississippi State College for Women, the first female public institution, opens.	Lewis Waterman invents the fountain pen.
1886	Newcomb becomes the first coordinate college when it associates with Tulane.	Grover Cleveland, 49, a bachelor when elected president, marries 21-year-old Frances Folsom.
1886	Harvard is the first college to do away with required chapel.	Coca-Cola is served at Jacob's Pharmacy in Atlanta, Georgia.
1890	Second Morrill Act, providing for black A&M colleges, is passed.	William Kemmler is the first man to die in the electric chair.
1892	The University of Chicago opens with a curriculum and academic departments similar to those of today's universities.	James Corbett knocks out John L. Sullivan for the heavyweight boxing championship.
1896	In *Plessy* v. *Ferguson*, the Supreme Court upholds segregated education.	Binney and Smith introduce crayons.
1901	College Board is founded; SAT is developed.	Theodore Roosevelt assumes the presidency after William McKinley is assassinated.
1904	First Rhodes Scholars named.	Edwin Porter's *The Great Train Robbery,* the first U.S. film, is released.
1905	President Theodore Roosevelt calls a White House conference in an attempt to reduce violence in college football.	The Industrial Workers of the World union is formed in Chicago.
1910	The National Collegiate Athletic Association is formed.	Halley's comet appears, its first visit since 1759. It will not be visible again until February 9, 1986.
1915	The American Association of University Professors is founded.	The first taxicab appears in New York City. The fare is 5 cents.

World War I to the Present, 1917–1988: Strengthening and Expanding

This period marked the continuation of trends established in the previous sixty years. The American goal of making higher education generally available was carried even further.

With the federal government bringing its legislative and financial weight to bear, women and members of minority groups made great advances toward educational equality. Community colleges came on the scene, offering a classroom seat and the opportunity for an associate degree to every high school graduate.

The idea of education as a complete experience, involving both classroom and extracurricular activities, became the norm. Athletics, both recreational and intercollegiate, grew rapidly. Clubs and organizations of all kinds flourished. But student involvement would not be limited to on-campus issues. As it turned out, student concern with external events resulted in a protest movement that was more extensive and divisive than anything that had gone before.

The period began with innovations in curriculum:

Swarthmore started an honors program, Reed introduced independent study, St. John's of Maryland embarked on its famous "Great Books" program, and survey courses appeared, most notably Columbia's Introduction to Contemporary Civilization.

Other colleges offered alternative forms of education. Sarah Lawrence in 1928 and Bennington a few years later broke from tradition by paying less attention to majors and grades and placing more emphasis on academic programs adapted to the needs of the individual. Other innovations, such as student-designed courses, new academic calendars, and interdisciplinary programs of study, soon followed.

The 1930s saw the United States in a deep economic depression. Colleges were concerned with keeping their enrollments up and their costs down. Yet even in a time of financial hardship, college attendance gradually increased. Apparently, Americans felt that education was the way to beat the Depression.

Full-time attendance dropped significantly as the young men went off to World War II. Most colleges were able to avoid hard times, however, as the government turned to them for officer training programs and war-related research.

The conclusion of World War II marked the end of nearly

twenty years of stagnation in higher education. The time was ripe for the democratic tide that had shaped so much of American higher education in the previous century to sweep across the country once more.

The Servicemen's Readjustment Act, commonly known as the G.I. bill, was signed

---

Beginning with the G.I. bill, federal aid to students increased dramatically in the post-WW II era.

---

by President Roosevelt on June 22, 1944. Second in importance only to the Morrill Act, the G.I. bill encouraged veterans to attend college by providing money for educational costs and living expenses. Existing colleges expanded and new colleges were formed to handle the veterans' demand for education. With the G.I. bill paving the way, federal student aid grew enormously. In the years after World War II, the federal government became the major source of money for students, its expenditure reaching $10-billion a year by 1988.

Besides the student aid dollars that flowed in, universities increasingly relied on federal research grants to pay for laboratories, equipment, and faculty salaries. The success of campus-based research projects during World War II convinced the federal government that it should direct its research money to colleges rather than create its own labs.

Assisted greatly by the intervention of the federal government, discrimination against women and minorities all but disappeared. The key pieces of federal legislation were the Civil Rights Act of 1964, which forbade discrimination in the use of public facilities, and Title IX, which prohibited sexual discrimination.

In the late 1960s and the early 1970s, student demonstrations were a dominant issue in higher education. Starting at Berkeley in 1964 as a protest against restrictions placed on political action groups, student concern about civil rights was soon combined with opposition to the Vietnam War. The result was a nationwide campus protest movement unparalleled in participation, disobedience, and—near the end—violence.

Extracurricular activities grew in importance throughout this time. After falling from favor in the Vietnam era, fraternities and sororities regained their popularity. Clubs of every imaginable variety were created. Whether students

wanted to learn karate, master ballooning, sing with a madrigal group, or campaign against nuclear war, there was an appropriate organization on campus.

Intercollegiate athletics became both more elitist and more broadly based. Top college football and basketball players shared the sports spotlight with professional athletes, and successful teams earned millions of dollars for their colleges. At the same time, women joined men on college playing fields. The NCAA expanded its sponsorship of athletic teams and organized championships in twenty men's and fourteen women's sports. Increased emphasis on athletics was not limited to intercollegiate teams—club sports and intramurals gained a widespread and enthusiastic following.

Community colleges were formed to complete the third leg of the American higher education system, along with liberal arts colleges and comprehensive universities.

The number of two-year colleges has increased sixfold in the last fifty years.

Before World War II there were only 200 two-year colleges, and they enrolled fewer than 10 percent of the undergraduates. A half century later, nearly 40 percent of all students were attending the nation's 1,200 community colleges.

As a result, today's college-bound students have a variety of options in America's extensive higher education system unmatched in any other country. College students can live at home and commute to a local two-year college; travel to another part of the country to a residential liberal arts college; or attend the state university, which offers a wide variety of undergraduate and graduate schools. They can pursue their educational objectives either as full-time students or by taking classes in the evening or on weekends.

With the 1980s drawing to a close, students once again are looking inward, toward their own campuses and their own futures. The pendulum has swung from the radicalism of the sixties to the conservatism of the eighties. As students have been for most of the 350 years of American higher education, the current generation is primarily concerned with improving its station in life by going to college.

Colleges themselves are increasingly organized like diversified businesses. Today the typical college is much more than a place where a professor imparts knowledge to a student. Colleges are hotels, restaurants, cultural and entertainment centers, and athletic facilities all rolled into one. Colleges operate museums, computer centers, publishing companies, and major research laboratories. Budgets run into the hundreds of millions of dollars. Colleges have marketing departments (called admissions) that sell their product to prospective consumers. Today American colleges are in a very competitive business, the business of education.

1917–1988

1917	Columbia announces the first Pulitzer Prizes.	The United States declares war on Germany.
1919	Columbia offers the first general education course.	Daily airmail service is established between New York and Chicago.
1920	Union (New York) goes on the air with the first licensed college radio station.	Tennessee ratifies the Nineteenth Amendment; women receive the right to vote.
1922	Swarthmore initiates an honors curriculum.	
1925	Trinity College of North Carolina changes its name to Duke in return for the income from a $40-million trust fund established by tobacco millionaire James B. Duke.	The Lincoln Memorial is dedicated. The National Spelling Bee is initiated by the *Louisville Courier- Journal*.
1928	Sarah Lawrence is founded as an alternative to the traditional academic program.	Robert Goddard launches the first liquid-fuel rocket.
1934	Olivet College in Michigan abolishes all credits and grades. Students need only reside on campus for three years and pass a general exam to graduate.	Wallace Carothers of Du Pont labs invents "polymer 66," later known as nylon.
1935	The New Deal's National Youth Administration is the first federal agency to give money to college students.	Huey Long, the populist governor of Louisiana, is assassinated in Baton Rouge.
1939	Boston College student Lothrop Withington Jr. begins the fad of goldfish swallowing.	Franklin D. Roosevelt becomes the first U.S. president to appear on television.

continued

1944	The Servicemen's Readjustment Act (G.I. bill) is signed by President Roosevelt.	D day. Allied troops land on Normandy beaches.
1950	Elements 97 and 98, berkelium and californium, are discovered at the Cal Berkeley cyclotron.	Minimum wage of 75 cents an hour goes into effect.
1954	The Supreme Court ruling in *Brown* v. *Board of Education* mandates the integration of colleges.	Polio vaccine and the contraceptive pill are introduced.
1955	The last of the military schools, the Air Force Academy, opens in Colorado Springs.	Bill Haley's "Rock Around the Clock" begins the rock and roll craze.
1956	The first black student enrolls at the University of Alabama. She is suspended after three days of near riots.	The last Civil War veteran, Albert Woolson, dies at age 109.
1960	Four black students from North Carolina A&T sit in at a Woolworth lunch counter in Greensboro to protest whites-only policy.	John Fitzgerald Kennedy is elected president.
1961	SDS, Students for a Democratic Society, is founded at the University of Michigan.	Fifteen hundred Cuban refugees land at the Bay of Pigs. All are killed or captured within three days.
1962	James Meredith begins classes at the University of Mississippi as federal troops hold back rioters.	Lt. Col. John Glenn orbits the Earth three times in the space capsule Friendship 7.
1964	The Civil Rights Act barring discrimination passed by Congress. The free speech movement begins at Berkeley.	U.S. warplanes bomb North Vietnam in response to attack on Navy destroyers in the Gulf of Tonkin.
1969	Oberlin opens the first coed dorm. After a 36-hour sit-in at Cornell, black students emerge from the student union armed with shotguns and other weapons.	The Apollo II mission: astronauts Neil Armstrong and Edwin Aldrin walk on the moon while Michael Collins orbits overhead.
1970	Students killed at Kent State and Jackson State; 448 colleges close.	The CIA attempts to prevent the election of Marxist Salvador Allende in Chile.

continued

1972	Title IX of the Higher Education Act prohibits sexual discrimination. One of its first effects is the expansion of women's athletics.	Police arrest four men in an attempted burglary at the Democratic National Headquarters at the Watergate complex in Washington, D.C.
1978	The Bakke decision: the Supreme Court supports the use of racial considerations in college admissions decisions.	President Carter authorizes a $1.6-billion loan to New York City to prevent bankruptcy.
1979	The U.S. Department of Education is created.	A nuclear accident occurs at the Three Mile Island reactor near Harrisburg, Pennsylvania.
1980	Average SAT scores rise after a seventeen-year decline.	The FBI's Abscam investigative operation uncovers illegal acts committed by thirty-one public officials.
1986	University of Georgia English professor Jan Kemp is awarded $2.5-million because she was fired after protesting favoritism toward student athletes.	The 100th birthday of the Statue of Liberty is celebrated in a four-day extravaganza.
1988	Stanford revises its Western culture course, replacing some classics with more work by women and minorities.	The U.S. experiences its worst drought of the century; farm prices surge.

The Development of an American University

Early colleges did not sprout fully grown from the American soil. They started slowly, usually as secondary schools (called seminaries or academies), later adding college-age students and college-level courses. In due time academic departments were expanded, graduate schools formed, and the faculty charged with conducting research as well as teaching. Once the academic side of the house was in order, administrators turned their attention to organizing collegiate athletics, student activities, alumni associations, and fund-raising campaigns.

continued

The growth of Indiana University is a good example of this historical pattern:

1816 The Indiana Constitution provides for a general system of education from high school to college.
1824 Indiana Seminary opens with one professor and ten students. It includes a preparatory department to teach high school courses.
1828 Indiana Seminary renamed Indiana College.
1838 Indiana College renamed Indiana University.
1842 Law school opens.
1854 The original college building is destroyed by fire.
1867 Indiana admits women. Student newspaper published. Baseball team plays first game.
1882 First Ph.D. degree granted.
1886 Men's football team started.
1890 Preparatory department abolished.
1891 Department of Physical Training for both men and women established.
1903 School of medicine established.
1906 Student center constructed from private subscriptions.
1913 Alumni association formed.
1917 ROTC established.
1920 Business school opens.
1933 South Bend extension center established.
1941 Indiana cyclotron becomes operational.
1949 Major expansion of campus housing takes place.
1963 Aerospace research center is started with NASA funding.
1968 University's 150th birthday fund drive announced.
1971 Intercollegiate athletics begin for women.
1973 Black culture center established.
1974 Administration of Indiana system reorganized to be more efficient.

Student Life in the Early Days

TYPICAL DAILY SCHEDULE

The following is an excerpt from the Plan of Education for Philadelphia College in 1756. The schedule is for the third term of the second year.

6:00 a.m. Morning Prayers
7:00 a.m. Breakfast
8:00 a.m. Lecture I   Moral Philosophy:
                               Fordyce's *Compendium*

Notes: Disputation continued. Fordyce well understood will be an excellent introduction to the larger ethic writers.

10:00 a.m. Lecture II   Natural Philosophy:
                               Rowning's *Properties of Body and Mechanic Powers*

continued

Notes: Declamation continued. Rowning as a general system may be supplied by larger works recommended for private study.

12:00 noon Lunch
  1:00 p.m. Lecture III   Classical and Rhetorical Studies:
                                Horace's *Art of Poetry,* Aristotle, Quintilian

Notes: During the application of the rules to these famous orations, imitations of them are to be attempted on the models of perfect eloquence.

5:00 p.m. Free Time
6:00 p.m. Dinner
7:00 p.m. Evening Prayers
8:00 p.m. Private Hours   Miscellaneous Studies:
                                Helsham's *Lectures,* Newton's *Philosophy,*
                                Cote's *Hydrostatics*

Notes: Holy Bible: To be read daily from the beginning to supply deficiences of the whole.

10:00 p.m. Lights Out

RULES OF STUDENT CONDUCT AND BEHAVIOR

These come from the University of Pennsylvania in 1801.

1. None of the students or scholars, belonging to this seminary, shall make use of any indecent or immoral language: whether it consist in immodest expressions; in cursing and swearing; or in exclamations which introduce the name of God, without reverence, and without necessity.

2. None of them shall, without a good and sufficient reason, be absent from school, or late in his attendance; more particularly at the time of prayers, and of the reading of the Holy Scriptures.

3. Within the walls of the building, none of them shall appear with his hat on, in presence of any of the Professors or Tutors; or, in any place, fail to treat them with all the respect which the laws of good breeding require.

4. The students of the Philosophical classes shall, each of them in succession, deliver an oration every morning in the Hall, immediately after prayers; the succession to begin with the senior class; and, in each of the two classes, to proceed in alphabetical order.

5. And if any student of the Philosophical classes, not prevented by sickness or other unavoidable necessity, shall twice successively neglect to appear in his turn, and pronounce his oration, as above directed; he shall be considered as guilty of a willful disobedience to the laws of the institution; and shall be suspended.

DRESS RULES

In the 1822–23 academic year, Harvard published these standards of dress: "The dress of the undergraduates shall be as follows: the coat of black, single-breasted, with a rolling cape square at the end, and with pocket flaps; waist reaching to the natural waist, with lapels of the same length; skirts reaching to the bend of the knee; three crows-feet, made of black silk cord, on the lower part of the sleeve of a Senior, two on that of a Junior, and one on that of a Sophomore."

The Education of Women

In 1837 Oberlin became the first U.S. college to admit women. Iowa State, in 1856, was the first coeducational public institution.

Even while proceeding with its bold experiment, Oberlin took elaborate measures to keep men and women apart. When members of opposite sexes attended classes together, they were separated by a wide central aisle. The library remained segregated until the 1890s, with different hours of operation for men and women. The chapel had separate seating until 1934.

Like Oberlin, other colleges had special rules pertaining to the presence of coeds on their campuses. For example:

Penn State (1891)
Men were required to receive special permission from the president and headmistress to meet with women socially. Women were forbidden to communicate out windows and through steampipes.

Stanford (1920s and 1930s)
Men were allowed to smoke, but there was a firm no-smoking rule for women. If a woman was discovered smoking, she was asked to leave the dormitory. For a second offense, she was required to withdraw. There was a dress code for women students. They were allowed to "wear bobbysox, or anklets, as far as the old Post Office, but stockings were obligatory beyond that point."

University of Washington (1896)
The catalog listed a number of different math courses with a note that young ladies could substitute music or art for these "male" subjects.

University of Arkansas (1872)
A rigid dress code was in effect which, among other things, stated: "Dresses of such fabrics as silks or satins will not be tolerated."

University of Florida (late 1800s)
The men wore uniforms and the women "plain dresses of blue,

trimmed with brass buttons, and a small Confederate cap on their heads."

South Carolina (1897)

A coed named Laura Bateman was elected president of the freshman class but was asked to resign because her sex made her unfit for the job.

The question of which was the first women's college is subject to debate. In the 1830s and 1840s there were a number of female academies that were more like finishing schools than colleges. A few of them, like Emma Willard and Mount Holyoke, offered some "higher education beyond reading, writing, embroidery, and French." The first women's college to be named as such was Wesleyan Female College of Georgia, founded in 1836. The first that offered courses on a par with male institutions was Elmira College for Women, which opened in 1855. The New York State Regents Board found that Elmira's curriculum "formed a justifiable basis for issuing the Bachelor's Degree."

It was Vassar, however, founded in 1865, that was the real pioneer of women's colleges. Thanks to Matthew Vassar's gift of $1-million and the leadership of President John Howard Raymond, Vassar set the standards for women's higher education. Since secondary schools did not offer women precollege courses, Vassar established its own preparatory department to bring its students up to speed. At the same time, Vassar worked with girls' high schools to raise their standards. It took a number of years, but eventually Vassar was able to admit women who had the same academic preparation as men. Following Vassar's example, Smith (1875), Wellesley (1875), and Bryn Mawr (1885) were founded during the next twenty years.

Even among these early leaders in female colleges, little thought was given to placing women on an equal educational footing with men. In 1870 Vassar's Raymond doubted if women had "the strength of brain" to be educated without destroying their feminine grace and delicacy. The "fact" that women were physically unable to receive the same education as men was widely accepted. For example, in 1873 Dr. Edward Clarke wrote that a woman could not be educated in the same way as a man and "retain uninjured health and a future secure from neuralgia, uterine disease, hysteria, and other derangements of the nervous system."

By 1900 the doors of many colleges, both coeducational and single-sex, were open to women. Increased access, however, did not mean equality of educational opportunity. It would be well into the twentieth century before numerous academic and social restrictions on women were lifted.

The Education of Blacks

In the 1820s a handful of New England colleges had one or two black students among their undergraduates. The first black graduate was Edward Jones of Amherst in June 1826. Eleven days later John Russwurm received his degree from Bowdoin. The first black woman graduate was Lucy Ann Stanton of Oberlin. On December 8, 1850, she received a Bachelor of Literature degree. In 1844 Lafayette became the first college to award a degree to a slave, David McDonogh. McDonogh had been sent north by his owner, John McDonogh of New Orleans, to be educated as a medical aide so he could accompany freed slaves sent to Liberia. But overall black graduates were few and far between. When the Civil War began there were only twenty-eight in the entire country.

As it was in coeducation, Oberlin was a pathfinder in making college available to blacks. In 1835, two years after it opened, Oberlin launched a policy of admitting students regardless of color. Oberlin's commitment to racial equality, initially encouraged by a strong antislavery feeling among its students, turned out to be financially profitable as well. The Tappan brothers, wealthy merchants from New York City, promised Oberlin a major gift if

By the end of the 1880s it was estimated that one third of the black graduates of predominately white colleges held Oberlin degrees.

it would admit blacks. By the end of the 1800s it was estimated that one third of the black graduates of predominantly white colleges held Oberlin degrees.

Prior to the Civil War the Institute for Colored Youth (later Cheyney) and Ashmun Institute (later Lincoln) opened in Pennyslvania, while Wilberforce University was founded in Ohio. Although they are generally regarded today as the first of the black colleges, none of the three originally offered an education beyond secondary school.

After the Civil War a number of northern church groups started colleges to educate freed slaves. Fisk in Nashville, Atlanta in Georgia, and Howard in Washington, D.C., were the most notable. Further expansion of black colleges had to wait until passage of the second Morrill Act in 1890, which made money available for "separate but equal" land-grant colleges for blacks. As a result, seventeen new black colleges were founded, joining another seventeen that had existed before 1890 but were included under the Morrill provisions.

While black colleges were becoming established, there was a gradual increase in the number of blacks attending predominantly white colleges. But progress in both areas was very slow. By 1900 it was estimated that there were only 2,500 black graduates in the entire country, along with 800 who were then in college. As the twentieth century progressed, enrollment of blacks increased steadily, reaching 90,000 by 1950, the eve of the abolition of legalized segregation. Although the percentage of black students attending black colleges has diminished greatly since World War II, until then 80 to 90 percent of all black graduates held degrees from black colleges.

In the late 1800s and early 1900s the debate went on about what form of college education was most appropriate for blacks, practical or general. The practical, or vocational, thrust was advocated by Samuel Chapman Armstrong of Hampton Institute and Booker T. Washington at Tuskegee. This academic program consisted of subjects like education, mechanics, and agriculture. On the other side, arguing for liberal arts, were W. E. B. Du Bois and his followers. Howard was one of the few black colleges to resist the Armstrong-Washington approach; it offered a broad-based curriculum from the very beginning.

It would take many years, but eventually Du Bois's educational philosophy gained acceptance. Today historically black colleges provide essentially the same courses as predominantly white institutions.

How Some Colleges Began

VIRGINIA

The University of Virginia was founded in 1819 by Thomas Jefferson as an academic demonstration of the democratic principles he saw in the new republic. Jefferson outlined the institution's purpose, designed its buildings, supervised construction (in his later years he did this through a telescope from his home at Monticello, a short distance from the campus), planned the curriculum, and recruited the first faculty. Never before or since has one man

been so involved in the founding of a college.

When UVA opened for classes in 1825, its curriculum was not restricted to training future teachers and preachers, but designed for leaders in commerce and public service as well.

Although other colleges (namely Penn and William and Mary) had university-like characteristics before Virginia opened, UVA is called the nation's first university because of its distinctive college system. Students could select a field of study in one of eight different schools—classics, modern languages, mathematics, natural philosophy, history, anatomy, moral philosophy, and law. Although a true elective system was still years away, within each school students were free to select courses and set their own pace of study. Virginia also broke new ground with its guidelines for faculty. There was considerable academic freedom; professors could select their own textbooks and teach controversial subjects without fear of reprisal.

MICHIGAN

The University of Michigan, based on a founding date of 1817 (as the Catholepistemiad of Michigania in Detroit), claims to be the first state-assisted college. At the time, the Catholepistemiad, whose name means "universal science," was more of a coordinating agency for secondary schools, although, starting in 1821, some college-level instruction was offered. The actual beginning of

Michigan as a university was when it moved from Detroit to Ann Arbor in 1837, the year Michigan became a state.

RADCLIFFE

Radcliffe College, an institution closely integrated with Harvard, never had a founder or a faculty of its own. Radcliffe started in 1879 as a nondegree program for women who lived in Cambridge and arranged for private tutoring with Harvard professors. In 1882 the informal setup was designated the Society for the Instruction of Collegiate Women. In 1894, when Harvard refused to absorb the society as an academic unit, it was incorporated as Radcliffe College.

BELOIT

Some colleges start out on shaky ground, but not Beloit College in Wisconsin. At first Beloit wasn't on any ground at all. It was founded in 1844 when seven men met in a stateroom aboard the steamer *Chesapeake* during a trip on Lake Erie. Because a majority of its founders, as well as its first president, were Yale graduates, Beloit was known as the "Yale of the West."

GRINNELL

If Horace Greeley had not said, "Go West, young man, go West," Grinnell College in Iowa might never have existed. The recipient of Greeley's famous advice was Congregational minister Josiah Bushnell Grinnell, who, as chairman of the Iowa legislative committee on education, was responsible for having tiny Iowa College of Davenport moved to the town of Grinnell in 1859 and changing its name to match the location. Grinnell was a main stop on the Underground Railroad in the years before the Civil War, serving as a temporary home for more than 1,000 slaves.

HOWARD

When its charter was drawn up in 1867, Howard patterned itself after the University of Michigan rather than after the typical black institute. Not only was the use of the name "university" significant, but the charter went on to specify that Howard would provide for the "education" rather than the "training" of students. A teachers' school was established first, but the trustees soon added departments of theology, law, medicine, and liberal arts. Howard's beginning as a university rather than a vocational institute is the main reason that today, more than a century after it opened, Howard is the only comprehensive university in the country that has a predominantly black constituency.

A sidelight on Howard's founding is that its charter was signed on March 2, 1867, by Andrew Johnson—a vehemently anti-Negro president—on the same day he vetoed the Reconstruction Act.

UCLA

UCLA, now the largest university in the U Cal system, was known as the "Southern Branch" of the University of California when it opened its doors in 1919. Its haughty northern colleagues at Berkeley thought it would never be more than a branch junior college and called it "the Twig."

NEW HAMPSHIRE

The state legislature organized the University of New Hampshire in 1866 under the provisions of the Morrill Act. The new institution did not have a home of its own, but was attached to Dartmouth College, New Hampshire's only institution of higher education at the time. For nearly thirty years Dartmouth provided faculty and the use of its library, classrooms, and laboratories to the fledgling agricultural college. In 1893, when a prosperous farmer from southern New Hampshire offered land and money, UNH moved to its present home in Durham.

WELLESLEY

Family misfortune played a major role in the beginning of Wellesley. Harry Durant, the son of Wellesley's founder, Henry Fowle Durant, died of diphtheria at age 8. The grief-stricken father left his career as a prosperous Boston lawyer and turned his attention to religion and education. The Durants established the college on 300 acres adjacent to their summer home, named Wellesley—land they had intended for young Harry's future estate.

CORNELL

Ezra Cornell and Andrew White were New York State senators in 1862 when Congress passed the Morrill Act. Each of them had a different idea about how New York should use the money it would receive from the sale of federal lands. Cornell was a farmer turned mechanic who lived in Ithaca. He came into great wealth when the telegraph lines he had built were formed into Western Union. Cornell believed in a new kind of university that would provide training in practical subjects for the children of laborers and farmers. In contrast, White was a gentleman scholar seeking to improve on the classical curriculum.

Rather than oppose each other, they decided to combine their educational philosophies into one institution. The college would be free of church influence and enroll all who qualified, regardless of sex, race, or family status. It would offer courses in agriculture and mechanics and, on an equal basis, courses in the classics, history, and literature. Within

either curriculum, students could select courses rather than have them prescribed. Built and operated along these lines, Cornell was a significant milestone in the development of American higher education, with a mixture of private and land-grant status, of traditional and modern curriculum, and of liberal arts and professional education.

NEW YORK UNIVERSITY

The first true urban university was New York University, which opened on October 1, 1832. Even at that time, New York City, with a population of 200,000, was the nation's largest city. It viewed itself as the "London of America" and, like large European cities, aspired to be home to a major university, one that would represent the spirit of the city: patriotic, business-oriented, nonsectarian, and democratic. Columbia was approached about adding useful subjects like modern languages, history, and natural science to its classical curriculum, but declined. Under the leadership of Albert Gallatin, former secretary of the treasury, a group was formed to found a "private university in the public service." When NYU opened, it offered something new in American education. Students could enroll in the full-time course that led to a diploma or pursue part-time study to learn job-related skills. Within the regular curriculum there was a further option. Students could master Greek and Latin as part of the classical course or take the English and scientific option.

DREW

Drew University in Madison, New Jersey, was founded in 1867 by Daniel Drew, a wealthy New York farmer. Drew made his fortune by buying cattle in upstate New York and driving them to the city. A clever businessman, Drew, rather than setting out water for the cattle as they made their journey, placed salt licks along the route. Just before nearing the market, Drew led his herd of thirsty cattle to water. The cattle drank profusely, increasing their weight a great deal before they were sold at "inflated" prices. The term "watered stock" originated with Drew's manipulations. Its connection with Wall Street came about a short time later when Drew, allied with Jay Gould and Jim Fiske, persuaded Cornelius Vanderbilt to pay $7-million for worthless Erie Railroad stock. Drew may have been the only major college benefactor to make his contribution in small bills.

U CAL DAVIS

The Davis campus of the University of California was founded in 1908 because California needed a school where young men could learn the practical aspects of dairy farming. The University of California at Berkeley bought the farm of Jerome Davis and established a branch of its agricultural college. From its start as literally a cow college, Davis has grown into a full-fledged member of the U Cal system, adding a college of letters and science, a graduate division, and schools of engineering, law, and medicine. To this day, however, UC Davis's agricultural roots are still evident. The Silo, built in 1908 as the world's most modern dairy barn, now houses a variety of student services and one of the largest recreational craft centers in the country.

ST. MARY'S (MARYLAND)

St. Mary's was a small two-year college located on the Chesapeake Bay when, in the late 1960s, St. Mary's County politicians appealed to the state legislature to approve its expansion to a four-year college. After some delicate political maneuvering, a compromise was suggested. If St. Mary's County officials would agree to give up the county's lucrative slot machines, the state would finance the conversion of the junior college to a full four-year institution. The agreement was struck, and today St. Mary's County, minus its one-armed bandits, is home to one of the better small public colleges in the East.

RICE

Perhaps the strangest story of all about the founding of a college was that of Rice Institute, now Rice University, in Houston, Texas. In 1839 William Marsh Rice, a merchant, moved his business from Massachusetts to Houston. After he had accumulated his fortune, Rice wrote a will that directed the bulk of his estate to go toward establishing a college.

But matters didn't go quite as Rice had planned. In 1891 an unscrupulous lawyer conspired with Rice's valet to chloroform the old man as he slept. After Rice's death, the attorney drew up a fake will that gave him control over Rice's estate.

Thanks to the diligence of Rice's friend and attorney, James A. Baker (the grandfather of former secretary of the treasury James A. Baker III), the scheme was exposed a short while later, but it took thirteen years for matters to be straightened out. Not until 1904 did the Rice trustees receive $4.6-million and begin construction of the science school Rice had envisioned.

In September 1912 Rice Institute opened with seventy-seven students. In accord with Rice's will, the institute was tuition-free, and it remained so until 1965. Even today the founder's desire to keep tuition as low as possible has been honored. Rice's 1987–88 tuition was $5,150, one of the lowest for a selective college.

An irony of the controversy over William Marsh Rice's will is that Howard Hughes, the reclusive billionaire whose will also was contested after his death in 1976, attended Rice in 1924.

3

HALLS OF LEARNING

GETTING INTO COLLEGE,
HONORS FOR HIGH SCHOOL SENIORS,
UNDERGRADUATE HONORS, STUDENT
ACCOMPLISHMENTS, FACULTY, MAJOR
AWARDS TO PROFESSORS, ACADEMIC
PROGRAMS

Getting into College

Higher education starts with a student choosing a college—except for a few hundred institutions that can afford the luxury of doing the choosing themselves. The difficulty of getting into college varies greatly—from institutions that practice open enrollment to those that select fewer than one in five applicants. Although only about 200 of 3,100 colleges accept fewer than 50 percent of their applicants, considerable national attention is paid to selective admission. Students who apply to these colleges are judged mainly on three academic characteristics—standardized tests, class rank, and admission essays.

STANDARDIZED TESTS

About one half of all U.S. colleges ask their applicants to take either the Scholastic Aptitude Test (SAT) or American College Testing Assessment (ACT). Colleges that don't use the tests for admission rely on them for counseling or placement. Regardless of how they are used, for many students, thinking about college and worrying about the SAT start at the same time.

In the annual ritual of sorting out some 1.6 million college-bound high school seniors among 3,100 institutions, the attention given to standardized tests, most notably the SAT, occupies a unique place in the American education system. Not only are SAT scores one of the factors that determine which students will be admitted, they also are used to award financial aid, to determine athletic eligibility, and to place students in college courses. How did these tests, the spoilers of an otherwise pleasant Saturday morning for millions of teenagers, come to occupy the position they have today?

The development of a single test to measure a student's ability to perform college-level work was a big step forward. Before the College Board was founded in 1901, each college had its own examination for admission. These tests covered different subjects and varied greatly in their level of difficulty. For example, Columbia's ancient geography exam asked the student to recite in order, beginning with Greece and going around the European continent, all the capes and rivers of Europe, giving both Latin and English names. Not only was it hard for a student to prepare for such tests, but two institutions might give their exams on the same date, forcing the applicant to make an early choice between colleges.

The move for one set of exams that would be acceptable to all colleges was led by President Nicholas Murray Butler of Columbia. After years of negotiations between secondary schools and colleges,

the first College Board test was given on June 17, 1901, to 973 candidates at sixty-seven test centers. Because they were set in their traditional ways of judging students' academic abilities, it took the majority of northeastern private colleges more than a decade to accept the SAT concept. For years many colleges continued to require their own tests along with the College Board exams. When Yale first adopted the SAT, it did so on the condition that the exams could be regraded by members of its own faculty.

After their slow and painful start, SATs are now taken annually by 1.8 million students who pay $20-million for the privilege. In addition about a million students take the ACT. The average combined math and verbal SAT score is 906; the average composite ACT score is 18.8. Student performance on the tests varies considerably by state. Which states do the best on these standardized admissions tests?

Mean SAT Scores of High School Seniors by State (1987)

Combined	Math and Verbal
1. New Hampshire	938
2. Oregon	928
3. Wisconsin*	926
4. Iowa*	922
5. Minnesota*	918
6. Maryland	914
Vermont	914
8. Connecticut	912
9. Delaware	910

COLLEGES WITH HIGH SAT SCORERS

For freshmen entering in 1986, these colleges enrolled the highest percentage of students with scores over 600.

	Percent over 600 Verbal		*Percent over 600 Math*
1. Deep Springs	100	1. Caltech	100
2. Harvard	80	Deep Springs	100
Yale	80	Harvey Mudd	100
4. Amherst	78	Webb	100
Williams	78	5. Cooper Union	99
6. Rice	76	MIT	99
7. Caltech	75	7. Carnegie Mellon	96
8. Stanford	74	Columbia (Engr)	96
9. Haverford	73	9. Rice	92
MIT	73	10. Stanford	91
Swarthmore	73		

Only two colleges have at least one third of their students scoring 700 or above on the verbal SAT. One is an illustrious four-year eastern college (Harvard) and one is a tiny little-known two-year western college (Deep Springs).

10. Massachusetts   909
*ACT scores converted to SAT equivalent.

CLASS RANK

Of freshmen entering in the fall of 1986, a number of colleges enrolled only the highest-ranking high school students.

	Percent in top 10 percent
1. Caltech	100
Deep Springs	100
U Cal Davis	100
4. Harvard	95
Harvey Mudd	95
U Cal Berkeley	95
7. Rice	91
Stanford	91
9. U Cal San Diego	90
U Cal Santa Barbara	90

Four University of California colleges appear on the list because their admission formula requires a student to rank in the top 12.5 percent of his or her class, except for a few spaces that are set aside for students with special qualifications.

Caltech has the most impressive record for enrolling students who rank number one in their class. About one third of the freshmen who entered Caltech in the fall of 1986 were high school valedictorians.

THE MOST SELECTIVE COLLEGES

For freshmen entering in 1986, these colleges admitted the lowest proportion of their applicants.

	Percent admitted
1. Curtis	9
2. Coast Guard Academy	10
Naval Academy	10
4. West Point	12
5. Air Force Academy	15
6. Merchant Marine Academy	16

ADMISSION ESSAYS

Next to taking the SAT, the most disconcerting part of applying to college is writing the admission essay. Fortunately for most high school seniors, the vast majority of colleges either have open enrollment or admit students on the basis of an SAT and class rank formula that doesn't include an essay. Colleges that do require essays ask the applicant to answer anywhere from one question to five or six. No matter how many questions are asked, admission offices seek the same information. What kind of values and accomplishments are important to the student and how well can he or she express them on paper? In the attempt to unlock the mind of an 18-year-old high school senior, essay questions come in four forms:

— Tell us about yourself.
— Tell us about something you like to do.
— Tell us why you want to go to our college.
— Tell us something about your intellect.

Here are examples of actual admission questions that fall into these categories.

— Which academic subject in school is most meaningful to you?
— How did you spend last summer?
— Tell us about a special interest, experience, achievement, or anything else you would like us to know about you.
— Given the authority to establish a holiday, what would you choose to commemorate? Briefly explain.
— You have been selected to spend an evening with any one person, living, historical, or fictional. Whom would you choose and why? What would you do that evening, what would you discuss, and what would you hope to learn from this unique opportunity?
— If you were asked to select an object that would represent our culture to a group of students living in the year 2988, what would you choose and why?
— If you were to describe yourself by a quotation, what would the quote be? Explain your answer.
— Early in the century, John Dewey, philosopher and educator, wrote, "It does not pay to tether one's thoughts to the post or use too short a rope." Do you agree or disagree?

The above questions come from a variety of selective colleges that seek well-rounded academic achievers. There is a different type of college, Ringling Brothers and Barnum & Bailey Clown College in Venice, Florida, that is looking for another kind of student. As might be expected, the Clown

College's essay questions take a different approach. For example:

— Do you get along with animals? With children?
— What does it take to make you mad?
— In one or two words describe how you enter a crowded room.

STUDENT RECRUITING

Years ago colleges used to sit back and let students come to them. Modern-day admission offices operate in a far different way. They are staffed with well-trained and highly motivated salespeople for their colleges. Mass mailings are sent to students whose names are acquired from search lists. Admission officers visit high schools and attend college nights. When potential applicants come to campuses they are greeted with tours, information sessions, and video presentations.

Some colleges have taken a cue from the advertising profession and employ well-known figures, either real or fictional, to attract potential applicants. For example, the Association of State Colleges and Universities uses Garfield the Cat in its promotional material, while Memphis State bills itself as the home of the 1987 Miss America, Kellye Cash.

ADMISSION TRYOUT

Hood College of Frederick, Maryland, has a unique admission procedure. During the fall Hood holds six morning seminars at which applicants get a hands-on introduction to college-level courses. After each seminar, the admission committee assesses a student's academic potential. If the result is satisfactory, the applicant receives an offer of admission later in the same day.

Honors for High School Seniors

NATIONAL MERIT SCHOLARS

Sponsored by the National Merit Corporation, businesses, and colleges, Merit Scholarships have been awarded yearly since 1958. The selection process begins with a Preliminary Scholastic Aptitude Test (PSAT) given during the fall of a student's junior year in high school. Based on PSAT scores, about 50,000 students are named Commended Students. Of this number 15,000 move along to become Semifinalists. After a review of high school records, about 14,000 Finalists emerge, and 6,000 of them ultimately receive scholarships. The typical scholarship is a one-year award for

continued

$2,000. Corporations and colleges may give larger scholarships and grant them for four years.

For 1983–87, the most National Merit Scholars enrolled in the following colleges:

	Total number of Scholars	Number sponsored by the college
1. Harvard	1,564	0
2. Texas	1,275	1,001
3. Rice	879	566
4. Yale	850	0
5. Princeton	823	0
6. Stanford	793	0
7. Texas A&M	716	530
8. MIT	606	0
9. Michigan State	574	431
10. Chicago	559	389

The first column shows the number of Merit Scholars who enrolled in the five-year period. The second column shows how many of these received their scholarships directly from a college that participates in the program. Harvard is the overall leader while Texas, largely on the strength of an extensive college-sponsored program, heads the public universities.

Looking at the number of Merit Scholars as a percentage of the freshman class, in 1987 Georgia Tech was first among public colleges and universities with 6 percent, while Harvard led the private list with 20 percent. Since the first Merit Scholar was named in 1958, Harvard has enrolled the most winners, while Michigan State and Texas lead among public universities.

NATIONAL ACHIEVEMENT SCHOLARS

This scholarship works the same way as the National Merit except that it is for black students. From 80,000 PSAT test takers, 1,200 are named Finalists and 700 receive scholarships. During four recent years, the following colleges have enrolled the most National Achievement Scholars:

	Total number of Scholars	Number sponsored by the college
1. Harvard	190	0
2. Stanford	125	0
Texas	125	52
4. Princeton	103	0
5. Georgia Tech	97	40
6. Yale	90	0
7. MIT	86	0
8. Michigan	64	48
9. Brown	63	0
10. Northwestern	61	42

WESTINGHOUSE SCIENCE TALENT SEARCH

Nearly as famous as the National Merit Scholarship program is the talent search sponsored by Westinghouse, known as the Nobel Prize for high school scientists. The purpose of this award is to discover and develop

---

Seventy percent of the Westinghouse winners have gone on to earn their Ph.D. or M.D.

---

scientific and engineering ability among high school seniors. The 1,300 entrants are judged first on the quality of an independent research project and then on test scores, grades, and an interview. Forty winners are chosen each year; they receive $140,000 in scholarships that range from $1,000 to $20,000.

The Science Talent Search is a very competitive program, and from among its 1,840 winners in forty-six years have come some of the United States' most outstanding scientists. An extraordinary 70 percent of the winners have gone on to earn Ph.D.'s or M.D.'s, and 55 percent are either college faculty members or physicians today. Westinghouse winners have also received five Nobel Prizes, two Fields Medals in mathematics, four MacArthur Fellowships, and twenty-four appointments to the National Academy of Sciences.

Through the 1987 competition the eleven colleges that have enrolled the most Westinghouse Science Talent Search winners are:

	Number of winners
1. Harvard	81
2. MIT	34
3. Princeton	28
Yale	28
5. Stanford	23
6. Caltech	15
Cornell	15
8. Washington (St. Louis)	8
9. Columbia	6
10. Penn	5
Rochester	5

Here is a sample of research projects submitted by the 1987 winners:

— Apolipoprotein A-I Metabolism in Humans with Familial Hypoalpha- lipoproteinemia Associated with Premature Coronary Artery Disease.
— Inca Megaliths Transport; Considerations in Manpower Requisition and Handling Techniques.
— Tilt Angles of Jovian Decametric Radiation.

KUDOS FOR KUOS

In January 1987 David Kuo was named a Westinghouse winner, and in April he accepted Harvard's offer of admission. In September 1987 David, class of 1991, joined brothers Mark, class of 1990, and John, class of 1989, at Harvard. Mark won the Talent Search in 1984 and John in 1985, the first time one family has produced three winners. The Kuos came to the United States from Taiwan in 1976 and have learned to speak English since their arrival.

Undergraduate Honors

There are a number of honors that students can achieve while they are undergraduates. The most notable awards are the Truman, Churchill, Marshall, and Rhodes scholarships and the Watson Fellowship.

HARRY S. TRUMAN SCHOLARSHIP

This award, normally given for two years, is for students entering their junior year in college. It is given to undergraduates who show outstanding potential for leadership in government or other public service. There are slightly more than 100 awards given each year, averaging 2 for each state, the District of Columbia, Puerto Rico, and the Trust Territories. The Truman Scholarship is worth a maximum of $6,500 annually. The colleges that have produced the most Truman recipients since the program began in 1977 are:

	Number of winners
1. Harvard	24
2. Yale	16
3. Stanford	14
4. Kansas State	10
Oberlin	10
Princeton	10
7. Chicago	9
8. Bowdoin	8
Michigan	8
Montana	8
Utah	8
Vanderbilt	8

When the number of Truman Scholars is adjusted for college size, Bowdoin has had the most winners, followed by Harvard and Oberlin, tied for second place.

Truman Scholarship winners do well in competition for the other major awards given two years later to graduating seniors. In the first ten years of the program's existence, Truman recipients went on to win sixteen Rhodes and twelve Marshall scholarships.

THOMAS J. WATSON FELLOWSHIP

The Watson Foundation (Thomas Watson was the founder of IBM) started its fellowship program in 1968. This award is limited to students from fifty colleges with enrollments under 2,800. Its purpose is to offer an honor similar to a Rhodes scholarship to students from smaller colleges. The Watson, however, has a different focus than the Rhodes. It is not given for a program of study at an English university, but for independent study anywhere in the world. A student's project must demonstrate commitment, significance, and imagination. Examples of winning projects are "Health Care Delivery to the Urban Poor" (Mexico), "Retooling the Steel Industry" (Japan), and "Effects of Acid Rain on the Fish Population" (Sweden). About seventy-five awards are made each year to college seniors. Each fellowship is worth $11,000. Colleges that have done well in the Watson competition during its nineteen-year history are:

	Number of winners
1. Wesleyan	46
2. Williams	45
3. Colorado	40
Pomona	40
5. Amherst	39
Oberlin	39
7. Davidson	36
Lawrence	36
Middlebury	36
Occidental	36
Swarthmore	36

CHURCHILL SCHOLARSHIP

This small program, started in 1961, chooses ten college seniors each year to do graduate work in the natural sciences, engineering, or mathematics at Churchill College of Cambridge University in England. The awards are usually for one year, although there is a special three-year grant that leads to a Ph.D. The scholarship covers tuition plus $2,500 for travel and living expenses.

Of the 250 Churchill awards given in the last twenty-five years, the leading colleges (in alphabetical order) are Brown, Caltech, Dartmouth, Harvard, MIT, Michigan, Michigan State, Princeton, Stanford, and Yale.

GEORGE C. MARSHALL SCHOLARSHIP

Established by the British government in 1953 to express its gratitude for the European Recovery Program (the Marshall Plan) after World War II, thirty scholarships are awarded annually to college seniors to undertake two years of study at any university in the United Kingdom. The award pays $15,000 per year. In selecting recipients, the Marshall committee weighs a student's academic record most heavily, but classroom work must be combined with good character and a variety of other activities and interests.

Through 1987, the colleges that have produced the most Marshall winners are:

	Number of winners
1. Harvard	141
2. Princeton	65
3. Yale	62
4. Stanford	25
5. U of California	22
6. Dartmouth	21
7. Brown	16
MIT	16
9. Bryn Mawr	15
Cornell	15

Of the 920 Marshall Scholars that have been named since 1954, many have gone on to make their marks in society.

1988 presidential candidate Bruce Babbitt is a former Marshall Scholar.

Among previous Marshall winners are former governor of Arizona and 1988 presidential candidate Bruce Babbitt; Ray Dolby, the inventor of the Dolby Sound System; and John Jay Iselin, president of the New

York PBS station and WNET-TV. Other winners include the presidents of Wellesley and Mount Holyoke, two recent recipients of MacArthur fellowships, a Pulitzer Prize–winning correspondent for the *New York Times,* and the United States Ambassador to Kuwait, who is assisted in his duties by his wife, also a former Marshall Scholar.

The thirty 1987 winners included twenty-three men and seven women from twenty-one different colleges. Harvard, with six scholars, was the leader, followed by Yale (three), Princeton (two), and Emory (two).

CECIL B. RHODES SCHOLARSHIP

This is the oldest and most prestigious award for undergraduates. The Rhodes Foundation was established in 1903 with £4,137,000 donated by Cecil Rhodes, a British colonial financier. The money from the trust finances thirty-two scholars from the United States (and others from abroad) each year to do graduate study at Oxford University in England. There have been a total of 2,468 winners in eighty-four years of Rhodes competition.

The selection process is the most rigorous of those for any prestigious scholarship. An applicant is asked to submit a résumé, a transcript, a 1,000-word essay, a photograph, and eight references. In addition there is a lengthy interview before a panel of former Rhodes recipients, first within the state and then at the regional level. Selection depends on academic and extracurricular achievements as well as highly moral character and a strong commitment to the welfare of society. Through 1987, colleges with the most Rhodes Scholars are:

	Number of winners		
1. Harvard	228	Reed	29
2. Yale	170	12. Air Force Academy	27
3. Princeton	160	North Carolina	27
4. West Point	61	Vanderbilt	27
5. Stanford	53	Williams	27
6. Dartmouth	52	16. Wisconsin	26
7. Virginia	39	17. Chicago	25
8. Brown	33	18. Oklahoma	24
9. Washington	31	19. Mississippi	23
10. Annapolis	29	Montana	23

Reed deserves special mention since it is the highest-ranking liberal arts college on the list and the size of its student body (1,100) is the smallest among the top twenty. If the colleges had been ranked on a per capita basis, Reed would stand fourth. Other small colleges that have fared well in the Rhodes competition are Williams, Sewanee, and Swarthmore.

continued

As might be expected of participants in a scholarship program that selects only a small fraction of the most outstanding college seniors, many Rhodes winners have gone on to successful careers. Among the more recognizable names are:

Letters

	College	Class	Field
Robert Penn Warren	Vanderbilt	1925	Poet
Daniel Boorstin	Harvard	1934	Historian, former Librarian of Congress

Television and film

Howard K. Smith	LSU	1937	TV newscaster
Kris Kristofferson	Pomona	1958	Movie actor

Government

James Fulbright	Arkansas	1925	Senator
Carl Albert	Oklahoma	1931	Senator
Byron "Whizzer" White	Colorado	1937	Supreme Court justice
Richard Lugar	Denison	1954	Senator
Paul Sarbanes	Princeton	1954	Senator
David Boren	Yale	1963	Senator
Larry Pressler	South Dakota	1964	Senator
Bill Bradley	Princeton	1965	Senator
William Clinton	Georgetown	1968	Governor
Tom McMillen	Maryland	1974	Congressman

Football All-Americans

Pete Dawkins	West Point	1958	
Pat Haden	USC	1974	
Thomas Neville	Yale	1971	

Bill Bradley and Tom McMillen also could have been listed in a sports category. Each was named an All-American in basketball and played professionally.

Like Boorstin, the new Librarian of Congress, James Billington, Princeton class of 1950, won a Rhodes scholarship as an undergraduate.

The 1987 Rhodes winners included eleven women, two blacks, and a Vietnamese refugee who attended the Air Force Academy. Hoang Nhu Tran, who fled Vietnam in 1975 with his family, was the first Vietnamese Rhodes Scholar. Tran majored in both biology and chemistry, had a 3.91 grade point average, and ranked second in his class. After he completed his studies at Oxford, Tran began a career as an Air Force flight surgeon.

One of the most remarkable Rhodes winners of recent years is Bonnie Lee St. John of National City, California, a Harvard graduate in the class of 1986. Bonnie, who is black, was an honor

continued

student and won three gold medals in skiing events at the 1983 Handicapped Olympics. Bonnie skis on one leg; she lost her other leg in a childhood accident.

Actually there is one college that is filled with Rhodes scholars— tiny Rhodes College of Memphis, Tennessee. Known as Southwestern at Memphis until 1984, Rhodes now has a distinguished name and is building an academic reputation to match.

TIME MAGAZINE COLLEGE ACHIEVEMENT AWARD

A straight-A student at Princeton majoring in international affairs is ranked as a top Olympic candidate in the heavyweight boxing division.

A Colorado College junior has written for scholarly journals on the causes of teenage suicide and is president of BACCHUS, an organization that promotes responsibility in the use of alcohol.

An applied physics major who attends Caltech, working on a NASA contract, recently designed a cargo transport to be used in support of space stations or manned bases on other planets.

These are 3 of the 20 students who were named the outstanding college juniors in the nation by *Time* magazine for 1986–87. In addition to the top 20, there were 80 other finalists, a total of 100 *Time*-designated "Leaders of Tomorrow."

The colleges that produced the most winners:

	Number of winners
1. Harvard	13
2. Dartmouth	6
Princeton	6
4. Barnard	4
Yale	4
6. Caltech	3
U Cal Berkeley	3

In addition, there were eleven colleges with two recipients each: the Air Force Academy, Annapolis, Claremont, Denison, Emory, Iowa, Morehouse, Nebraska, Northwestern, UCLA, and Wellesley.

KERR WRITING PRIZE

The Sophie Kerr Prize for outstanding writing, worth $30,000, is the largest undergraduate literary award in the United States. The award is not widely known because it is restricted to students enrolled at Washington College in Chestertown, Maryland. In keeping with one of its primary educational goals—to teach every student to write well— Washington College uses the interest from the $500,000 Sophie Kerr bequest to bring famous literary figures to campus and to sponsor the prize. The 1987 winner was Susan DePasquale, a senior from Towson, Maryland, who carried a double major in English and political science.

ACADEMIC HONORARY SOCIETIES

The first Phi Beta Kappa chapter was founded at William and Mary in 1776. Originally a social fraternity, it had all the characteristics of a secret society—ritual, an oath of fidelity, a grip, a motto, and a badge. By 1873 Phi Beta Kappa had changed from a fraternal club to an honorary society for students with academic distinction. Today it has about 200,000 living members.

Vassar opened the first Phi Beta Kappa chapter at a women's college in 1889.

Centre College of Danville, Kentucky, with an enrollment of 800, is the smallest institution with a Phi Beta Kappa chapter.

In 1886 Cornell was the first university to have a chapter of the equivalent of Phi Beta Kappa for scientists—Sigma Xi. Students with a strong academic record and an aptitude for scientific research are eligible for election. Today, Sigma Xi has approximately 175 chapters and 115,000 active members.

For engineers, the academic honor society is Tau Beta Pi, which began at Lehigh in 1885. Tau Beta Pi is about the size of Sigma Xi, with 125 chapters and 125,000 members.

ON MY HONOR

It is not uncommon for a college to have an honor system that governs the taking of examinations. Under such a code, students sign a pledge that they will not cheat and they will report classmates who do. In 1779, William and Mary established the first honor system of this type.

Phi Beta Kappa began at William and Mary in 1776.

The University of Virginia, in 1842, initiated the first honor code that regulated a number of different aspects of campus life. UVA's honor system was based on the concept of mutual trust that is assumed to exist among members of a university community. It went beyond merely regulating examinations and banned lying, cheating, and stealing among students. Today, almost 150 years later, Virginia is still governed by essentially the same honor code.

The twentieth century finds college honor codes alive and well. Agnes Scott of Decatur, Georgia, has one of the most extensive. Students are honor bound to obey all rules, both inside and outside the classroom. Although mailboxes are left open and dorm rooms are rarely locked, theft is almost nonexistent. Exams are self-scheduled and unproctored. Even the trickiest part of an honor code, the provision that students turn in other students who are observed breaking the code, is followed without hesitation.

Caltech has an honor system that is highly valued and carefully observed. It is described in one sentence, "No one shall take unfair advantage of any member of the Caltech community."

Other colleges noted for their comprehensive honor codes are Haverford and Bryn Mawr. The service academies have strict honor codes based on military regulations that define conduct unbecoming an officer candidate. Many other colleges have strong religious affiliations, and their honor codes, founded on the teachings of the church, encompass virtually every aspect of student life.

Student Accomplishments

YOUNGEST

The youngest student to graduate from a four-year college was Jay Luo, who was 12 years old when he received a B.S. in mathematics from Boise State

The youngest college graduate was twelve when he received his B.S. from Boise State.

in Idaho on May 16, 1982. Jay enrolled in Boise State at age 9 after only 2½ years of formal education, having skipped both junior and senior high school. His SAT scores placed him above the 80th percentile on the verbal test and above the 98th percentile in math. He graduated cum laude after taking courses in advanced calculus, linear programming,

and engineering physics. If all goes well, Jay should be able to get his driver's license within a year or two after he finishes his doctoral studies.

The previous record for the youngest college graduate was held by 14-year-old Merrill Wolf, who received a B.A. in music from Yale in 1945.

VIETNAM MEMORIAL

An extraordinary accomplishment by a college student was Yale senior Maya Ying Lin's 1981 entry in the design contest for the Vietnam Memorial. Lin won the $20,000 first-place prize in the largest competition in architectural history, which received over 1,400 submissions. A month before she entered the Vietnam Memorial contest, Lin had submitted her project for a course grade at Yale. Her teacher, Andy Burr, gave Lin a B. Professor Burr also submitted a design for the Vietnam Memorial, but it finished well below Lin's entry in the contest.

YOUNG GENIUS

Dave Stuart, a member of the class of 1989 at Princeton, won a MacArthur "genius" grant of $150,000 just prior to entering Princeton as a freshman. Stuart, 18 years old when he was honored, was the youngest person ever to win a MacArthur award and is considered one of the world's foremost authorities on deciphering Mayan hieroglyphics.

PULITZER PRIZE

John Filo was a student at Kent State in 1971 when he took a photograph of a student who was shot and killed by National Guard soldiers called to the Kent State campus by the governor of Ohio. Later that year Filo's photograph won a Pulitzer Prize.

RADIO

While attending Columbia from 1909 to 1913, Edwin Armstrong made a major contribution to the science of communication. In his junior year Armstrong invented the radio feedback circuit that allowed homemade crystal and earphone sets to be replaced by speaker-equipped receivers. Armstrong's breakthrough led to the era of mass-produced radios.

PHOTOGRAPHY

Edwin Land experimented with light polarization when he was a Harvard student from 1928 to 1932. He invented a substance that he named Polaroid, which allowed light passing through it to vibrate in only one plane so objects could be seen clearly without glare. After graduation Edwin Land went on to found the Polaroid Land Company.

Faculty

THE EARLY DAYS

In the 1700s and early 1800s, colleges paid their faculty little more than the barest wage.

When the University of Michigan first opened in Detroit in 1817, its yearly pay scale was President, $25; Vice President, $18.50; Professor, $12.50; Instructor, $25. The faculty members were encouraged to take second jobs to make ends meet.

Ironically, while college professors were treated poorly in financial terms, they were highly respected members of society, often receiving special privileges because of their positions. Through most of the 1700s, professors and tutors were exempt from taxes. They also were not required to enter the military, fight fires, or serve on juries. At William and Mary there was even a tie-in with government. The law specified that two representatives of the Virginia House of Burgesses were to be William and Mary faculty members.

FIRST LECTURER

The first faculty member to give a lecture was William Small of William and Mary in 1760. Previously, tutors and professors simply read from textbooks and asked students to memorize their assignments. Professor Small was a teacher of physics, metaphysics, and math who not only lectured but also introduced classroom demonstrations in physics. One of his students was Thomas Jefferson, who used Small as a model for the type of professor he later hired at the University of Virginia.

LONGEST TENURE

The record is believed to be the sixty-eight-year term (from 1913 to 1981) of chemistry professor Joel Hildebrand of U Cal

---

Professor Joel Hildebrand taught at Berkeley for 68 years.

Berkeley. In 1981, at age 100, Professor Hildebrand was still conducting first-rate experiments on the molecular structure of water and publishing articles in scientific journals. When reporters came to interview Professor Hildebrand on the occasion of his 100th birthday, they found him in the backyard of his house chopping wood. He died in 1983 at age 102.

The previous record holder for a faculty member with the longest tenure was Alpheus Spring Packard, who taught ancient languages at Bowdoin from 1819 to 1884, a span of sixty-five years.

Although not a record holder, Carl Seashore was landlocked at the University of Iowa from 1897, when he first taught psychology, until 1946, when he retired at age 80 as acting dean of the graduate college. Seashore established the field of speech pathology, designed the audiometer that is still used to measure hearing, and developed the Seashore music ability test.

MOST VERSATILE

Because of his esteemed language ability, in 1777 John Smith of Dartmouth was appointed "Professor of English, Latin, Greek, Chaldee, etc., and such other languages as he shall have time for." He was paid £100 per year, half in money and half in goods. When he complained of his low salary, President Wheelock gave Smith an acre of land on which to build a home.

YOUNGEST

Charles Louis Fefferman was 22 years old in 1971 when he was named professor of mathematics at the University of Chicago, the youngest full professor ever at a U.S. college.

Fefferman started reading math textbooks at age 9, mastered elementary calculus by 11, and graduated from the University of Maryland at age 17. After moving from Chicago to Princeton in 1974, Fefferman became the first recipient of the National Science Foundation's Waterman Award at age 27, was the youngest person ever to win the Fields Medal in mathematics, and was elected to membership in the National Academy of Sciences at age 30. And what does one of the world's foremost mathematicians actually do? Fefferman mostly sits and thinks, usually about geometric shapes or relationships rather than numbers.

FIRST WOMAN

The first female faculty member was Rebecca Mann Pennell of Oberlin in 1853. Professor Pennell taught classes in geography and natural history.

NOTABLE WOMAN PROFESSOR

The 1800s were a rather inhospitable time for women in higher education. Although the number of woman undergraduates rose greatly in the second half of the century, it was rare to see a female professor. Given such a climate, the accomplishments of Ellen Swallow Richards, Massachussetts Institute of Technology class of 1873, were extraordinary. MIT's first woman graduate, Richards was appointed an instructor in sanitary chemistry. She soon became a full professor and embarked on a distinguished academic career that included founding the fields of home economics and environmental science, coining the word "ecology" along the way.

HYMN WRITER

Katherine Lee Bates was an English professor at Wellesley from 1885 to 1925 and wrote a number of books and plays while there. However, she is best remembered for the writing she did while on vacation in the Rocky Mountains. On a mountaintop in Colorado, Bates wrote the national hymn, "America the Beautiful."

HONORED BY CONGRESS

George Washington Carver, professor of agriculture at Tuskegee Institute in the early 1900s, is the only college faculty member to have a day named after him. To honor his achievements in transforming southern agriculture, in 1944 Congress designated January 5 as George Washington Carver Day.

SALARIES

The American Association of University Professors (AAUP) publishes a yearly report that shows average faculty salaries at more than 2,000 colleges.

For 1987–88, median salaries at all types of institutions were:

Professor	$47,400
Associate professor	35,300
Assistant professor	29,200
Lecturer	25,470
Instructor	22,090
Median–all ranks	37,000

The highest paid are professors at doctorate-granting institutions, who have an average salary of $52,950. The lowest paid are lecturers at two-year colleges, who earn about $19,510.

In 1987–88, the universities that paid their full professors the most were Rockefeller ($77,400), Harvard ($73,200), Stanford

($70,800), Caltech ($69,900), Princeton ($67,800), Yale ($67,700), and MIT ($66,600). Rockefeller is an upper-division medical school with a faculty consisting primarily of physicians and research scientists.

Highest Paid

Although less than the earnings of top football and basketball coaches, the $306,000 paid by the University of South Carolina to Jihan el-Sadat for three semesters of teaching in 1985 and 1986 is believed to be the highest salary on record for a faculty member. Mrs. Sadat, the wife of slain Egyptian leader Anwar Sadat, taught a course in women's studies as a visiting professor.

While Mrs. Sadat earned about $9,000 per lecture, South Carolina, like other colleges, often pays even higher amounts to attract "star" lecturers or famous commencement speakers. For example, public-television commentators James Lehrer and Robert MacNeil each received $37,500 to lecture twice a semester and Bill Cosby was paid $25,000 for a

---

In the fall of 1986, Gary Hart was paid $32,000 for two lectures at the University of Florida Law School. His 1987 contract was not renewed.

---

commencement address. In the fall of 1986 Gary Hart was paid $32,000 for two lectures at the University of Florida Law School. His 1987 contract was not renewed.

ACTING UP IN CLASS

The lecture style of a typical professor can be rather routine—a stack of notes, a piece of chalk, and the endless hope of getting the class to care as passionately about the subject as he or she does.

Now and then a professor will make an extraordinary effort to arouse the class to the point where learning can occur spontaneously. John Rassias of Dartmouth, Kevin Byrne of Gustavus Adolphus, and Sarah Short of Syracuse are three professors who have gained notoriety for their creative and entertaining teaching methods.

One day dressed in a silver wig and a blue velvet costume as Montesquieu, another time sporting the white uniform, apron, and cap of a village butcher, Rassias transforms his classroom into a French theater in which both he and his students are the performers. The concept is called the Dartmouth Intensive Language Model and the idea is to drop students into a foreign culture, teaching by spur-of-the-moment emotional reactions rather than through grammar and pronunciation drills. Rassias's revolutionary method has proven so successful that organizations as diverse as the Peace Corps and the New York

City Transit Police have called on him to conduct language training.

Associate Professor of History Byrne uses a similar approach at Gustavus Adolphus. At various times he plays characters such as Thomas Jefferson, John D. Rockefeller, or a 1960s radical, all in an effort to draw his students "into the act" so they will ask serious and difficult questions of the historical figures. Byrne finds his role playing helps break down academic apathy and brings students into contact with history in new and exciting ways.

Sarah Short, professor of nutrition at Syracuse, explains her unorthodox teaching

---

What student could ignore a professor who, dressed in a blond wig, silver jacket, and exotic beads, rides a motorcycle into the classroom?

---

methods by simply stating, "If I don't get their attention, I can't teach them." And she does get their attention. What student could ignore a professor who, dressed in a blond wig, silver jacket, and exotic beads, rides a motorcycle into the classroom? Or a teacher who turns a lecture into a multimedia event complete with flashing lights, slide shows, and rock music? Or someone who presents herself as a living blackboard with chemical formulas painted on her arms and legs? But Short's lectures are

Professor Byrne as Thomas Jefferson.

more than just showmanship, they include substance as well. For her teaching excellence, Professor Short has been designated one of Syracuse's outstanding faculty members and honored with a teacher/scholar award.

CHRISTMAS GIFT

Occasionally students give a popular professor a Christmas present, but seldom does the teacher reverse the process. One who bestows a gift on his class is Professor of Business Administration George Gazmararian of Alma College, in Alma, Michigan. Mr. Gazmararian's yearly present consists of a list of stocks that he expects will do well in the year ahead. The stocks are all high risk and sell for less than $10 per share. In seven of the nine years Gazmararian has played stock market Santa Claus, better than 75 percent of his picks have increased in value. Although Professor Gazmararian is an expert in the stock market, he is, after all, human. In 1983, a year in which he gambled on high-tech companies, his stocks dropped 52 percent.

TRACK RECORD

Faculty members often deal in esoteric topics that are seldom heard of outside of academic journals. But occasionally professorial knowledge focuses on subjects of popular interest. Two professors of economics, Richard Quandt of Princeton

and Peter Asch of Rutgers, recently published *Racetrack Betting: The Professor's Guide to Strategies.* Quandt and Asch designed a computer program that compared hundreds of actual betting records at two New Jersey tracks and simulated thousands more. Their conclusion: there is no surefire way to make money, but bettors can increase their odds of winning by following a conservative strategy. This means staying away from long shots and exotic combination bets, putting money on favorites to finish second or third, and betting on horses whose odds fall during the last few minutes before post time.

KERMIT THE PROFESSOR

The famous Muppet character Kermit the Frog was named for Theodore Kermit Scott, a professor of philosophy at Purdue. Scott grew up in Leland, Mississippi, with Muppet creator Jim Henson, who used Scott's middle name for the green amphibian.

DIRTY TRICK

In 1937 the Ohio River flooded, causing extensive damage to the city of Cincinnati. Students at the University of Cincinnati spent weeks cleaning up the dirt and debris that covered their campus. The flood motivated geology professor Nevin Fenneman to write what is believed to be the shortest final exam question ever. It consisted of one word, "Mud." The teacher told the class to write everything they knew about it.

FACULTY POLITICIAN

Hubert Humphrey was an assistant instructor of political science at Louisiana State in 1939–40, an assistant professor at Minnesota in 1940–41, a visiting professor at Macalester in 1943–44, a full professor at Macalester in 1969–70, and a part-time teacher of social science at Minnesota in the same year.

TEACHING IS FOR THE BIRDS

Hope College professor Eldon Greij is chairman of the biology department and specializes in courses on ornithology. In 1985, after six years of work, he published a magazine, *Birder's World,* for casual bird-watchers as well as serious birders. The only magazine in the country devoted entirely to birds, it features noted birding authority Roger Tory Peterson as an editorial adviser. The first issue was sent to 14,000 subscribers.

AAUP

The American Association of University Professors, with 52,000 members, is the largest organization that represents the interests of faculty members. AAUP sets nationwide standards for protecting academic freedom

and establishing tenure rules. The AAUP also has set up a legal defense fund to assist faculty members who sue their employers in defense of academic freedom.

UNDERGROUND FACULTY

Union College in Schenectady, New York, has its own cemetery, which has been in use since 1863. The college continues to offer its faculty the privilege of burial in the college plot. Three former Union presidents as well as fifty faculty members are buried there.

UPSETTING EXPERIENCE

One of the most illustrious college faculty members of all time was Louis Agassiz, the Swiss naturalist who was professor of zoology and geology at Harvard from 1847 to 1873. Among Stanford students Agassiz was known not so much for his academic accomplishments but for the remark made when a statue of him fell over during the San Francisco earthquake of 1906, "Agassiz was great in the abstract but not in the concrete."

MOST FAMOUS PROFESSOR

The honor goes to Jimmy Carter, thirty-ninth president of the United States, who is a distinguished professor at Emory. Carter gives a series of lectures for three days each month.

For a full-time faculty member, the most recognizable name is that of Carl Sagan, professor of astronomy at Cornell. Professor Sagan has written three best-selling books and hosted the "Cosmos" TV series on the Public Broadcasting System.

DISTINGUISHED FACULTY

Caltech's faculty of 265 includes 61 members of the National Academy of Sciences and 29 members of the National Academy of Engineering. In both societies, the percentage of Caltech faculty who have been made members is the highest in the nation.

BEST FACULTY EVER?

Many universities have attracted famous scholars and scientists to their faculty. Which college had the strongest academic department of all time? It's hard to imagine a more illustrious group of professors than Caltech's physics department in the late 1920s and early 1930s.

Led by physicist Robert Millikan, a Nobel Prize winner for his experiments with electrons, the department included Nobelists Albert Michelson, Henrik Lorentz, and Albert Einstein. Also on the staff was future Nobel laureate William Shockley and other famous scientists like Paul Epstein, Richard Tolman, and J. Robert Oppenheimer.

FACULTY FACTORY

In the fifty years following the founding of Johns Hopkins, one of the nation's earliest universities in 1876, 1,440 students received Ph.D.'s. By 1926, 1,000, or 70 percent, of these scholars were serving on the faculties of other colleges. In the same year a list of the most eminent American men of science was published. Among this group of famous scientists, nearly 25 percent were Hopkins alumni.

GUEST LECTURER

In 1909 Sigmund Freud made his only visit to the United States to lecture at Clark University in Worcester, Massachusetts. At first Freud turned down Clark's invitation, but he later changed his mind when Clark increased his travel allowance and promised him an honorary degree. During one of his lectures Freud was asked to talk about sex, but he refused to comment.

TELEPHONE

Alexander Graham Bell was on sabbatical leave from his position as professor of oratory at Boston University when he invented the telephone in 1876. Actually, he didn't have to go far to complete his experiments. He demonstrated the first working telephone in Boston at MIT's Society of Arts.

TELEGRAPH

Another famous developer of communication equipment was a professor, and, like Alexander Graham Bell, his academic field was different from his area of scientific interest. Samuel F. B. Morse invented the telegraph at NYU's University Building in 1838 while he was a professor of sculpture and painting.

FACULTY AFFIRMATIVE ACTION

The Evergreen faculty is one of the most egalitarian in the nation. At Evergreen there is no tenure or academic rank. Perhaps the absence of a formal structure leads to increased opportunity for women and members of minority groups. Forty percent of Evergreen's faculty members are women and 15 percent come from minorities; these are among the highest percentages of any college in the country.

LONGEST TITLE

Reverend Peter Gomes of Harvard probably has the longest title of any college faculty member. Officially he is known as the "Preacher to the

S.F.B. Morse's Allegorical Landscape of New York University.

University and Ernest Plummer Professor of Christian Ethics and Morals."

Miami's McGuffey.

ALL-TIME BEST-SELLER

While James Oscar McKinsey's *Accounting Principles* has sold 7 million copies, he doesn't hold the record as the best-selling faculty author. That achievement belongs to William Holmes McGuffey, a professor at Miami of Ohio when he wrote his famous series of textbooks, the *McGuffey Readers*. First published in the 1830s, this series of books taught five generations of American schoolchildren to read. McGuffey was known as the "Schoolmaster of the Nation," and 125 million copies of his books have been sold.

Miami University

BEST-SELLING TEXTBOOKS

In spite of rapid advances in modern methods of transmitting knowledge, the old-fashioned college textbook remains at the heart of the education process.

There have been a number of textbooks, some more than fifty years old, that have stood the test of time and sold millions of copies. Among this elite group, the best-sellers and their faculty authors are:

Textbook/author	Year published	Copies sold	Edition
Accounting Principles James O. McKinsey, Chicago	1929	7 million	15th
Economics Paul Samuelson, MIT	1948	3 million	12th
History of Art H. W. Janson, NYU	1962	3 million	3rd
Introduction to Psychology Ernest Hilgard, Stanford	1962	3 million	9th

continued

Harbrace College Handbook John Hodges, Tennessee	1941	2.8 million	10th
Basic Marketing E. Jerome McCarthy, Michigan State	1960	2.5 million	9th

Major Awards to Professors

NOBEL PRIZE

The most prestigious award a faculty member can receive is the Nobel Prize. Given yearly by the Nobel Foundation in Stockholm, Sweden, awards are made in physics, chemistry, medicine, literature, economics, and peace. The winner receives a cash grant of $340,000 and a gold medal.

Here are lists of winners who were teaching at American colleges when they won the award.

Physics

Year	Recipient	Faculty member at . . .
1907	Albert Michelson	Chicago
1923	Robert Millikan	Caltech
1927	Arthur Compton	Chicago
1936	Carl Anderson	Caltech
1939	Ernest Lawrence	U Cal Berkeley
1944	Otto Stern	Carnegie Tech
	Isidor Rabi	Columbia
1945	Wolfgang Pauli	Princeton
1946	Percy Bridgman	Harvard
1949	Hideki Yukawa	Columbia
1952	Felix Bloch	Stanford
	Edward Purcell	Harvard
1955	Willis Lamb	Stanford
	Polykarp Kusch	Columbia
1956	John Bardeen	Illinois
1957	Tsung-Dao Lee	Columbia
1959	Emilio Segre	U Cal Berkeley
	Owen Chamberlain	U Cal Berkeley
1960	Donald Glaser	U Cal Berkeley
1961	Robert Hofstadter	Stanford
1963	Eugene Wigner	Princeton
	Maria Goeppert-Mayer	U Cal San Diego
1964	Charles Townes	MIT
1965	Julian Schwinger	Harvard
	Richard Feynman	Caltech
1967	Hans Bethe	Cornell
1968	Luis Alvarez	U Cal Berkeley
1969	Murray Gell-Mann	Caltech
1972	John Bardeen	Illinois
	Leon Cooper	Brown
	J. Robert Schrieffer	Penn

continued

1975	James Rainwater	Columbia
1976	Burton Richter	Stanford
	Samuel Ting	MIT
1977	John Van Vleck	Harvard
1979	Sheldon Glashow	Harvard
	Steven Weinberg	Harvard
1980	James Cronin	Chicago
	Val Fitch	Princeton
1981	Nicolaas Bloembergen	Harvard
	Arthur Schawlow	Stanford
1982	Kenneth Wilson	Cornell
1983	Subrahmanyan Chandrasekhar	Chicago
	William Fowler	Caltech

In physics, Harvard leads with seven Nobel Prize winners, followed by Caltech, Columbia, Stanford, and U Cal Berkeley with five each.

Chemistry

Year	Recipient	Faculty member at ...
1914	Theodore Richards	Harvard
1934	Harold Urey	Columbia
1946	James Sumner	Cornell
	John Northrop	Rockefeller
	Wendell Stanley	Rockefeller
1949	William Giauque	U Cal Berkeley
1951	Edwin McMillan	U Cal Berkeley
	Glenn Seaborg	U Cal Berkeley
1954	Linus Pauling	Caltech
1955	Vincent DuVigneaud	Cornell
1960	Willard Libby	UCLA
1961	Melvin Calvin	U Cal Berkeley
1965	Robert Woodward	Harvard
1966	Robert Mulliken	Chicago
1968	Lars Onsager	Yale
1972	Stanford Moore	Rockefeller
	William Stein	Rockefeller
1974	Paul Flory	Stanford
1976	William Lipscomb	Harvard
1979	Herbert Brown	Purdue
1980	Paul Berg	Stanford
1981	Roald Hoffmann	Cornell
1983	Henry Taube	Stanford
1984	R. Bruce Merrifield	Rockefeller
1986	Dudley Herschbach	Harvard
	Yuan Lee	U Cal Berkeley
1987	Donald Cram	UCLA

In chemistry, Rockefeller University and U Cal Berkeley have five Nobelists, Harvard has four, and Cornell and Stanford have three each.

continued

Medicine

Year	Recipient	Faculty member at . . .
1912	Alexis Carrel	Rockefeller
1930	Karl Landsteiner	Rockefeller
1933	Thomas Morgan	Caltech
1934	George Whipple	Rochester
	George Minot	Harvard
	William Murphy	Harvard
1943	Edward Doisy	Saint Louis
1944	Joseph Erlanger	Washington (St. Louis)
	Herbert Gasser	Rockefeller
1946	Hermann Muller	Indiana
1947	Carl Cori	Washington (St. Louis)
	Gerty Cori	Washington (St. Louis)
1952	Selman Waksman	Rutgers
1953	Fritz Lipmann	Harvard
1954	John Enders	Harvard
	Frederick Robbins	Western Reserve
1956	André Cournand	Columbia
	Dickinson Richards	Columbia
1958	George Beadle	Caltech
	Edward Tatum	Rockefeller
	Joshua Lederberg	Wisconsin
1959	Severo Ochoa	NYU
	Arthur Kornberg	Stanford
1961	Georg Von Bekesy	Harvard
1962	James Watson	Harvard
1964	Konrad Bloch	Harvard
1966	Peyton Rous	Rockefeller
	Charles Huggins	Chicago
1967	Haldan Hartline	Rockefeller
	George Wald	Harvard
1968	Robert Holley	Cornell
	Har Khorana	Wisconsin
1969	Max Delbruck	Caltech
	Salvador Luria	MIT
1971	Earl Sutherland	Vanderbilt
1972	Gerald Edelman	Rockefeller
1974	George Palade	Yale
	Christian de Duve	Rockefeller
1975	David Baltimore	MIT
	Howard Temin	Wisconsin
1978	Daniel Nathans	Johns Hopkins
	Hamilton Smith	Johns Hopkins
1979	Allan Cormack	Tufts
1980	Baruj Benacerraf	Harvard
1981	Roger Sperry	Caltech
	David Hubel	Harvard
	Torsten Wiesel	Harvard
1985	Michael Brown	Texas
	Joseph Goldstein	Texas

continued

| 1986 | Stanley Cohen | Vanderbilt |
| 1987 | Susumu Tonegawa | MIT |

In medicine, Harvard is again first with eleven, followed by
Rockefeller with eight and Caltech with four.

Economics

Year	Recipient	Faculty member at . . .
1970	Paul Samuelson	MIT
1971	Simon Kuznets	Harvard
1972	Kenneth Arrow	Harvard
1973	Wassily Leontief	Harvard
1975	Tjalling Koopmans	Yale
1976	Milton Friedman	Chicago
1978	Herbert Simon	Carnegie Mellon
1979	Theodore Schultz	Chicago
	Arthur Lewis	Princeton
1980	Lawrence Klein	Penn
1981	James Tobin	Yale
1982	George Stigler	Chicago
1983	Gerard Debreu	U Cal Berkeley
1985	Franco Modigliani	MIT
1986	James Buchanan	George Mason
1987	Robert Solow	MIT

In economics, Harvard, Chicago, and MIT are tied for first with
three each.

Literature
Among the winners of the Nobel Prize for Literature only three
were college faculty members at the time of the award: Saul Bellow
(Chicago), 1976; Czeslaw Milosz (U Cal Berkeley), 1980; and
Joseph Brodsky (Columbia), 1987.

Peace
Only three American recipients of the Nobel Peace Prize were
college faculty members when they won the award. Ralph Bunche
(1950) was teaching at Harvard, Linus Pauling (1963) was professor
of chemistry at Caltech, and Elie Wiesel (1986) was a professor at
Boston University. Linus Pauling's Peace Prize was his second
Nobel; he also won the 1954 award in chemistry. Nicholas Murray
Butler, who received the Peace Prize in 1931 for his work in
promoting the Kellogg-Briand Pact, was president of Columbia at
the time.

Nobel U.
Harvard deserves the title of "Nobel University." It has the most
faculty members in three of the four scientific categories—physics,
medicine, and economics. Its total winners number twenty-five,
nearly twice as many as any of the runner-up colleges can claim:

continued

Rockefeller (thirteen), U Cal Berkeley (eleven), and MIT, Chicago, and Caltech (nine).

First U.S. Nobelist

Albert Michelson was the first American to win a Nobel Prize. Michelson received the honor in 1907 for developing optical precision instruments. Michelson had a long and distinguished academic career. In 1881 he was the first professor of physics at Case School of Applied Science (later Case Western Reserve), and he was chairman of the physics department at Clark in 1889 before taking up positions at the University of Chicago and Caltech.

Nobel Prankster

Nobel laureates aren't usually known as practical jokers. An exception is Richard Feynman, Caltech professor of physics until his death in February 1988. Feynman was a master at breaking lock and safe combinations. During World War II, while he was working at the Los Alamos labs, Feynman gave officials fits by opening top secret safes and leaving "Guess Who?" notes inside them.

Double Winner

John Bardeen, a physics professor at Illinois, is the only American to win two Nobel Prizes in the same field. Bardeen won in both 1956 and 1972 for his research on semiconductors.

PULITZER PRIZE

The Pulitzer Prizes, endowed by publisher Joseph Pulitzer and administered by Columbia University, are awarded annually in journalism, letters, and music. In the last ten years a number of winners in fiction, history, biography, poetry, nonfiction, and music were college faculty members.

Fiction

Year	Winner	Work	Faculty member at . . .
1978	James Alan McPherson	*Elbow Room*	Virginia
1981	John Kennedy Toole	*A Confederacy of Dunces*	Southwestern Louisiana
1983	Alice Walker	*The Color Purple*	Brandeis
1984	William Kennedy	*Ironweed*	SUNY at Albany
1985	Alison Lurie	*Foreign Affairs*	Cornell
1987	Peter Taylor	*A Summons to Memphis*	Virginia

History

Year	Winner	Work	Faculty member at . . .
1978	Alfred D. Chandler Jr.	*The Visible Hand: The Managerial Revolution in American Business*	Harvard

continued

1979	Don E. Fehrenbacher	*The Dred Scott Case: Its Significance in American Law and Politics*	Stanford
1980	Leon F. Litwack	*Been in the Storm So Long*	U Cal Berkeley
1981	Lawrence A. Cremin	*American Education: The National Experience, 1783–1876*	Barnard
1982	C. Vann Woodward	*Mary Chestnut's Civil War*	Yale
1983	Rhys L. Isaac	*The Transformation of Virginia, 1740–1790*	Princeton
1985	Thomas K. McCraw	*Prophets of Regulation*	Harvard
1986	Walter A. McDougall	*The Heavens and the Earth*	U Cal Berkeley
1987	Bernard Bailyn	*Voyagers to the West: A Passage in the Peopling of America on the Eve of the Revolution*	Harvard
1988	Robert Bruce	*The Launching of Modern American Science 1846–1876*	Boston U

Biography

Year	Winner	Work	Faculty member at ...
1978	Walter Jackson Bate	*Samuel Johnson*	Harvard
1982	William S. McFeely	*Grant: A Biography*	Mount Holyoke
1984	Louis R. Harlan	*Booker T. Washington*	Maryland
1985	Kenneth Silverman	*The Life and Times of Cotton Mather*	NYU
1986	Elizabeth Frank	*Louise Bogan: A Portrait*	Bard
1987	David Garrow	*Bearing the Cross: Martin Luther King, Jr., and the Southern Christian Leadership Conference*	CUNY
1988	David Herbert Donald	*Look Homeward: A Life of Thomas Wolfe*	Harvard

Poetry

Year	Winner	Work	Faculty member at ...
1978	Howard Nemerov	*Collected Poems*	Washington (St. Louis)
1979	Robert Penn Warren	*Now and Then: Poems 1976–1978*	Yale
1980	Donald Justice	*Selected Poems*	Iowa
1982	Sylvia Plath	*The Collected Poems*	Smith
1983	Galway Kinnell	*Selected Poems*	NYU
1985	Carolyn Kizer	*Yin: New Poems*	Stanford
1986	Henry Taylor	*The Flying Change*	American
1987	Rita Dove	*Thomas and Beulah*	Arizona State
1988	William Meredith	*Partial Accounts*	Connecticut College

continued

Nonfiction

Year	Winner	Work	Faculty member at . . .
1978	Carl Sagan	*The Dragons of Eden*	Cornell
1979	Edward O. Wilson	*On Human Nature*	Howard
1980	Douglas R. Hofstadter	*Gödel, Escher, Bach: An Eternal Golden Braid*	Indiana
1981	Carl E. Schorske	*Fin-de-Siècle Vienna: Politics and Culture*	Princeton
1984	Paul Starr	*Social Transformation of American Medicine*	Harvard
1986	J. Anthony Lukas	*Common Ground*	Harvard

Music

Year	Winner	Work	Faculty member at . . .
1979	Joseph Schwantner	*Aftertones of Infinity*	Rochester
1980	David Del Tredici	*In Memory of a Summer Day*	Boston University
1982	Roger Sessions	*Concerto for Orchestra*	Princeton
1984	Bernard Rands	*Canti del Sole*	U Cal San Diego
1986	George Perle	*Wind Quintet IV*	CUNY-Queens
1987	John Harbison	*The Flight into Egypt*	MIT
1988	William Bolcom	*Twelve New Etudes for Piano*	Michigan

NATIONAL ACADEMY OF SCIENCES

Considered by faculty members to be second in importance only to receiving a Nobel Prize, election to the National Academy of Sciences is a great honor for a college professor.

A private organization founded in 1863, the academy consists of 1,523 members elected because of their lifetime achievements in physical or social science.

Professor Daniel Gorenstein supervised a group of 100 mathematicians who took over 30 years to solve a complex algebra problem.

If the accomplishment of a recent appointee, math professor Daniel Gorenstein of Rutgers, is any indication of the level of work required to be named a member of the academy, the honor is well deserved. Professor Gorenstein supervised a group of 100 mathematicians who took over thirty years to solve a complex algebra problem. The 15,000-page solution is the longest in mathematics history.

The leading colleges, based on the faculty member's affiliation when appointed to the academy:

	Number of members
1. Harvard	115
2. MIT	85
3. U Cal Berkeley	84

4. Stanford	77
5. Caltech	54
6. Yale	50
7. U Cal San Diego	45
8. Chicago	43
9. Cornell	38
Wisconsin	38

NATIONAL MEDAL OF SCIENCE

From its inception in 1962 until 1987, there have been 225 recipients of the National Medal of Science. The Medal of Science is the nation's highest award for achievement in science and technology. Some of the illustrious scientists who have won the award are Theodore von Karman, Vannevar Bush, John Bardeen, Albert Sabin, Linus Pauling, Wernher von Braun, Edward Teller, James Van Allen, and Michael De Bakey.

One hundred seventy-four members of college faculties have won the National Medal of Science. Based on the recipient's institution at the time the award was given, here are the leading colleges:

	Number of members
1. Harvard	17
Stanford	17
3. MIT	12
U Cal Berkeley	12
5. Caltech	10
6. Illinois	8
Princeton	8
Rockefeller	8
9. Columbia	6
Wisconsin	6

WATERMAN AWARD

Each year the National Science Foundation gives the Alan T. Waterman Award to an outstanding young researcher in the fields of science, math, or engineering. Established in 1975, this prestigious award includes a medal and stipends of up to $500,000 for research and advanced study.

Through 1987, both Columbia and Princeton have had three Waterman winners. Two members of Harvard's faculty have received the award, and one each came from UCLA, U Cal Berkeley, Stanford, and Ohio State.

MACARTHUR GRANTS

The MacArthur Foundation of Chicago gives so-called "genius" grants to creative individuals. The amount of the awards, varying from $30,000 to $70,000 a year for five years, are intended to set winners free from the necessity of earning a living and allow them to concentrate on their areas of expertise.

The $2.7-billion charitable foundation was established by John D. MacArthur, an eccentric billionaire who earned his fortune in insurance and real estate. Although the genius grant program has brought considerable notoriety to the MacArthur Foundation, the awards account for only 10 percent of the $100-million the foundation gives away each year.

Including the 1987 awards, the MacArthur program has been in existence for six years. During that time there have been 223 winners. The majority of the recipients have been faculty members at American universities. The following list shows the colleges at which recipients were teaching when they were honored.

	Number of grants
1. Harvard	16
2. Princeton	11
3. Chicago	10
Stanford	10
U Cal Berkeley	10
6. MIT	7
7. U Cal San Diego	6
8. Caltech	5
Columbia	5
NYU	5

A MacArthur winner in 1984, Bill Irwin of New York, was a faculty member at a different kind of college. Irwin is a professional clown and teaches at Ringling Brothers and Barnum & Bailey Clown College. His subject is physical comedy— how to move your body to make people laugh.

PROFESSOR OF THE YEAR

The Council for Advancement and Support of Education in Washington, D.C., selects a Professor of the Year from 800 nominations. Since the award was first given in 1981, the winners have been:

1981 Mary Eleanor Clark, Professor of Biology, San Diego State
1982 Anthony Aveni, Professor of Anthropology and Astronomy, Colgate
1983 Peter Beidler, Professor of English, Lehigh
1984 Charles Pine, Professor of Physics, Rutgers

1985 William Marvin Bass, Professor of Anthropology, Tennessee
1986 Rosemarie Tong, Associate Professor of Philosophy, Williams
1987 Ralph Ketcham, Professor of Political Science, Syracuse

YOUNG INVESTIGATOR AWARDS

The National Science Foundation's Presidential Young Investigator Awards are intended to help universities attract faculty members who might otherwise pursue nonteaching careers. Two hundred awards worth $25,000 per year for five years are given annually. Private corporations may add money to the government grant. With a matching gift, a young scientist can receive as much as $100,000 annually.

From the beginning of the program in 1984 through the 1987 awards, the following colleges have had the most Presidential Young Investigators.

	Number of recipients
1. U Cal Berkeley	43
2. Stanford	33
3. MIT	32
4. Illinois	28
5. Princeton	25
6. Cornell	24
7. Texas	22
Wisconsin	22
9. Carnegie Mellon	20
10. Washington (Seattle)	19

SLOAN AWARDS

The Alfred P. Sloan Foundation of New York awarded its 1987 grants to ninety young scientists, aged 28 to 36, in chemistry, math, economics, and neuroscience. Each winner receives $25,000 at a time in his or her career when teaching demands are most pressing and research grants are difficult to obtain. MIT had the most recipients with five, followed by Stanford, Harvard, Chicago, and Columbia with four and Johns Hopkins, Colorado, Caltech, Illinois, Princeton, and Purdue, three each.

GUGGENHEIM FELLOWSHIPS

In the sixty-third annual competition in 1987, the John Simon Guggenheim Memorial Foundation awarded 273 fellowships worth well over $6-million. The recipients were chosen "on the basis of unusually distinguished achievement in the past and exceptional promise for future accomplishment." The research topics ranged from the abstruse ("The Solution of Large Sparse Systems of Linear Equations" or "Studies in Perturbative Quantum Chromodynamics") to the commonplace ("A Critical History of Popular Music" or "The Evolution of Flowers").

The colleges that had the most 1987 Guggenheim Fellows:

	Number of Fellows
1. Princeton	9
2. Harvard	8
UCLA	8
Yale	8
5. Cornell	7
Penn	7

7. Chicago	6
Columbia	6
Stanford	6

SEARLE SCHOLARS

In 1987 eighteen biomedical researchers were named Searle Scholars by the Chicago Community Trust. Each scholar received a grant of $80,000 to support a three-year research project. The eighteen winners were affiliated with sixteen different colleges. The only institutions that had more than one scholar were Northwestern and the University of California at San Francisco, with two apiece.

Academic Programs

INNOVATIVE COLLEGES

Although 350 years have passed since the first American college was founded, higher education remains structured in a way that is remarkably similar to the system that was imported from England and later altered somewhat by influences from Germany. A core curriculum, a professor imparting knowledge to a class of students, examinations to mark progress, grades to rank students, and four years of study for a bachelor's degree are all characteristics that remain from the earliest days. While there have been a number of significant changes, for the most part these have occurred not in the basic structure but in offering access to more students and adding new courses and new schools. In spite of the strong influence of tradition, however, a few colleges have come up with new ways to teach students. These innovative colleges tend to follow a common principle: give students the responsibility of arranging for their own education and reduce the emphasis on tests, grades, and lockstep movement from one class to the next. Among America's innovative colleges are:

St. John's

St. John's is a small college (enrollment 400) in Annapolis, Maryland, with a sister institution in Sante Fe, New Mexico. The entire curriculum at St. John's consists of 130 classic books of Western civilization. The first year is devoted to Greek authors, the second year books from the Roman and medieval periods, the third year readings in the seventeenth and eighteenth centuries, and the fourth year literature from the 1800s and 1900s. Since many of the Great Books are read in their original language, St. John's students must be competent in Greek and French. The music department requires all students to sing in the St. John's chorus and to perform simple Bartók pieces on the piano. Except for a once-a-week lecture for all students, class meetings consist of seminars with twenty students and two faculty members.

Bard

Located on the Hudson River 90 miles north of New York City, Bard (originally an experimental school of Columbia University) divides itself into two distinct colleges. Lower College teaches basic cultural literacy, while Upper College promotes independent scholarship and research. No grades are given, but students must pass an oral examination given by a panel of three faculty members before they are permitted to enter Upper College. The senior year academic requirement is a yearlong research project equivalent to a master's thesis.

Even more unusual than the education Bard offers is the academic program at Bard's branch campus, Simon's Rock, in Great Barrington, Massachusetts. Simon's Rock is the only four-year college in the country designed for students of high school age. Simon's Rock seeks to enroll intelligent but underachieving eleventh and twelfth graders who feel that their high schools do not keep up with their academic abilities and interests. While some of Simon's Rock students stay for four years, most of them transfer to other colleges after they've earned an associate degree.

Evergreen

Evergreen of Olympia, Washington, is unique among innovative colleges because it is a public institution. Nearly closed down in 1972 when the state legislature took exception to its academic liberalism (no grades, no majors) and its hippie life-style, Evergreen now seems secure in its distinctive approach to learning. It may be more than a coincidence that Evergreen's political problems subsided when former governor Bob Evans became president of the college in 1977. While Evergreen has steadfastly held to its original purpose, it has not been immune to the careerist trend of the 1980s. Evergreen's publications now talk about a curriculum that deals with "real life" issues and boast about the college's 88 percent success rate in placing students in jobs after graduation.

Alverno

Alverno, a Catholic women's school in Milwaukee, takes a different approach to nontraditional education. Alverno does not follow the typical progressive approach with do-it-yourself liberal arts, but instead stresses relevancy, imagination, and innovation. Alverno's courses are taught in corporate style. Grades are out, assessment is in. Students aren't taught English or math, but communication, analysis, and problem solving. With relevancy as the key word in both course content and teaching methods, Alverno students are readily employable—nearly every one finds a job in her major field within six months after graduating.

Bennington and Sarah Lawrence

Located in Vermont, Bennington is known for the distinctive education it offers, its rich tradition of creative arts, its high cost (the highest tuition in the country), and its unconventional image. Bennington assumes its students will learn for the rewards of learning itself, with no need for grades or a structured curriculum. Most of Bennington's 600 undergraduates are involved in creative writing, dance, drama, music, or visual arts.

Sarah Lawrence, in Bronxville, New York, follows a similar educational philosophy. Sarah Lawrence was started in 1928, four years before Bennington, and its goal was to break from the academic orthodoxy that dominated American higher education. For sixty years Sarah Lawrence has held true to its pioneer spirit— "to shift the base of college education from the acquisition of a well-ordered body of information to the flexible use of materials and information for the best development of each individual."

FOREIGN STUDY

Boston University started the first foreign study program in 1875 when it arranged with universities in Athens and Rome that they would teach courses for which BU would give students academic credit.

Michigan State has the largest overseas study program. In a typical year, Michigan State sends nearly 1,000 students abroad to study sixty different subjects in eighteen countries. This strong tradition may explain why more Peace Corps volunteers come from Michigan State than any other college.

Based on the percentage of the student body that studies abroad, the most active colleges are Earlham, St. Lawrence, Lewis and Clark, and Dartmouth, each with a participation rate of about 60 percent.

Junior-year-abroad programs started with the University of Delaware in 1923, when a group of its students attended the University of Paris.

FIELD STUDY

Beloit College has one of the oldest anthropology departments in the country. In 1930, Beloit sent an expedition of professors and students to Algeria on an archaeological dig. This was the first time that college students received academic credit for fieldwork off campus.

LEARNING AND WORKING

Cooperative education, or "co-op," is an arrangement that allows students to alternate

The idea of cooperative education originated at the University of Cincinnati.

periods of classroom work with paid employment. Co-op has the dual advantages of providing money for college and enabling students to learn job skills that will be useful upon graduation. The University of Cincinnati originated the idea in 1906 and today is still among the most active co-op practitioners in the nation.

The largest co-op program is run by Northeastern University in Boston. In 1986 Northeastern placed 9,400 students with 2,400 different employers. The average earnings were $7,100. After graduation, over one third of the co-op students stayed on to work full-time. Drexel in Philadelphia is another noted co-op college, with 98 percent of its students participating.

A college whose curriculum consists entirely of co-op education is the General Motors Institute. Now separate from the General Motors Corporation, GMI is a private college at which every student combines an engineering major with work for a corporate sponsor. As a result of its selective admissions and strong academic program, a high percentage of GMI's graduates go on to management positions in business.

Among liberal arts colleges, Antioch, of Yellow Springs, Ohio, has the largest co-op program.

CONTINUING EDUCATION

A major aspect of the democratization of American colleges after World War II was the increased attention paid to continuing education. Continuing education (also called adult or lifelong education) is a special program in which the student, normally occupied full-time with work or raising a family, arranges to take a reduced course load at convenient hours. Continuing education can lead to a degree, but most often the courses are taken for self-improvement or job advancement. Study may take place on campus, by mail, or through extension centers.

Although NYU established a part-time nondegree program when it opened on October 1, 1832, the first formal continuing

The first formal continuing education program started at Penn State in 1898.

education program started at Penn State in 1898. In 1986–87 more than 140,000 students were enrolled in continuing education at the various branches of the Penn State education system.

UCLA operates the largest continuing education program on a single campus, each year offering 4,500 courses to about 100,000 students.

NYU was the first college to have an evening school. In 1853,

NYU began to give evening instruction in chemistry, civil engineering, design, modern languages, philosophy, political economy, and literature.

One of the first colleges to offer courses for adult students was Columbia in 1891. Today Columbia's program is called the School of General Studies. Famous people who have studied in this school are Amelia Earhart, David O. Selznick, Ira Gershwin, Sandy Koufax, Telly Savalas, John O'Hara, Jacob Javits, Isaac Asimov, Pat Boone, and two Nobel laureates—Baruj Benacerraf and Simon Kuznets.

EDUCATIONAL OUTREACH

The University of Alaska at Fairbanks is involved in research dealing with the frontier of space. UAF scientists studying the characteristics of the upper atmosphere have made major advances in missile defense systems, polar communications, and high-altitude aircraft navigation techniques. Working on a frontier of a different sort is UAF's cross-cultural educational outreach. This program brings education to Alaskan natives, nearly all of whom live in villages that have fewer than 500 inhabitants and are inaccessible by road. The UAF faculty members who work in the program are like the circuit-riding teachers of the Old West. When they can't get to a village on horseback, they use dogsleds, boats, planes, or snowmobiles to complete their educational rounds.

In the continental United States, Berea College in Kentucky runs an extension program to educate the poor families of southern Appalachia. When this rural outreach program first started in the early 1900s, Berea teachers traveled to the backcountry on pack mules loaded with books. The inhabitants of isolated villages heard lectures on mountain agriculture, sanitation, and disease prevention. Today Berea is deeply involved with the Rural School Improvement Project, which places teachers of proven ability in mountain country schools.

ADVANCED PLACEMENT

The Kenyon Plan was the forerunner of the Advanced Placement testing program of the College Board. In 1951, Kenyon College president Gordon Chalmers revised the rules of the Kenyon curriculum so that able students could complete the requirements for a bachelor's degree in less than four years. The next year Chalmers called on the College Board to administer advanced placement tests centrally so that a uniform standard could be established across the country. A group of high school teachers was asked to join the effort so courses could be designed to prepare students for the AP

exams. In 1987 the College Board's AP Program gave exams in twenty-six subjects to 260,000 students.

FIRST ELECTIVES

Charles Eliot, elected president of Harvard in 1869, is credited with introducing the elective system to American higher education. Eliot believed that all nonvocational college courses had academic value if properly taught and studied. In a thirty-year period, Eliot changed the Harvard curriculum from one in which the same courses were specified for every student in the same class to a system of free electives except for required English and foreign language courses during freshman year.

FOREIGN LANGUAGES

In the middle 1830s Kenyon College in Gambier, Ohio, was the first to offer modern foreign languages. Up to that time only classical languages like Greek, Latin, and Hebrew were taught.

FIRST PRECEPT

When Woodrow Wilson became president of Princeton in 1905, he observed that for a great majority of students, "residence here meant a happy life of comradeship and sport interrupted by the grind of perfunctory lessons and examinations." Wilson's solution to the lack of close interaction between students and faculty was the creation of a precept, a small academic gathering in which the preceptor guided students in a two-way academic discussion. Over time the idea spread to other colleges, and today small discussion-oriented classes are a common and highly effective means of teaching.

ONE COURSE AT A TIME

Colorado College calls it the Block Plan, while at Cornell (Iowa) it is known as OCAAT, or One-Course-at-a-Time. Under this unique educational arrangement, a student takes one course for 3½ weeks nine times a year. Between minisemesters, the student is given a four-day break to relax or to take part in special activities.

JAN PLAN

In 1962 Colby College of Waterville, Maine, was the first to initiate the January program of independent study termed the "Jan Plan," or the 4-1-4 academic calendar. The one-month semester is time set aside for students to define their talents, goals, and aspirations by learning outside the classroom through such activities as exploring foreign countries or investigating career possibilities.

SUMMER SCHOOL

Mount Union College in Alliance, Ohio, was the first

college to spoil students' vacations when it opened a summer school in 1870.

THESIS TOPICS

Students at many universities spend a good part of their senior year buried in the library trying to get a handle on the academic monster known as the thesis. While the content of many theses has been known to produce a yawn or two (a recent paper at Texas A&M was "A Survey of the Parasites of the Cotton Fleahopper in Its Wild Habitat"), some recent titles are more likely to make the reader sit up and take notice.

Optics in a Coffee Cup: A Study of Caustics and Catastrophes (Physics)

To Dream the Impossible Dream: Contamination and Trace Metal Analysis of Hair (Chemistry)

Just Give Me a Cold Damp Corner: A Study of Solitude in the Monastic Tradition from Antony to Benedict (Medieval Studies)

Spoked Bike Wheels (Civil Engineering)

Getting Around the Old Bastards: Congressional Appropriations Committees (Politics)

The Message of Star Trek: Science Fiction as Political Art (Politics)

Cheap Thrill Politics (Politics)

Purple Swans and Violet Sheep (Independent Study)

There's No Business Like Shaw Business: The Plays of George Bernard Shaw (English)

How Much of Your Face Can I See at Once? (Psychology)

The Dancing Bee (Biology)

Father Knows Best (Classics)

Facts Only Confuse the Truth (Comparative Literature)

The Newspaper Boy (East Asian Studies)

The Kosher Jesus (Religion)

Still Ironing Curtains (Slavic Languages)

We + They = Us (Sociology)

STUDENT NICKNAMES FOR COURSES

Virtually every college has a geology course students have labeled "Rocks for Jocks." Beyond this time-honored sobriquet, what other names do students have for their courses?

Texas A&M
Literature for Children	Kiddie Lit
Introductory Chemistry	Cowboy Chemistry

Princeton
Female Literary Tradition	Chick Lit
Astronomy 103	Astrogut
Music 103	Clapping for Credit

Rochester
National Security Policy	Bombs and Rockets
World Population and Resources	Food and Famine

Fairfield
Astronomy I	Lost in Space

Harvard
Human Behavioral Biology	Sex
Modern Art and Abstraction	Spots 'n' Dots
American Architecture Since 1700	Gas Stations
The Concept of the Hero in Hellenic Civilization	Heroes for Zeros (as a gut course taken by athletes)
Nordic History	Sub-Zero Heroes
Literature of Social Reflection	Guilt
Monuments of Japan	Rice Paddies
Folklore and Myth	Bedtime Stories
Introductory Electronics	Wires and Pliers

Georgia Tech
Introduction to Ceramic Engineering	Bricks for Kicks

Chicago
Self-Culture and Society	Self-Torture and Anxiety
Professional and Academic Writing	Little Red Schoolhouse

NAMES OF REAL COURSES

Anyone who has attended college is familiar with courses that virtually all institutions have in common, such as English Composition, American History, Calculus, and Introductory Psychology. But not all courses are quite so ordinary. Here are actual courses offered by various colleges in 1986–87:

Texas A&M
Unsteady State Processes

Carleton
Aquatic Sculpture

Wisconsin
Tree Fruits
Hunters and Gatherers
Zen and Martial Arts
Animal Parasites of Human Beings

Maryland
Introduction to Underwater Archeology

Rochester
Existentialism and Rock 'n' Roll
MTV: Music and Culture
Couples Communication
Psychology of Academic Success

Harvard
Sound and Hearing

Carnegie Mellon
Thinking

Washington (St. Louis)
Physics for Poets

Arizona State
The Aerodynamics of Frisbee Throwing

Brown
Rock 'n' Roll Is Here to Stay
A Perfect 10: The Man's Woman

Scripps
Reading, Writing and Thinking

Michigan
The Good Life
Roman Decadence
Waves and Beaches
Dinosaurs and Other Failures
Construction Uncertainty
Antenna Theory
Hormone Action
Epic and Saga
Organized Camping

HIPPOCRACY

"Hippopotamus Hydrostatics: the use of water to effect temperature control in Hippopotami." This was a course description that might have been found in a catalog at the University of Rochester in 1962. It all turned out to be an elaborate joke put on by Rochester biology majors. The students founded a Department of Hippopotamus Studies, complete with faculty assignments and a course catalog.

PRESIDENTIAL THESIS

A ponderous thesis title, submitted by a Harvard politics major in 1940, was "Appeasement at Munich: The Inevitable Result of the Slowness of the British Democracy to Change from a Disarmament

Policy." Published commercially under the title *Why England Slept,* it earned $40,000 in royalties that the author donated to the town of Plymouth, England, which was bombed during World War II. The author of the thesis was John F. Kennedy.

BEST-SELLING THESIS

William F. Buckley's successful book *God and Man at Yale* originally was written as his senior thesis.

COMPREHENSIVE EXAMS

In 1913 Whitman College in Walla Walla, Washington, was the first college to require all students to pass a comprehensive exam, and the approach hasn't changed in seventy-five years. Current Whitman undergraduates must pass both an oral and written examination in their major subject. Oral exams, before a faculty panel, run from 1 to 3 hours, and written tests can be as long as 5 hours. These requirements are in addition to a senior thesis.

IT'S NOT EDUCATION, IT'S TRAINING

In October 1971 Adelphi University of Garden City, New York, was the first college to offer courses on a railroad train. The $246 course fee did not include train fare. Given the reputation of Long Island Rail Road trains to run late, it is assumed the students had ample time to complete their lessons.

A STEAK IN ONE'S EDUCATION

Far from modern high-tech education that teaches robotics, particle physics, and molecular biology is the meat management program at Sul Ross State in Alpine, Texas. Sul Ross offers a degree in meat science. Courses are given in livestock slaughter, sausage manufacturing, carcass evaluation, and meat chemistry.

ART AND SCIENCE, SCIENCE AND ART

Poets and physicists aren't often seen breaking bread together. Some colleges, recognizing the different worlds that literary and scientific types frequent, offer courses to bridge the gap. For example, Washington University in St. Louis has an introductory science course called Physics for Poets.

Santa Clara's efforts extend in the opposite direction with Poetry for Engineers. The course is taught by Santa Clara's president, William Rewak, who uses authors such as Robert Frost and T. S. Eliot to encourage engineering majors to put their calculators aside and let their imaginations run loose.

A GOOD DEAL

This college's motto is "Make a Blue Chip Investment in Your Future." No, it's not the Harvard or Stanford Business School. It is a branch of New Jersey's Atlantic Community College, the Casino Career Institute in Atlantic City. The institute teaches the fundamentals of blackjack, craps, roulette, and baccarat. The Casino Institute's course in slot machines is not about levers and gears but about microprocessors. While gamblers still refer to modern slots as one-armed bandits, they are actually one-armed computer bandits. The final exams in the dealing courses are called auditions. Students must demonstrate their classroom knowledge at the gaming table, with the staff of the institute acting as the gamblers.

4

BEYOND THE CLASSROOM

LIBRARIES, COLLECTIONS, UNIVERSITY PRESSES, MUSEUMS, COMPUTERS, RESEARCH

Libraries

It is said that the three key ingredients of a college are students, teachers, and books. From Harvard's initial collection of only 400 books, college libraries have grown to become massive enterprises comprising millions of books, periodicals, and microfilms.

FIRST LIBRARY

There is only one book left from the first library opened at Harvard in 1638, and that is a matter of luck. After a 1764 fire destroyed the Harvard library, it was thought that every volume was lost. Fortunately *Christian Warfare Against the Devill, World, and Flesh* survived because a student had forgotten to turn the book in when it was due.

Along with the oldest library, Harvard has the honor of the

first librarian, "library-keeper" Solomon Stoddard, appointed in 1677.

FIRST LIBRARY BUILDING

Until 1840 a college library usually consisted of a room set aside within the main academic building that held a modest collection of books. On May 6,

The first college library building.

1840, the University of South Carolina opened the first separate college library building in the United States. It was designed by noted southern architect Robert Mills, and its Federalist style was derived from the famous Fireproof Building in Charleston. Part of the building fund was set aside to purchase books, and by 1850 South Carolina had accumulated 18,400 volumes, the largest collection in the South. Although it is no longer used as the main

university library, the building is still standing today and is a National Historic Landmark.

COSTS

A well-stocked and well-staffed library is an integral part of a good college, but libraries are expensive to operate. For example, Stanford's 1986–87 library costs were $23-million, about 7 percent of the total operating budget. The cost to purchase and process one book was $60, and to subscribe to a scientific journal, $175.

MOST OVERDUE BOOK

Library records at the University of Cincinnati show that the 1805 book *Medical Reports of the Effects of Water, Cold and Warm, Remedy in Fever and Febrile Diseases, Whether Applied to the Body or Used Internally,* by James Currie, was checked out in 1823. It was 145 years overdue when returned on December 7, 1968, by the borrower's great-grandson, Richard Dodd. If the fine were two cents a day, it would have cost $1,053.60. Fortunately for the younger Dodd, the fine was waived.

THE GREAT LIBRARIAN

Andrew Carnegie, the Scottish philanthropist who made millions in the steel industry, donated $57-million to establish 2,800 libraries around the country. Ironically, although Carnegie was a major benefactor

LARGEST

The centerpiece of the largest college book collection is the Widener Library at Harvard. It alone holds more than 3 million volumes. But if it were not for an iceberg, this magnificent structure might never have been built. The money for the library was given by Mrs. Eleanor Widener in memory of her son Harry, who perished when the Titanic struck an iceberg and sank in the North Atlantic with the loss of 1,500 lives on April 16, 1912.

The ten largest college libraries as of January 1, 1987, were:

		Volumes
1.	Harvard	11,284,170
2.	Yale	8,391,707
3.	Illinois	7,190,443
4.	U Cal Berkeley	7,031,934
5.	Michigan	6,019,919
6.	Texas	5,753,629
7.	Columbia	5,625,925
8.	UCLA	5,625,521
9.	Stanford	5,598,363
10.	Cornell	4,865,137

The largest library in the United States is the Library of Congress, with 20,957,228 volumes. (If the entire U Cal system is counted as one library, its nearly 23 million volumes are the most.) Other libraries of comparable size to major research university libraries are the New York Public Library, with 6,056,320 volumes, and the Boston Public Library, with 5,806,895. Among institutions that do not have major graduate schools, Dartmouth College has the largest library, with 1,664,847 volumes. For two-year colleges, Anchorage Community College is the leader, with 447,189. The fastest-growing library is UCLA, which increased its holdings by 257,027 books in 1987.

of the college that bears his name, Carnegie Mellon in Pittsburgh, he never established a library on the school's campus. It wasn't until 1961, nearly sixty years after it was founded, that Carnegie Mellon received a gift from Mr. and Mrs. Roy Hunt to construct a main library building so the various departmental collections could be brought under one roof.

SMILING ABE

On display at the Lovejoy Library at Southern Illinois in Edwardsville is a rare portrait of a beardless, smiling Abraham Lincoln painted by Alban Conant just before the 1860 election. On seeing the painting Mrs. Lincoln exclaimed, "Oh, that's just the way he looks. I hope he will look like that after

money for a book in those days. The purchase turned out to be a good one; today *Birds of North America* is worth $300,000.

A WAGONLOAD OF BOOKS

In 1811, after John Browne founded Miami University in Oxford, Ohio, he made a trip east to raise money for a library. His visit with James Madison at the White House was unproductive, but a member of Congress gave him a five-volume history of Ireland. Proceeding northward, he received $5 from the president of Princeton and two books and $10 from John Adams. After two months of effort, Browne returned to Ohio with a wagonload of books and $700. Unfortunately, a few weeks later while crossing the Little Miami River, Browne's wagon overturned and he drowned.

the first of November." As matters turned out, there wouldn't be any more smiling portraits of Lincoln.

GOOD BUY

In 1836 the first book purchased for the University of Michigan library was J. J. Audubon's *Birds of North America*. After considerable debate, the Regents authorized $970 for its acquisition, a large sum of

CARD CATALOGS

Before computer access completely replaces the familiar card catalogs, with their little white 3 x 5s filed in row after row of wooden drawers, the world should recognize the ingenuity of Otis Hall Robinson, an 1861 graduate of the University of Rochester. Robinson invented the hole in the cards for the rod to go through. This simple but brilliant idea made library catalogs available to students and faculty, since librarians no longer had to worry about the cards becoming disarranged.

WATER, WATER, EVERYWHERE

In the flood of November 1985, librarians at Hollins College in Roanoke, Virginia, saw much of their collection go down the drain, literally. Swelled by 12 inches of rain in five days, the banks of Carvin's Creek overflowed and poured into the basement and subbasement of Fishburn Library. Some 30,000 of the college's total collection of 234,000 volumes were destroyed, and another 20,000 books were damaged. Many of the 20,000 were saved by quick thinking on the part of the Hollins librarians. They arranged for the Roanoke Fish and Oyster Company to donate special boxes and refrigerator space so the books could be quick-frozen. Thousands more books were placed on the library's patio with their pages fanned out to dry in the sun.

In all, 40,000 books were destroyed, but the plight of Hollins brought a great deal of support from others. Boston College donated 30,000 duplicate books from their library, hundreds of local citizens signed up for the "Adopt a Book" program to nurse a waterlogged book back to health, and Hollins received flood-restoration gifts totaling $1.3-million.

After the flood—at Hollins.

Despite all the damage it caused, the flooding was not without its light moments. During the cleanup, the Hollins librarians ran a waterlogged-book-title contest. The three finalists were *The Creek Also Rises, 20,000 Leagues Under the Library,* and *Slime and Punishment.*

Special Libraries and Collections

MUSIC

UCLA's Rubsamen Music Library houses some 98,000 books, 55,000 music scores, 250,000 pieces of sheet music, 35,000 recordings, and the personal collections of many composers. The music library also contains more than 400 non-Western instruments.

Besides UCLA, the three largest music collections and music research libraries are the Peabody at Johns Hopkins, the University of Illinois Music Library, and the Sibley at the University of Rochester.

Indiana University has a huge collection of 7,000 wax cylinders (the type used on Edison's original gramophone) on which are recorded rare folk music from African tribes, Eskimos, and American Indians. Many of the tribes have disappeared, and Indiana's collection is the only record of their songs and chants.

FILM

The UCLA Film Archive is the largest collection of films on a college campus. It contains more than 20,000 movies and short subjects and 27 million feet of Hearst Metrotone News film dating back to 1895. Under a grant from the National Endowment for the Arts, the UCLA archive is preserving old movie prints by transferring them from unstable nitrate film to a more durable medium. Along with its movie relics, UCLA also maintains the largest collection of television programs on kinescope, telefilm, and videotape. These include dramatic, comedy-variety, documentary, and public affairs programs broadcast since 1947.

BOSTON UNIVERSITY

At its Mugar Memorial Library, Boston University has established the Twentieth Century Archives, one of the largest collections of its kind in the world. It contains the personal papers and memorabilia of more than 1,400 contemporary public figures. Among those included are Stewart Alsop, Samuel Beckett, Ella Fitzgerald, Robert Frost, Theodore Roosevelt, George Bernard Shaw, Martin Luther King Jr., Isaac Asimov, Al Capp, Sam Shepard, and Alexander Woollcott.

VIRGINIA

The Barrett Library of American Literature at the University of Virginia includes first editions and manuscripts of nearly all major American writers from the Colonial period to the present. Poe, Hawthorne, Twain, Crane, Whitman, Dos Passos, Faulkner, and Frost are some of the authors represented. Another special library at UVA, the McGregor, emphasizes major southern historical figures. The McGregor has the papers of Jefferson, Madison, and Monroe, as well as those of many other Virginia statesmen and politicians.

NORTHWESTERN

The internationally known Herskovits Library of African Studies is located at Northwestern University in Evanston, Illinois. It features one of the most extensive collections of books on Africa, including all disciplines and many different languages. The Herskovits Library provides academic support to Northwestern's Program in African Studies, the first such program in the United States.

MICHIGAN

The Clements Library of Americana at the University of

Michigan contains, along with many other rare books, an original copy of Christopher Columbus's letter to Queen Isabella telling about his discovery of America.

PRESIDENTIAL LIBRARIES

Three colleges are home to presidential libraries. The first U.S. president to establish his library on a college campus was Lyndon Johnson at the University of Texas. Next came the Gerald Ford Library at Michigan, followed by a collection of Jimmy Carter's papers and memorabilia at Emory. Until mid-1987 it looked as though the Reagan library would be built at Stanford, but faculty objections caused a change in plans.

MISCELLANEOUS LIBRARY COLLECTIONS

Due to the generosity of H. Ross Perot, the University of Texas at Austin now has one the country's largest collections of early English-language books and manuscripts. With a value of at least $15-million, the collection contains nearly 1,500 pieces dating from 1475 to 1700. Among the valuable items are the first book printed in English, *Recuyell of the histories of Troye,* by Roul Le Fevre, and the first editions of books by Chaucer, Milton, and Thomas Hobbes.

Although Texas's early English holdings are significant,

the largest such collection at a U.S. college is the Bienecke Rare Book and Manuscript Library at Yale. Known for the size of its resources (half a million books and 1.5 million manuscripts) in British and European literature and history, the Bienecke also displays spectacular individual items like the Gutenberg Bible, the Cloverdale Bible, the Bay

---

Three of the forty-eight known copies of the complete Gutenberg Bible are owned by American universities.

Psalm Book, and a first edition of *Pilgrim's Progress*.

The Nettie Lee Benson Latin American Collection, part of the University of Texas library system, has been described as "one of the world's most important libraries on Latin America." Started in 1921, the Benson Collection now contains 510,000 books, periodicals, and pamphlets; 2 million pages of manuscripts; and 18,000 maps and other materials. Not only does the Benson Collection serve as a valuable research center for University of Texas students and faculty, it also attracts scholars from all over the United States as well as foreign countries.

The largest collection on poets Robert Browning and Elizabeth Barrett Browning is at Baylor's Armstrong Library.

UCLA's Elmer Belt Library of Vinciana, widely regarded as one of the nation's finest, includes a rare facsimile of

Leonardo da Vinci's notebooks and some 15,000 other articles.

Lake Forest College in Illinois has an extensive collection of ghost stories. A former Lake Forest trustee, Hugo Sonnenschein, believed in ghosts. When he died in 1981 Sonnenschein left the college hundreds of books and periodicals on spirits. The collection of shivery tales includes stories by Ambrose Bierce, Arthur Conan Doyle, and Edgar Allan Poe.

Nearly 60,000 pieces of material pertaining to *Gone with the Wind* author Margaret

---

Nearly 60,000 items pertaining to* Gone with the Wind *author Margaret Mitchell are housed at the University of Georgia's library.

Mitchell are contained in a special collection within the University of Georgia library.

The Mark Twain Project at the Bancroft Library of the University of California at Berkeley houses the richest collection of Mark Twain materials in the world. It includes 600 manuscripts (many never published), thousands of letters, dozens of scrapbooks, and hundreds of photographs. The Mark Twain Project plans to issue Twain's works in a seventy-volume set, of which seventeen volumes have been published. The project leaders are taking care to heed Twain's advice to editors of his material: "Any editor to whom I submit my manuscripts has an undisputed right to delete anything to which he objects, but God Almighty himself has no right to put words in my mouth that I never used."

One of the most popular tourist attractions on the Berkeley campus, also located in the Bancroft Library, is the famous Plate of Brass that was said to have been left near San Francisco in 1579 by Sir Francis Drake when he circumnavigated the globe on his ship, the *Golden Hind*. The public's fascination with this ancient treasure has not diminished since 1979 when it was shown that the Plate of Brass was an elaborate hoax. On close examination, metallurgists discovered the brass was of a type that did not exist in the 1500s and the edges of the plate had been cut by a modern machine.

Of the forty-eight known copies of the complete two-volume set of the Gutenberg Bible, three are owned by colleges—Texas, Harvard, and Yale. Texas purchased its copy in 1978 for $2.4-million. In December 1987, a Gutenberg Bible was sold for $5.4-million.

University Presses

BEST-SELLERS

The primary purpose of a university press is to print scholarly works that expand knowledge in the various academic disciplines. While such books rarely sell more than 5,000 copies, now and then an academically oriented book will catch on. The best-sellers in this category are two books from the University of Chicago Press: Kate Turabian's *A Manual for Writers of Term Papers, Theses, and Dissertations* (5.4 million copies) and Richmond Lattimore's translation of *The Iliad of Homer* (1.3 million). Other scholarly books that have done well are another Chicago title, *The Structure of Scientific Revolutions*, by Thomas Kuhn (670,000), and Princeton University Press's *I Ching*, by C. F. Baynes and R. Wilhelm (555,000).

In recent years university presses have moved beyond their traditional academic orientation and are publishing novels, biographies, and other books intended for the popular market. This modern-day split personality of many university presses is illustrated by two works recently published by the University of Chicago. One is titled *Rhythmic Gesture in Mozart* and the second *The Eater's Guide to Chinese Characters*, a book for Chinese food lovers who prefer to read untranslated menus.

continued

In the trade category, university press best-sellers are:

Fiction	Title	Press	Copies sold
John Kennedy Toole	A Confederacy of Dunces	LSU	800,000
Tom Clancy	The Hunt for Red October	Naval Institute	360,000
Stephen Coonts	Flight of the Intruder	Naval Institute	260,000

Nonfiction			
H. B. Howell	Better Farm Accounting	Iowa State	800,000
William Kershner	Student Pilot's Manual	Iowa State	657,000
Norman McLean	A River Runs Through It	Chicago	136,000
Eudora Welty	The Collected Stories of Eudora Welty	Harvard	127,000

John Kennedy Toole committed suicide in 1969, apparently out of frustration at not being able to get *A Confederacy of Dunces* published. Eleven years later his mother was successful in convincing LSU to come out with the book. Of the 800,000 copies *A Confederacy of Dunces* has sold, 750,000 are the paperbacks that LSU arranged for Grove Press to print.

One novel that "got away" from a university press was . . . *And Ladies of the Club,* by Helen Hoover Santmyer. When an original printing of 2,000 books by the Ohio State University Press didn't sell very well, the rights were transferred to Putnam, which later sold 335,000 copies.

In addition to the 1981 Pulitzer Prize won by *A Confederacy of Dunces,* the LSU Press published *Flying Change* by Henry Taylor, the winner of the 1986 Pulitzer in poetry. The University of Chicago Press also has garnered a number of major awards, including three National Book Awards, two Carey-Thomas Awards, and a Pulitzer Prize.

OLDEST

Founded in 1878, the Johns Hopkins Press is the oldest college press in continuous operation. Since it first printed the *American Journal of Mathematics,* Hopkins has published over 2,700 journals and books.

LARGEST

The largest university press is that of the University of Chicago, with sales of 22 million volumes since it began operations in 1894. In second position is MIT, with 8 million copies sold. The University of Chicago Press has been so successful that the *Chicago Tribune* dubbed it the "King of the Least-Sellers."

Looking at the number of new titles published in 1986, the most productive university presses were:

	Number of titles
1. Princeton	151
2. Yale	140
3. U of California	137
4. Chicago	130

	Number of titles
5. MIT	122
6. Indiana	117
7. Cornell	114
8. Harvard	106
Johns Hopkins	106

The totals for the University of California Press, which is located in Berkeley, include all nine campuses of the system. For single universities, Princeton, Yale, and Chicago tend to publish the most new titles.

Museums

College museums serve two purposes. They function as extended classrooms in which students can study subjects like paintings, artifacts, and animal fossils. They also provide a valuable cultural and educational resource for the local community.

ART MUSEUMS

Often overshadowed by large city museums, college art collections are a treasure waiting to be discovered. American college museums house some of the finest works of art in the country. Focusing primarily on education rather than public display, these museums tend to be somewhat smaller and less well-known than major attractions like New York's Metropolitan Museum of Art or Chicago's Art Institute.

Oldest

Founded in 1832, the Yale University Art Gallery is the oldest university museum in the Western Hemisphere. Yale started its collection with a group of more than 100 paintings of the Revolutionary period by Colonel John Trumbull.

Oberlin

Called by the director of the Cleveland Art Museum the number one art museum for a college of its size (and third to Harvard and Yale among all college and university museums), Oberlin's Allen Museum has a collection of over 10,000 works of art. Most notable are Dutch paintings of the seventeenth century, nineteenth- and twentieth-century European and American paintings, contemporary art, a large number of prints including works by Dürer and Rembrandt, and a group of 1,500 Japanese woodcuts. The Allen's *Saint Sebastian,* painted by Hendrik Terbrugghen in 1625, is valued at more than $2.5-million and has been called one of the country's thirty best works of art.

Smith

Of equal stature to Oberlin in the small-college art world is the museum at Smith College in Northampton, Massachusetts. Called a world-class artistic resource, the Smith art museum began in 1879 with the $100 purchase of *In Grandmother's Time* by Thomas Eakins, an artist who was little known at the time. In 1911 a group of undergraduates donated a Rembrandt etching, and a Rodin bronze followed in 1914. Today the museum is especially noted for its nineteenth- and twentieth-century French and American paintings.

UCLA

Although Harvard and Yale are acknowledged as having the two finest university art museums, a 1987 announcement that UCLA had reached an "agreement in principle" with Norton Simon to receive his world-renowned art collection appeared to put UCLA in a position to overtake them both. This treasure, valued at $750-million, would be the largest gift ever made to a university and would give UCLA the preeminent college-based art collection in the world. The Simon works include Raphael's *Madonna and Child with Book,* Francisco de Zurbarán's *Still Life: Lemons, Oranges, and a Rose,* and Picasso's *Woman with Book.* Now, however, the agreement is stalled amidst legal complexities, making the eventual disposition of the Simon collection uncertain. Even without the Simon collection, UCLA's Wight museum is noted for its internationally recognized exhibitions, including African Art, The Nature of Japan, American Impressionism, and Painters of Italian Life.

Part of the Wight is the Grunwall Center for the Graphic Arts. This center contains approximately 30,000 prints, drawings, and photographs from the thirteenth through the twentieth centuries.

Harvard

Until the Simon gift to UCLA is made final (if ever), Harvard will continue to rank first among university art museums. Harvard has three major museums: the Fogg, the Busch-Reisinger, and the Sackler. Together these museums house some 100,000 works of art, a university collection that equals those of many major city museums.

The Fogg Art Museum was founded in 1891. Its present building is a large four-story structure with a beautiful interior that has two floors of galleries surrounding an Italian Renaissance courtyard. On view are masterpieces of Western painting and sculpture, including works by Rubens, Poussin, Van Gogh, Cézanne, and Pollack.

The Busch-Reisinger's major strength is in twentieth-century German, Swiss, Russian, and Scandinavian works, including masterpieces by Munch, Klee, Nolde, Feininger, and Klimt. The Busch-Reisinger is also noted for its medieval and Renaissance sculpture and its eighteenth-century porcelain from Germany and Austria.

The Arthur M. Sackler Museum contains Harvard's collection of Oriental, ancient, and Islamic art. Among its outstanding holdings are the world's finest display of Chinese jades and Chinese cave reliefs.

Yale

Like Harvard, Yale has more than one major art museum. The Yale University Art Gallery consists of two sections, one built in 1928 to resemble an Italian Gothic palace and the other a modern building designed in 1953 by Louis Kahn. The Art Gallery's holdings represent virtually all national schools and important periods in art history. Included are the first collection of Italian Renaissance art ever displayed in America, over 600 Greek and Roman vases, antiquities from a Roman excavation, African sculpture, pre-Columbian art, and American painting and decorative arts.

The Yale Center for British Art, opened in 1977, is the result of a gift by Paul Mellon. The Yale Center houses the largest collection of British art outside England—more than 1,200 paintings, 10,000 drawings, 20,000 prints, and 20,000 rare books. It is especially strong in works by Hogarth, Constable, and Turner.

North Carolina

The South boasts the University of North Carolina's Ackland Art Museum. The Ackland opened in 1958 with a modest collection of prints, some eighteenth- and nineteenth-century furniture and ceramics, and a few works of art. During the next twenty-five years the collection grew rapidly, and now it has earned both a regional and national reputation. The focus of the Ackland is broad, covering the entire history of Western art from ancient Egypt to the present. Paintings and sculpture of the nineteenth century are well represented, including works by Gilbert Stuart, Delacroix, Rodin, and Degas. The print collection, with more than 6,000 works, covers the history of printmaking from the fifteenth to the twentieth century.

Kansas, Nebraska, Wisconsin

In the Midwest, the Spencer Museum of Art at the University of Kansas houses a collection of 25,000 art objects. The Spencer's holdings are especially strong in seventeenth- and eighteenth-century German art, American painting, nineteenth-century Japanese prints, and contemporary Chinese art.

Another notable Midwestern art museum is the Sheldon Memorial Art Gallery at the University of Nebraska in Lincoln. It has a number of major pieces that show the development of American art from the eighteenth century to modern times. Included are nineteenth-century landscape artists; impressionists, modernists, and realists from the twentieth century; and a collection of recent sculpture. Featured artists are Thomas Cole, Georgia O'Keeffe, Frank Stella, and Edward Hopper. Designed by Philip Johnson, the building itself is a work of art.

In the upper Midwest the Elvehjem Museum of Art at the University of Wisconsin–Madison includes over 10,000 works of art, ranging from 2300 B.C. to the present. These include sculpture, prints, drawings, and decorative arts from the fifteenth through the twentieth centuries as well as nineteenth- and twentieth-century European and American paintings. Of special note are the collections of Indian miniatures, Japanese prints, and Russian icons and paintings. Attached to the Elvehjem is the Kohler Art Library. With over 80,000 volumes, it is the largest public university art library in North America.

Berkeley

In the San Francisco Bay Area, U Cal Berkeley has a distinguished collection. Berkeley's most famous acquisition is the world's largest collection of the works of twentieth-century abstract expressionist Hans Hofmann. Other modern Americans on display are Mark Rothko and Willem de Kooning. Berkeley also shows seventeenth-century works by Peter Paul Rubens, nineteenth-century paintings by Cézanne and Rousseau, and pieces from the twentieth century by Joan Miró and Fernand Léger.

Stanford

If it weren't for the San Francisco earthquake, Stanford's original art museum, built in 1891, would be the largest

---

Stanford's original art museum was destroyed by the Great San Francisco Earthquake.

---

college museum in the United States. The museum measured 650 feet by 330 feet and contained 300,000 square feet of display area. The huge structure housed a variety of collections, ranging from Egyptian antiquities to American Indian objects. Unfortunately, the 1906 San Francisco earthquake put an end to the museum. Eighty percent of the building was destroyed or made useless. When the university turned to the reconstruction of its campus after the earthquake, the museum's remains were allowed to fall into further disrepair. It wasn't until 1954 that Stanford started to revive its art department. It now has an art museum for collections, including one of the world's finest displays of Rodin sculpture, and a separate gallery for exhibits.

Cornell's art museum.

OUTDOOR ART

Not all the important works of art on college campuses are inside buildings. For hundreds of years campuses have been home to outdoor sculpture, but until recently the works usually were limited to statues that honored notable Americans or college founders. In the last two decades colleges have moved from statuary to sculpture, commissioning artists to create modern works that add variety and beauty to the existing mixture of green space, walkways, and buildings.

The University of Houston has one of the largest collections of outdoor art. It consists of thirty-one different pieces placed at various locations on its 500-acre campus. Artists such as Richard McDermott Miller, Reuben Nakian, and Gerhard Marcks are featured. A major reason for Houston's extensive sculpture collection is a Board of Regents rule that 1 percent of the cost of a new building must be set aside to purchase works of art.

UCLA has an impressive display but, unlike Houston, does not spread the artwork around the campus. It is contained in the Franklin D. Murphy Sculpture Garden, set on 5 acres of rolling campus. Among UCLA's seventy pieces of twentieth-century sculpture are works by Rodin, Matisse, Calder, Moore, and Miró.

In Regents Plaza at the University of Michigan stands a 1½-ton cube sculpture by Bernard Rosenthal that is so precisely balanced that it can be turned by hand. Tradition says that the president has to spin the cube each morning to start the university.

The largest outdoor sculpture on a college campus is the 28-foot-diameter, 25-ton World Globe at Babson College in Wellesley, Massachusetts. It shows the major features of the Earth, including cities, mountain ranges, rivers, and ocean contours. Like the planet it represents, the globe is set at an angle of 23.5 degrees from the vertical and rotates about its axis.

Because public art "belongs" to the people, they often hold strong views of what they like and what they don't. In Carleton's collection is a recent addition by Harvard artist Dimitri Hadzi called *The Carleton Arch*. Hadzi says the work is his best piece of sculpture and that it "will serve as a didactic reference, providing a link to history and focus for the future."

Others have a different opinion. A Carleton staff member thinks it "looks like a Transformer—not the electrical kind, but the toy."

Princeton has a small but distinguished collection, with pieces by Nevelson, Picasso, and Lipchitz. But even famous sculptures are not immune to the

Hadzi's arch, at Carleton.

irreverent perspective from which college students occasionally view the world. Princeton undergraduates have labeled Henry Moore's highly regarded *Oval with Points* the "Donut with Teeth."

NATURAL HISTORY MUSEUMS

Kansas

The Dycke Museum of Natural History at the University of Kansas is the number one tourist attraction in the state. The Dycke is noted for one of the largest diorama exhibits in the world, a vast sweep that shows North American plants and animals, and for the mounted body of the Seventh Cavalry horse, Comanche, the only living thing found on the battlefield after the Indian massacre of Custer and his troops at the Little Big Horn.

Florida

The University of Florida has the largest natural science museum in the South, with collections concentrated on Florida, the Caribbean, and South America. Designed to look like a southeastern Indian ceremonial mound, the museum resembles Mayan pyramids perched on the edge of a ravine.

ARCHAEOLOGY AND ANTHROPOLOGY MUSEUMS

Seeking to record and preserve thousands of years of human accomplishment, American colleges exhibit some of the most important archaeological and anthropological collections in the United States.

University of Pennsylvania

Penn's University Museum has extensive collections from nearly every part of the world. Over the past hundred years, students and faculty members from Penn have gone on more than 300 expeditions, and they brought back many of the artifacts that are now on display. Penn is world famous for its holdings in Egyptian art and archaeology, including statues from workshops in Abydos, architectural elements from the royal palace at Memphis, and reliefs from the chapel of Kapure.

Michigan

The Kelsey Museum of Archeology at the University of Michigan is known for its Near Eastern and Mediterranean collections. In 1985 archaeologists from Michigan caused a stir when they unearthed a women's religious shrine at Paestum in Italy. Because so little is known about secret women's cults in ancient Rome, the discovery sparked considerable interest about the role of women in antiquity and the nature of their religious practices.

SPECIAL MUSEUMS

Arctic

The Peary-MacMillan Arctic Museum at Bowdoin is unique among college museums. It is named for and features members of the classes of 1877 and 1898 at Bowdoin, Arctic explorers Robert Peary and Donald MacMillan. On April 6, 1909, Peary became the first man to reach the North Pole.

The schooner Bowdoin.

MacMillan assisted Peary in this famous feat and later made twenty-six Arctic voyages on the schooner *Bowdoin.* The museum re-creates the famous trip to the pole and includes a number of exhibits that show the people and animals of the Arctic.

Naval
Included in the collection of the Naval Academy Museum in Annapolis are ship models, marine paintings by Edward Moran, the table from the battleship *Missouri* on which the World War II surrender of Japan was signed, Commodore Oliver Hazard Perry's flag from the Battle of Lake Erie, and the personal effects of famous naval officers John Paul Jones, Decatur, Farragut, and Dewey.

Moon Rock and Meteorites
Even though there is a federal law against owning a piece of the moon, a fragment of moon rock

is part of Texas Tech's Southwest Collection. With unjustified bureaucratic assurance, NASA officials say they can account for all of the moon rocks on earth. In the meantime, Texas Tech plans to keep its lunar treasure on display.

When it comes to gathering material from outer space, Arizona State leads all other colleges. The ASU Center of Meteorite Studies has 1,200 specimens, the second largest in the United States (after the Smithsonian Institution).

Computers

Scientists at major research universities have a critical need for large computers that store vast quantities of data and perform millions of operations per second. Computers are needed to do mathematical calculations that are virtually impossible to perform by any other means, solving problems ranging from microscopic to global.

Inside a human cell, a few microns in diameter, there are forty-six chromosomes containing from 50,000 to 100,000 genes. Within these genes are strings of DNA that carry the blueprints for cell reproduction. Supercomputers will be used to analyze how 3 to 5 billion base pairs of DNA control the way the body functions.

Perhaps the biggest mathematical problem facing scientists today is to learn how atmospheric forces affect climate and weather. As an example of the complexity of the calculations involved, it would take a supercomputer, running day and night, three to five years to accurately measure the effects of pollutants on the depletion of the earth's ozone layer.

Fortunately for colleges, computer manufacturers like IBM and Digital make their new lines of large machines available at discounts, and colleges in the market for a supercomputer usually can count on the federal government to pay a good portion of the cost.

At the personal computer level, many colleges have made arrangements with companies like IBM, Apple, and Zenith for their students to buy microcomputers at greatly reduced prices. From the smallest to the largest machines, colleges have been enthusiastic users of the newest technology the industry has to offer.

LARGEST NUMBER-CRUNCHER

Until the new ETA-10 becomes fully operational, the University of Minnesota has the most computing power of any college.

SUPERCOMPUTERS

A number of colleges have access to the largest computers made today. The fastest machines among the latest generation of computers can make approximately 1 billion calculations per second.

Colleges that have supercomputers are listed below. While the supercomputers are located at the colleges mentioned, they are usually tied into a network that allows a number of institutions to have access to the computer at the same time.

	Type
Alabama at Huntsville	CRAY X-MP/24
U Cal Berkeley	CRAY X-MP/14
*U Cal San Diego	CRAY X-MP/48
*Carnegie Mellon/Pittsburgh	CRAY X-MP/48
Colorado State	CYBER 205
*Cornell	IBM 3090/600E
Florida State	CYBER 205 (ETA 10)
Georgia	CYBER 205
*Illinois	CRAY X-MP/48
Kentucky	IBM 3090-300
Michigan	IBM 3090-400
Minnesota	CRAY-2 (two), CYBER 205
Mississippi	CYBER 205
Ohio State	CRAY X-MP/24
*Princeton	CYBER 205 (two) (ETA 10)
Purdue	CYBER 205
Texas	CRAY X-MP/24

*National Science Foundation Supercomputer Center

This is primarily due to an arrangement the university has with Cray Corporation, the largest manufacturer of supercomputers, conveniently located in Minneapolis. The university has two CRAY-2s and a CYBER 205 made by Control Data Corporation. One of Minnesota's CRAY-2s, has a memory of 2 billion bytes and a speed of 1 gigaflop (a billion floating-point operations per second). This machine alone has the storage capacity of over 15,000 Apple Macintoshes. (With all their mathematical muscle, supercomputers are

MICROCOMPUTERS

In 1983 Stevens Tech, Clarkson, and Drexel were the first colleges to require all students to purchase personal computers. In the same year, Dallas Baptist asked its students to buy a Radio Shack 100, a small battery-operated portable computer. Virginia Tech in Blacksburg, Virginia, was the first public college to require certain students to have a computer. Thirteen more institutions had initiated a similar requirement by 1987.

	Model required
Bentley	Hewlett-Packard Portable Plus
Clarkson	Zenith Z-100
Dallas Baptist	Radio Shack 100
Drew	Epson QX-16
Drexel	Apple
Harvard Business School	IBM PC
Indiana Tech	Apple
LeTourneau	Zenith Z-121
Mississippi State Veterinary College	Apple
New Jersey Tech	Philips P3100
Polytechnic University	Texas Instruments CC40
South Dakota School of Mines	Internal design
Stevens	DEC PC 350
Vermont (engineering, math, and business)	AT&T PC-6300
Virginia Tech (engineering and computer science)	IBM or Apple
Air Force Academy	Zenith Z-248
Annapolis	Zenith Z-248
West Point	Zenith Z-248

In addition to these eighteen colleges, there are many others at which computers are not required but where students are encouraged to purchase them voluntarily. Colleges that have a high percentage of students with their own microcomputers are Dartmouth, Colby (Maine), Franklin and Marshall, Lehigh, Sweet Briar, Washington (Maryland), Stanford, and Houston.

Drexel, with an estimated 10,000 Apple Macintoshes (all versions) owned by students and faculty, has the largest number of personal computers on a college campus.

actually quite small. The CRAY-2's "brain," its central processing unit, can fit into a briefcase. The central processing unit and memory are contained in a cabinet about the size of a double-door refrigerator.)

The newest advance in computers is the ETA-10 manufactured by ETA Systems, a branch of Control Data Corporation. The ETA-10 is being installed first with four processors and then upgraded to eight processors in 1988. The ETA-10 with eight processors is expected to be able to make 10 billion calculations per second.

In May 1987, Florida State received the first ETA-10, the most powerful supercomputer in the United States. It will be featured in the Supercomputer Computational Research Institute financed by the U.S. Department of Energy, the state of Florida, and ETA Systems. After a six-month trial period, Florida State plans to trade in its CYBER 205 and switch operations to the ETA-10. Florida State will have access to 35 percent of the computer's time, with the remainder going to outside groups. The John von Neumann Supercomputer Center at Princeton received the next ETA-10 in March 1988 and by 1989 should phase out its two CYBER 205s.

COMPUTER U.

The Air Force Academy has perhaps the most comprehensive computer environment of any college. Each cadet is issued a Zenith Z-248 that can be used on its own or linked with the academy's mainframe. The majority of the faculty use computers in classroom instruction. Graphics terminals and specially designed software are a common teaching device, with uses that range from the physics department's simulations of experiments to the teaching of foreign languages through a videodisc technique.

Dartmouth, with 90 percent of its students owning Apple computers, is nearly as computer-intensive as the Air Force Academy. Each dorm room is wired with cable ports that allow the Macs to hook into a campuswide network that offers such conveniences as message boards and access to the library catalog. Students either use their Macs as stand-alone computers or as remote terminals for Dartmouth's large Honeywell mainframe.

Instead of urging students to buy their own personal computers, some colleges have taken a different approach—establishing sophisticated networks that link hundreds of terminals and microcomputers to a powerful central computer. For students and faculty members whose computational needs fall in between the capacity of very large or small machines, a few dozen midsize computers are added. Colleges that have a well-developed form of this method of academic computing are Carnegie Mellon, Brown, and MIT.

COMPUTER DEVELOPMENT

Besides being major users of both large and small computers, colleges have been home to many of the scientists who helped develop modern computer technology.

Iowa State

At Iowa State in 1939, Professor John Atanasoff and his graduate assistant, Clifford Berry, constructed the first electronic digital computer. It was called ABC, the Atanasoff and Berry Computer. Atanasoff and Berry successfully defended their patent in a seven-year court battle against a counterclaim by Sperry that its ENIAC was the first computer.

Iowa State's ABC computer.

Harvard

The Mark I was developed in the early 1940s, not long after the ABC. This large machine, measuring 50 feet by 8 feet, was really a gigantic calculator whose sequences were controlled by instructions coded on a punched paper tape. Calculations were made by switching electromagnetic relays.

Pennsylvania

The ENIAC (Electronic Numerical Integrator and Computer), the first fully electronic digital computer, was invented at Penn's Moore School between 1943 and 1945. The project was financed by the U.S. Army, which needed a better way to construct firing and bombing tables. One of ENIAC's first uses was to make calculations for the Manhattan Project. The machine (which contained 18,000 vacuum tubes and filled a large room) performed 300 multiplications per second, making it 1,000 times faster than the Mark I.

MIT

From 1949 to 1963, MIT scientists were at the forefront of new computer technology. MIT's Whirlwind computer was the first to operate in real time. In 1953, internal magnetic core memory was added to the Whirlwind. A few years later, time-sharing and plain language programs were developed in MIT research labs.

THE FUTURE OF SUPERCOMPUTERS

Today the University of Illinois, through its Center of Supercomputing Research and Development, is the leader in conducting research on new computer designs. Present supercomputers like the CRAY-2, although equipped with large memories and able to execute instructions with astounding speed, are somewhat inflexible in the range of operations they can perform efficiently. In an attempt to overcome these deficiencies, scientists at Illinois are constructing an experimental supercomputer, the Cedar system, that combines many individual processors, the mathematical brains of the computer. With its radically new design, the Cedar system will permit numerous operations to take place at the same time, a technique known as parallel processing. The intended outcome is a new breed of supercomputer that, without a loss of speed, will be able to deliver high-level performance over a wide range of problems.

In addition, Illinois researchers are designing new computer software programs that will be able to take advantage of Cedar's shared memory principle and provide more power and flexibility than programs currently on the market.

COMPUTER PROGRAMS

Some of today's most widely used computer languages were developed at colleges. Intermediate PL was developed at Michigan, and BASIC originated at Dartmouth. Many of the programs that are used to govern the way the computer works, like U Cal Berkeley's UNIX, are the products of college research.

Plato, the first interactive computer-based learning system, was invented by Professor Donald Bitzer at the University of Illinois in 1962. Plato evaluates a student's answers to questions about the subject matter and then adjusts its level of instruction so the material is neither too hard nor too easy. Currently Plato is the country's most popular educational software, and its development is being continued in cooperation with Control Data Corporation.

Research

When professors are not in the classroom, they are usually conducting research. Many colleges require their faculty members to do more than teach; they also are expected to further knowledge in their field and publish the findings. As a result, thousands of important scientific advances have emerged from research conducted at universities. Here is a sample of faculty research accomplishments.

AVIATION

Around the turn of the century, two years before the Wright brothers' flight at Kitty Hawk in 1903, Santa Clara's John Montgomery developed an "aeroplane." He was the first to fly a heavier-than-air machine, a glider with gull-shaped wings. Montgomery continued with improvements in gliders while the Wright brothers experimented with engine-powered flight.

While Montgomery was doing his work, Professor Albert Zahm of Notre Dame and Catholic University, the founder of modern aeronautical science, designed the first wind tunnel and the first successful helicopter.

It was at Caltech that Theodore von Karman developed the principles that made jet flight possible.

Conducting research in a different type of flight, mechanical engineering professor Joel Hollenberg of Cooper Union has analyzed the conditions that cause the air flow around a sphere to change from smooth to turbulent about two thirds of the way along its intended path. The sphere in question is not an object in space, but rather a baseball. Professor Hollenberg constructed a computer model of the forces that surround a knuckleball that enables him to explain why the pitch behaves the way it does. Now batters would like Professor Hollenberg to help them figure out how to hit the erratic pitch.

SPACE AND ROCKETS

Scientists at the University of New Hampshire designed the first man-made object to leave the solar system. After fifteen years of travel, the Pioneer 10 craft with its cosmic ray detectors passed by Pluto and into outer space in 1987.

James Van Allen of the University of Iowa installed instruments on the Explorer I spacecraft that led to his discovery of the Van Allen radiation belts.

When a suit costs $100,000, it should fit right and wear well. That's the expectation NASA has of Georgia Tech's School of

---

Georgia Tech's School of Textile Engineering is under contract to supply space suits to NASA's astronauts.

Textile Engineering, which is under contract to supply space suits to astronauts. Making space suits is no easy task; the suits must carry their own atmosphere and still be flexible enough so that an astronaut can perform a variety of precise movements.

In 1945, at the conclusion of World War II, the federal government brought Wernher Von Braun and his fellow German scientists to the White Sands Proving Ground to help the United States develop rockets along the lines of the successful German V-2. That project eventually grew into New Mexico State's Physical Science Laboratory, which today operates with an annual budget of $110-million and a staff of 850.

Robert Hutchings Goddard, professor of physics at Clark University in Worcester, Massachusetts, from 1914 to 1942, is known as the "Father of Modern Rocketry." By 1941 Goddard and his assistants had launched thirty-four liquid-fuel rockets, many to a high altitude. At the outbreak of World War II, Goddard offered his expertise to the War Department, but the military discounted the rocket's value as a weapon and instead assigned Goddard to do research on internal combustion engines. In Goddard's lifetime of rocket research, he received 214 patents, developed gyroscopic steering, and built guidance and landing devices. He also was one of the first to write of jet-propelled aircraft and interplanetary travel.

MEDICINE

In 1952 a polio epidemic struck the United States, killing more than 3,000 people and seriously affecting another 60,000. In 1954, while working at the University of Pittsburgh's Virus Research Lab, Dr. Jonas Salk introduced an experimental polio vaccine. In 1959, Albert Sabin, a professor at the University of Cincinnati, discovered a live-virus polio vaccine that could be taken orally. Within ten years, the two forms of immunization introduced by Salk and Sabin reduced the incidence of polio by more than 95 percent.

In 1895, about the time Wilhelm Conrad Roentgen announced his discovery of the X ray, Frank Austin, an engineering instructor at Dartmouth, was using a "picture machine" to detect metal objects placed inside a cigar box. Shortly before Roentgen published his paper on X rays, Austin unsuccessfully tried to interest the medical profession in using his equipment to diagnose bone fractures.

One of the more publicized advances in medical research was the first artificial heart, a Jarvik-7, that was implanted in 61-year-old Barney Clark by Dr. William DeVries on December 2, 1982, at the University of Utah hospital. Clark died in 1983 after surviving for 112 days. The operation was made possible by the pioneering work done by the Utah Institute of Biomedical Engineering in the development of artificial organs.

Cisplatin, the best-selling anticancer drug in the United States, was discovered at Michigan State in the mid-1960s by Dr. Barnett Rosenberg and his associates.

The University of Minnesota was the site of the world's first open-heart surgery, performed by Dr. Christiaan Barnard.

Johns Hopkins's world-famous Schools of Medicine and of Hygiene and Public Health have made numerous contributions to society. The Nobel Prize–winning discovery of restriction enzymes that gave birth to the genetic engineering industry took place at Johns Hopkins. Other accomplishments by Hopkins faculty include the first direct blood transfusion, the development of cardiopulmonary resuscitation (CPR), and the first "blue baby" operation, which opened the way to modern heart surgery.

The first open-heart surgery, by Dr. Christiaan Barnard, was performed at the University of Minnesota hospital in 1954. Today Minnesota is recognized as the organ transplant center of the world.

Like the Minnesota scientists, medical researchers at the University of Mississippi have made a number of breakthroughs in human organ transplants. In 1963 they transplanted the first human lung and a year later accomplished the initial chimpanzee-to-human heart transplant.

Professor Thomas Starzi at the University of Pittsburgh medical school developed the procedure for liver transplants. Since 1981 Pitt's Center for Liver Transplants has performed nearly 1,000 operations.

The University of Florida developed Bioglass, the first man-made material that can bond with human tissue. One of the many applications of this ceramic product is to replace damaged middle ear bones so hearing can be restored.

AGRICULTURE

In 1877 Michigan State botanist William Beal was the first person to cross-fertilize corn to increase yield. Since that time, scientists at MSU have created more than 200 new plant varieties in an effort to increase production and improve quality. Some of the bean varieties Michigan State has developed are ingredients of the famous U.S. Senate bean soup served in the Capitol lunchroom.

Agricultural researchers at the University of Massachusetts have developed instruments to measure the quality of cranberry color. Since the price farmers receive for their cranberries is based on color—the redder the berry, the higher the price—these advances have been of major importance to the Massachusetts cranberry industry, the state's number one cash crop.

The navel orange was developed at U Cal Riverside.

Penn State is the world leader in research on the growth and processing of mushrooms.

It's not a sophisticated laboratory with expensive instruments and computer support, it is only a piece of land totaling less than an acre. Nevertheless, the Morrow Plots, located on the campus of the University of Illinois at Urbana-Champaign, are a National Historic Landmark. More than a century old, the plots comprise the oldest agricultural experimental station in the United States and the longest-term cornfields anywhere. Experiments at the Morrow Plots developed new varieties of

hybrid corn and raised average corn yield from 30 bushels per acre to 120 bushels.

George Washington Carver conducted his famous agricultural experiments from 1896 to 1943, while he was a professor at Tuskegee Institute in Alabama. When he arrived at Tuskegee, Carver found the soil depleted because cotton was the sole crop. In looking for a way to restore mineral content, he discovered that peanuts and sweet potatoes could produce high yields while regenerating the soil. Carver then set out to find uses for the new crops. His experiments produced more than 300 by-products of the peanut and sweet potato, including medicines, fertilizers, dyes, and plastics. Carver's work in crop diversification, soil building, and the elimination of plant diseases is credited with revolutionizing the South's agricultural economy. While all this was going on, Tuskegee apparently received its money's worth from its distinguished professor. In his forty-seven-year tenure, Carver never accepted a raise above the $1,500 Booker T. Washington paid him when he first came to the college.

PHYSICS

Caltech physicist John Schwartz developed the "superstring"

theory of matter that is helping scientists achieve Einstein's goal of linking the basic forces of the universe. In 1963 fellow Caltech faculty member Maarten Schmidt discovered the nature of quasars.

The famous Michelson-Morley experiment took place at what is now Case Western Reserve in Cleveland in 1887. Conducted by professors Albert Michelson and Edward Morley, the experiment showed that the speed of light is unaffected by the Earth's motion. By disproving the theory that light was a wave phenomenon, Michelson and Morley set the stage for modern physics, including the theory of relativity and quantum mechanics.

Penn State physics professor Erwin Mueller invented the world's most powerful microscope, and in 1955 he was the first person to see an atom.

In January 1987, researchers at the University of Houston and the University of Alabama in Huntsville, in an effort led by Houston's Ching-Wu Chu, produced a superconductive

Houston's Ching-Wu Chu.

ceramic compound that lost all resistance to electricity when it was cooled to –283 degrees F. Wire or other electrical conductors made from the compound can transmit electricity over great distances without a loss of power. The relatively warm temperature at which superconductivity can now occur (fifty years ago it was thought that absolute zero, –460 degrees F, was needed) will make it possible to manufacture superconductors at much lower cost. Practical applications of this breakthrough are advanced magnetic imaging machines for medical diagnosis, electric motors a tenth of their present size, and a new generation of smaller and faster supercomputers.

Professor Henry Abarbanel's explanation sounds simple enough: "Suppose you've just poured yourself a cup of coffee and added cream. If mixing the cream into the coffee were governed by simple linear processes, you would be able to 'unmix' it. But because the process is nonlinear, the mixing is effectively irreversible. The intermixing is so complete, you can't turn it around." The field is nonlinear science, and Professor Abarbanel of the University of California at San Diego is one of the country's leading experts. Experiments in nonlinear science have important implications for tracking ocean currents, learning more about weather patterns in the atmosphere, and constructing plasma physics fusion reactors.

ELECTRONICS

Arizona State scientists have grown some of the largest pure crystals of gallium arsenide, the material from which semiconductors are made. In another ASU laboratory, researchers have made the world's smallest transistor.

Scientists at Illinois (working with General Electric) have developed the world's fastest transistor. Its gallium-arsenide gate is $\frac{1}{100,000}$ of an inch long and can switch 230 billion times per second.

BIOLOGY AND CHEMISTRY

Faculty members at the University of Wisconsin have an impressive record in discovering vitamins. Vitamin A, vitamin B complex, the ultraviolet irradiation of vitamin D, and niacin all were isolated and identified at Wisconsin.

Caltech's Max Delbrück conducted the studies of bacterial viruses that led to a new branch of biology called molecular genetics.

The periodic table shows 103 elements, starting with hydrogen and ending with lawrencium. Every element beyond uranium (number 92) was discovered at Cal Berkeley by Nobel laureates Glenn Seaborg and Edwin McMillan and a team of scientists. The elements are

The last eleven elements of the periodic table were discovered at Cal Berkeley.

neptunium, plutonium, americium, curium, berkelium, californium, einsteinium, fermium, mendelevium, nobelium, and lawrencium. Many of these heavy elements are very unstable and have little practical value because of their short half-lives. Americium is an exception. It is a stable element, and tiny particles of it are used as the sensory material in smoke detectors.

ENVIRONMENT

In 1974 two researchers at U Cal Irvine, F. Sherwood Rowland and Mario Molina, discovered that the freon from aerosol spray cans was damaging the Earth's ozone layer. Their work, for which they won major environmental awards, eventually led to the banning of fluorocarbon propellants.

Michigan State zoologist George Wallace provided Rachel Carson with the title for her best-selling book, *Silent Spring.* In the early 1960s, Wallace observed that in the springtime robins were dying on campus in great numbers. He traced the cause of their death to earthworms that had been contaminated by the DDT applied to the soil to treat Dutch elm disease. The process Wallace discovered, called biomagnification, was a major advance in the field of environmental science.

SOCIAL SCIENCES

Columbia was primarily responsible for the development of the social sciences, including the oral history movement, as a modern field of scholarship through the work of faculty members Jacques Barzun, Lionel Trilling, and Mark Van Doren.

CLIMATE

The University of Wisconsin has a research building that can duplicate any climate. Inside the Biotron, built in 1966, scientists can manipulate the temperature, moisture, light intensity, barometric pressure, and pollutant level. The Biotron is normally used for studying subjects such as altitude sickness, windchill effects, and biological clocks. But occasionally the lab is used for tests that do little to better the condition of mankind. For example, the Biotron has been used to see whether the ink in fountain pens will flow in polar regions.

Penn State has the most meteorology majors and has one of the country's most advanced weather forecasting facilities.

SEX

Indiana University houses the Kinsey Institute for Research in Sex, Gender, and Reproduction. Alfred Kinsey published his two classic books, *Sexual Behavior in the Human Male* (1948) and *Sexual Behavior in the Human Female* (1953), while he was a biologist at the institute that bears his name.

Gregory Pincus, faculty member at Clark and codirector of the Worcester Foundation for Experimental Biology, was the senior scientist on the team that in 1960 developed Enovid-10, or, more commonly, the Pill.

WASH-AND-WEAR ARTERIES

In the 1950s the North Carolina State School of Textiles applied its expertise in the garment industry to the advancement of medical research. Using a converted necktie-making machine, NC State scientists manufactured synthetic arteries made from Dacron polyester. These knitted arteries, which have the desirable properties of elasticity and flexibility, have been used successfully in human tissue transplants.

THE ATOMIC AGE

The initial atom bomb research was done in 1942 in the University of Wisconsin's Sterling Hall. In April 1943, the federal government asked the university to move its bulky atom smasher and staff of ten to a top-secret laboratory where they would be joined by hundreds of other scientists, all focused on developing the bomb in the shortest possible time. The top-secret laboratory turned out to be located in Los Alamos, New

Mexico, and the effort became known as the Manhattan Project.

Columbia University researchers, particularly its three Nobel Prize–winning physicists, Enrico Fermi, I. I. Rabi, and Polykarp Kusch, were the first to split the uranium atom, build an atomic pile, and discover heavy water.

RADAR

It has been said that radar won World War II—the atom bomb only ended it. Radar was developed at the wartime Radiation Laboratory at MIT.

The name "Radiation Laboratory" was selected to mislead people into thinking the project dealt with nuclear physics, a nonmilitary subject at the time. The lab eventually grew to include nearly 4,000 scientists and support staff, who developed 150 different types of radar sets as well as the Loran navigation system. The Rad Lab was by far the largest research effort ever conducted on a campus. Not only did radar turn the tide of the war, but the success of the Rad Lab set a precedent for the federal government to turn to colleges when it wanted to sponsor major research projects.

ALUMINUM

An Oberlin graduate and faculty member were responsible for devising a practical and inexpensive method for manufacturing aluminum. On

February 23, 1886, less than eight months after graduating from Oberlin, 22-year-old Charles Martin Hall, working with professor of chemistry Frank Jewett, produced pure aluminum by passing electric current through a solution of

Oberlin's inventive Charles Martin Hall.

sodium aluminum fluoride. To produce aluminum in quantity, Hall formed the Pittsburgh Reduction Company, later renamed Alcoa. After he died in 1914, Oberlin received $16-million from Hall's estate.

PERMANENT WAVE

In the early 1930s, Penn biologist David Goddard discovered that protein structures can be broken down and re-formed into new shapes. Professor Goddard's experiments later led to the "permanent wave" in hairstyling.

K2 NUMBER ONE?

Schoolchildren are taught that Mount Everest is the tallest mountain in the world. But University of Washington astronomer George Wallerstein says that may not be so. During an expedition to Himalayan peak K2 in the summer of 1986, Professor Wallerstein took along an instrument that made very precise measurements of signals from a Navy navigation satellite. This surveying technique showed K2 to be 29,064 feet above sea level compared to Everest's currently estimated height of 29,028 feet. But geography textbooks don't have to be changed just yet. Dr. Wallerstein is unwilling to call K2 the highest point on earth until he has a chance to measure Everest by the same method.

MOST WIDE AWAKE

Under a $500,000 grant, Yale professor Gary Schwartz determined that the smell of lavender scored the highest among fragrances that make people alert. Runners-up were lemongrass, peppermint, and eucalyptus.

MISCELLANEOUS

Dr. Robert Cade, University of Florida professor of medicine and kidney researcher, devised a formula for a drink to overcome dehydration and replace the body's loss of salts. It was first tested on University of Florida football players who experienced fluid losses while playing in the hot Florida sun. Designed to be taken internally, the drink received considerable publicity during the 1986 professional football season when it was used externally on the head of New York Giants coach Bill Parcells. The drink is Gatorade, named after the Florida mascot, the Gator.

Technicolor was developed in 1921 by MIT graduate Herbert Kalmus. If he hadn't named his invention after his alma mater, today's moviegoers would be viewing films in Kalmuscolor.

In 1958 Georgia Tech swimming coach Fred Lamoe invented "drownproofing." This technique is now commonly taught in swimming courses. Many colleges require students to successfully demonstrate this form of water survival before they can pass the physical education requirement.

Research Facilities

OBSERVATORIES AND PLANETARIUMS

Astronomy is an area of science that is carried out almost exclusively by college researchers. Caltech is the preeminent institution in the field. Besides operating a number of large telescopes on its own, Caltech also joins with other colleges to manage observatories for the National Science Foundation.

Oldest Observatory
The Hopkins Observatory at Williams College, built in 1836, is the oldest college observatory in the nation.

Largest Telescope
Caltech operates the largest optical telescope, the 200-inch Hale at Palomar Mountain. Telescopes like the Hale are able to see 14 billion light-years into space. Such distances are almost

beyond comprehension when one considers that the sun, at 93 million miles, is a mere 8 light-minutes from the Earth.

In partnership with the University of California, Caltech has begun construction of the 10-meter-diameter Keck telescope on Mauna Kea in Hawaii. When completed, in 1991, at a cost of $87-million, it will be the world's largest.

The National Observatory
The largest observatory is Kitt Peak on the Papago Indian Reservation near Tucson,

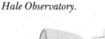

Hale Observatory.

Arizona, which is administered by the University of Arizona. These seventeen universities participate in Kitt Peak's operation:

Arizona	Michigan
Caltech	MIT
Chicago	Ohio State
Colorado	Princeton
Harvard	Texas at Austin
Hawaii	U of California
Illinois	Wisconsin
Indiana	Yale
Johns Hopkins	

Kitt Peak has sixteen separate telescopes, including the Mayall 158-inch optical reflector, the second largest in the United States. Although the Mayall telescope weighs 375 tons, it is so precisely balanced that a ½-horsepower motor is used to move it. Kitt Peak is also the location of the McMath Solar Telescope, the largest telescope in the world devoted exclusively to observing the sun.

Space Telescope

Under the direction of Johns Hopkins, the seventeen-member astronomy group mentioned above is developing the Hubble space telescope, which will orbit the Earth above the hazy layer of the atmosphere and provide mankind with its first look at the edge of the universe. This 94-inch mirror is designed so space shuttle astronauts can replace its components.

Radio Telescopes

Observing light that is visible to the human eye is not the only way to learn about the heavens. Stars emit radio waves that can be "heard" on giant antennas. The colleges involved in the National Radio Astronomy Observatory in Green Bank, West Virginia, are Columbia, Cornell, Harvard, Johns Hopkins, MIT, Penn, Princeton, Rochester, and Yale.

The largest movable radio telescope, a football field–sized installation at Green Bank, can observe objects undetectable by optical telescopes. This device is able to record such weak signals that, by comparison, a snowflake hitting the ground makes a loud noise.

The largest radio telescope in the world is operated by Cornell University in Puerto Rico.

The largest radio telescope in the world is operated by Cornell University in Arecibo, Puerto Rico. This gigantic ear measures 1,000 feet across and covers 18 acres. The telescope, located in a natural bowl between two mountains, is stationary but is able to scan the entire sky through a movable feed system. In a November 16, 1974, effort to communicate with life in outer space, the Arecibo telescope beamed a coded message towards the M13 galaxy, 20,000 light-years away. The message consisted of the numbers 1 to 10, a DNA helix, the Earth's population, the shape of the human body, and the position of Earth in the solar system.

College Telescopes

At the other end of the spectrum from these gigantic telescopes are many smaller observatories on college campuses. Used for both teaching and research, one of the best facilities is the Gale Observatory at Grinnell. The observatory has a 24-inch Cassegrain reflector telescope with sophisticated features like automatic pointing, programmable tracking, remote control, external computer linkage, and advanced spectrography. This telescope is currently being used for a major study of the brightness and color of a group of variable stars as well as for regular course work.

No southern college has a larger device than the 30-inch reflector at the Agnes Scott observatory. This telescope, although it does not have the sophisticated computer support of Grinnell's Gale telescope, is remarkable for a small women's college with an enrollment of less than 600. While primarily used for the education of Agnes Scott students, it is also open to the local community and to students at neighboring Georgia Tech, who are permitted to cross-enroll to take astronomy courses.

Stonehenge West

It is light-years away from modern observatories with their 13-foot-diameter reflector telescopes, but it is an observatory nevertheless. At the University of Missouri in Rolla, students under the leadership of

Morehead Planetarium, at North Carolina.

Professor Joseph Senne have constructed a working half-scale model of England's Stonehenge. By one modern-day measure of success, this human eye–powered observatory has proved to be a very popular attraction. Missouri Stonehenge T-shirts are best-sellers in the bookstore.

Planetariums

The oldest major college planetarium in the United States is the Morehead Planetarium at the University of North Carolina in Chapel Hill, which opened on May 10, 1949. (Major planetariums are those with a seating capacity of 200 or more and a celestial dome with at least a 50-foot diameter.) Other colleges with major planetariums are Michigan State, the Air Force Academy, Colorado, Arizona, De Anza, and Eastern Kentucky.

From 1960 through the mid-1970s, the Morehead was the location of star-recognition and orbital mechanics courses for NASA's astronauts. The planetarium was adapted so that the astronauts could sit in a space capsule simulator and observe the sky for the exact date and time of their launch.

PHYSICS LABS

What are cyclotrons, accelerators, supercolliders, and atom smashers, and why are they important? These machines all have essentially the same function—to generate large bursts of electricity that accelerate nuclear particles to extremely high speed. Magnetic fields are used to control the path of the particles so they strike each other repeatedly. When collisions occur, the inner part of the atom is exposed, revealing information about the basic composition of matter. By observing the results of such experiments, physicists hope to find out what matter is made of and what holds it together.

Fermilab

The Fermilab (named after Enrico Fermi), operated by the U.S. Department of Energy in cooperation with the University of Chicago and a consortium of fifty-five universities, is located in Batavia, Illinois, 35 miles west of Chicago. The Fermilab has the nation's largest accelerator, called the Tevatron, a 4-mile-long, 10-foot-high underground collider that generates 2 trillion electron volts. This tremendous charge of energy causes a series of reactions that help scientists learn more about the subatomic makeup of matter—the quarks, gluons, and antiquarks that comprise protons and antiprotons. While atoms are slam-dancing below the earth's surface, the Fermilab's 6,800 acres have a peaceful appearance. Part of the grounds are used as grazing land for a herd of buffalo.

Stanford Linear Accelerator

Three miles west of Stanford's main campus sits a 2-mile-long linear electron accelerator, operated under contract with the Department of Energy. The giant machine can produce a 30-million-volt electron beam that travels nearly 2 miles through a pipe 4 inches in diameter. The high-energy collisions that result allow scientists to learn about atomic particles. Nobel Prize–winning professor of physics Burton Richter discovered the psi particle here.

A new circular atom smasher, the Stanford Linear Collider, with a circumference of 1½ miles, has been added to the facility. This device forces beams of electrons and positrons to collide to produce the Z particle. Physicists have speculated that the Z particle is the key to linking the fundamental forces of nature.

Cyclotron

Presently under construction at Michigan State is the world's most powerful cyclotron, the K800. This machine will enable researchers to perform previously impossible experiments. MSU already has in operation the first superconducting cyclotron. On the way is the world's first superconducting cyclotron specifically designed for the treatment of cancer.

Plasma Physics

Experiments at the Princeton Plasma Physics Lab do not break atoms apart but instead join them together. A machine named the Tokamak Fusion Test Reactor, the only one of its kind in the United States, confines plasma (not blood plasma, but a heated gas) by use of a magnetic field. At 100 million degrees C, electrons in the plasma fuse and release vast amounts of energy. Different from a fission reaction, which uses radioactive material, fusion produces energy without the risks associated with conventional nuclear reactors.

In April 1987 Princeton scientists were able to heat plasma to 250 million degrees C, the highest temperature ever reached in a laboratory (by contrast, the center of the sun is a mere 15 million degrees C). It is anticipated that by 1990 the Tokamak will be able to generate as much energy as it receives. But even when the break-even point is reached, harnessing the fusion process to generate abundant and inexpensive energy will be many years away. It is estimated that it will take billions of dollars and thirty to forty years before utility companies will be able to operate cost-effective fusion power plants.

Nuclear Reactor Model

The University of Maryland has a 1:500-scale working replica (without the uranium) of a nuclear reactor, the type that malfunctioned at Three Mile Island. This model, unique for a college campus, can be used to find out what happens when things go wrong in an operational nuclear reactor.

The Johns Hopkins Applied Physics Lab

Founded during World War II, the Hopkins lab now employs 2,700 scientists, engineers, and support staff who are engaged in applied and basic research. The APL's work ranges from an argon laser for eye surgery and a rechargeable cardiac pacemaker to the design of an air defense network and ballistic missile guidance systems.

Argonne Laboratory

Superlatives abound at the Argonne National Laboratory, operated by the University of Chicago for the Department of Energy. Scientists at Argonne are doing research like designing the world's most intense X-ray beam to "watch" chemical and biological processes as they take place; producing the nation's most powerful source of pulsed neutrons for detecting differences in energy as small as 70 millionths of an electron volt; and operating a one-of-a-kind high-voltage electron microscope that permits the observation of radiation damage as it takes place.

But not all the work at Argonne is in superscience. Ongoing projects of a more practical nature include testing new battery designs that will make electric cars practical and developing a way to cool homes inexpensively in the summer with ice frozen during the winter.

MORE RESEARCH LABS AND CENTERS

Jet Propulsion Lab

One of the largest of all college laboratories is the Jet Propulsion Lab, which is administered for NASA by Caltech. Scientists at the JPL, operating with an $800-million budget, have built and guided many of the nation's unmanned spacecraft, including the nation's first satellite, Explorer I, and the Voyager craft that passed by Uranus in January 1986.

Earthquake Centers

Caltech also operates a seismology lab that measures earthquake tremors. The Richter scale for measuring the intensity of earthquakes was developed in 1935 by Charles Richter, a Caltech professor of geology.

Scientists at California universities were shaken when the National Science Foundation decided to locate its Earthquake Engineering Center at the State University of New York at Buffalo rather than on the West Coast. Apparently the number of tremors experienced by the states in question, 15 in New York compared to 4,421 in California since 1900, were not a factor in the selection. The decision is under appeal.

A mover and shaker at the University of California at San Diego is Gil Hegemier, professor of applied mechanics and engineering. With the help of an $835,000 grant from the National Science Foundation, Professor Hegemier and his staff are erecting a structural systems laboratory, the only one in the United States. The facility will enable researchers to measure the effects of simulated earthquakes on full-size buildings, some as high as five stories. Prior to the UCSD laboratory, research had to be done with scale models or on a computer. Professor Hegemier's experiments will result in the construction of buildings that are better able to resist the forces of an earthquake.

Oceanography

The University of California at San Diego operates the largest marine science center at a

Scripps' Flip *in action.*

college, the Scripps Institution of Oceanography, which has a budget of $63-million and a staff of 1,100. Research is conducted in areas such as the composition of the ocean bottom, waves, currents, the nature of plankton, and the habits of marine mammals. UC San Diego recently opened a new Ocean Sciences Center to serve as a laboratory for research scientists as well as a public aquarium. Scripps operates four research ships, including *Flip*, named for its unique characteristic of submerging its bow to stand on end.

On a February 1987 expedition aboard the research submersible *Alvin*, Scripps oceanographers were the first to observe an active underwater volcano. The scientists said the journey was like visiting a strange new world similar to an abstract painting by Miró or Picasso. They observed beautiful red terraces, shimmering water, and a new species of fish with a huge mouth, blue eyes, and front legs.

The other top college marine science facilities are the Rosenstiel School of Marine and Atmospheric Science at the

Super Science

The days when individual scientists would toil away in their laboratories trying to discover a new particle or find a cure for a disease may be numbered. The federal government, by far the largest source of college research funding, is now throwing its weight behind large and expensive engineering research centers. There are now thirteen such centers financed by the National Science Foundation.

	Research field
Brigham Young	Advanced combustion
Carnegie Mellon	Engineering design
Colorado	Optoelectronic computing
Columbia	Telecommunications
Delaware	Composites manufacturing
Illinois	Semiconductor microelectronics
Lehigh	Large structural systems
Maryland	Systems research
MIT	Biotechnology engineering
Ohio State	Net shape manufacturing
Purdue	Intelligent manufacturing
UCLA	Hazardous-substance control
U Cal Santa Barbara	Robotic systems

By the end of 1988 the Reagan administration expects to have twenty-one science centers operating with an annual budget of $50-million. The program also encourages the sharing of costs by industrial companies that benefit from the research.

University of Miami and Columbia's Lamont-Dougherty Laboratory. Researchers at Rosenstiel have discovered that a 2° to 5°F change in the southern Pacific Ocean temperature in the fall can mean the difference between a mild and a harsh winter three months later in the United States.

The Long Marine Laboratory of the University of California at Santa Cruz excels in the study of marine mammals. It has a number of outdoor tanks where whales can be observed, and it maintains a branch on Año Nuevo Island, one of the largest seal and sea lion habitats on the Pacific Coast.

CORNELL'S AND MIT'S RESEARCH CENTERS

Cornell is home to six national research centers, the most of any college. They are:

Center for Theory and Simulation in Science and Engineering
High Energy Synchrotron Source
Laboratory of Nuclear Studies
Mathematical Sciences Institute
National Astronomy and Ionosphere Center
National Research and Resource Facility for Submicron Structures

Cornell's submicron facility, the only national lab of its kind, looks at very small interactions and dimensions. Scientists conduct research in areas such as nanoelectronics, in which they work with objects smaller than one millionth of a meter.

When it comes to the number of laboratories in which it is involved, MIT is unrivaled in the scope of its scientific experimentation. A sampling of some of MIT's thirty-nine labs and centers includes:

Artificial Intelligence Laboratory
Francis Bitter National Magnet Laboratory
Center for Materials Science and Engineering
Center for Transportation Studies
Laboratory for Information and Decision Systems
Microsystems Research Center
Plasma Fusion Center

SOME UNUSUAL CENTERS AND LABS

Not all research conducted at colleges is of the high-tech variety. Experiments also go on in more commonplace areas. Examples are:

Arizona	Laboratory of Tree Ring Research
Auburn	National Center for Asphalt Technology
Mississippi State	Optimum Pest Management Program
Nebraska	Tractor Test Lab
North Carolina State	International Potato Center
Northwestern	Traffic Institute
Utah	Laboratory of Coal Science

5

LIFE ON CAMPUS

STUDENT ACTIVITIES, FESTIVALS AND TRADITIONS, STUDENT PRANKS, FRATERNITIES AND SORORITIES

Student Government

THE EARLY DAYS

The first examples of self-government in which college students had a say in making their own rules occurred at Amherst in 1883 and Bryn Mawr in 1892. While the decisions of the Amherst senate were subject to veto by the president, Bryn Mawr students were given the authority to establish their own standards of conduct. There had been a number of earlier attempts at giving students the right to regulate their behavior, but they were limited in scope and short in duration. In the 1820s students at Virginia, Amherst, and Colgate practiced rudimentary forms of self-government. Later on, in the mid-1800s, undergraduates at Vanderbilt, Pennsylvania, and Chicago formed committees to keep order in the dormitories, and student advisory groups appeared at Vermont, Princeton, Virginia, Wesleyan, and Bates. A formal student government structure was established at the University of Illinois in 1867, but students voted to end the experiment in 1883.

WITTY WISCONSINITES

While most student government organizations take their responsibilities seriously, once in a while student apathy sets the stage for a joke party to be elected. One such group of playful politicians was the Pail and Shovel Party at the University of Wisconsin. As president and vice president of

The Pail and Shovel party gave Wisconsin students "what they wanted."

the student government from 1978 to 1980, Jim Mallon and Leon Varjian did everything they could to mix lunacy and politics. To "give the students what they wanted," Mallon and Varjian placed 1,000 pink plastic flamingos on Bascom Hill, built a replica of the Statue of Liberty emerging from the ice on Lake Mendota, and organized a "boom box" parade down Madison's State Street.

The name of the party, Pail and Shovel, came from Mallon and Varjian's campaign promise that, if elected, they would convert the student government's $70,000 budget into pennies, dump them in front of the library, and let the students collect the money with pails and shovels.

The hard-fought campaign included mudslinging—literally.

Mallon and Varjian set up cardboard likenesses of their opponents and invited supporters to throw mud at them.

To the disappointment of many students, an attempt to help them solve their academic problems was unsuccessful. Pail and Shovel's suggestion that all university clocks run backwards (so classes would be over before they began) was not received cordially by the Wisconsin administration.

Such tongue-in-cheek political antics are not a new idea. As far back as 1874, at the University of Illinois, the Dead Beet Party, running as an amusing alternative to the serious slate of candidates, finished second to the incumbent student government.

Student Newspapers
OLDEST

The *Dartmouth Gazette* began in 1799, although then it was a commercial newspaper published in the town of Hanover. In 1839 the *Gazette* moved onto campus as a weekly.

The first issue of the *Ohio Literary Focus* was printed in 1826 at Miami of Ohio. A weekly, the *Literary Focus* was published by three professors with some help from students. Composed as a literary journal, the *Focus* was not really a student newspaper. The *Miami Student,* first published in 1867, would have been able to make such a claim, but it was soon reduced to a monthly printing schedule.

The oldest true student newspaper is the *Yale News,* which brought out its first issue on January 28, 1878, and has been published daily during the school year ever since.

ODDEST NAME

The student newspaper at the University of Rhode Island is called *The Good 5-Cent Cigar.*

Yearbook

LONGEST OVERDUE

The publication of the 1966 Grinnell (Iowa) yearbook

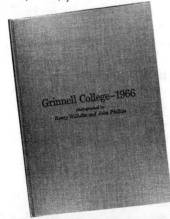

Grinnell College–1966
photographed by
Henry Wilhelm and John Phillips

was delayed twenty years, finally appearing in the spring of 1986. Back in the turbulent 1960s, Grinnell president Leggett thought pictures of students at a pot party were potentially libelous. He also did not care for the photo caption, "Marijuana is fun, cheap, less harmful than alcohol, and it doesn't produce hangovers."

Literary Magazine

Beginning in 1984 the Coordinating Council of Literary Magazines in New York has made an award to the best student literary magazine. In 1985 and 1986 the council gave an additional prize for the magazine with the best design. In each of those years *cold drill* of Boise State was the winner. It comes in a loose-leafed, boxed format that allows for considerable creativity: for instance, 3-D comics with glasses, cassettes, photo portfolios, and even scratch 'n' sniff poems. The title, *cold drill,* comes from a mining tool used to uncover deposits of precious minerals that are otherwise inaccessible.

Humor Magazines

The earliest efforts to put college humor on paper were two 1830 publications at Princeton, *The Thistle* and *The Chameleon.*

The year 1876 saw the founding of the most famous campus satire magazine, the *Harvard Lampoon*. The *Lampoon* has published the two all-time best-selling issues ever printed by a college humor magazine. Its 1966 parody of *Playboy* sold more than 500,000 copies, and the 1986 takeoff on *USA Today* sold 350,000.

The Columbia *Jester*, started in 1901, has had a number of student editors who later became famous literary figures, including Bennett Cerf, class of 1920, and Herman Wouk, class of 1934. Ivy League humor magazines, however, were not the only ones to spawn writers. James Thurber started on the Ohio State *Sundial*, Art Buchwald on Southern Cal's *Wampus*, and Peter Maas on Duke's *Dukes 'n' Duchesses*.

Radio

FIRST STATION

Union's WRUC has a strong claim to the distinction of being the first college radio station to go on the air; it signed on at 8 p.m. on October 14, 1920, for an evening music series. The

Union's radio station, WRUC, may have been the first U.S. station of any kind to broadcast regular programming, preceding KDKA in Pittsburgh by two weeks.

newspaper headlines the next day read: "College students give concert by radio telephone." In fact, WRUC may have been the first U.S. radio station of any kind to schedule regular programming, preceding the pioneering KDKA of Pittsburgh by two weeks.

While Union may have the oldest licensed college station, the University of Wisconsin's 9XM was the first to broadcast. A student working in the lab of physics professor Earle Terry designed a vacuum tube powerful enough to make voice

transmission possible. In 1917, 9XM broadcast locally from Professor Terry's office. Two years later the call sign was changed to WHA, and the Wisconsin student station has been on the air ever since. Although WHA's initial broadcasts were much more informal than WRUC's, there is a certain amount of truth to their slogan, "the oldest station in the nation."

The first FM radio station, the University of Illinois's WIUC, came on the air on September 1, 1941. In 1954 the station's call letters were changed to WILL-FM.

The first college FM stereo station was WKCR of Columbia in 1945.

MOST EXTENSIVE PARTICIPATION

WBCR, Beloit College's 130-watt FM radio station, is the most popular extracurricular activity on campus. More than 100 students (1 out of 10 of Beloit's undergraduates) are involved with the station.

LARGEST AUDIENCE

In the winter of 1987 WHUR-FM, owned by Howard University but operated by professionals, was the number-five rated commercial radio station in Washington, D.C., with an average daily audience of 455,000.

WHUR, however, is not really a student-run radio station. According to the Intercollegiate Broadcasting System, the college stations with the largest audiences are Fordham (WFUV), Columbia (WKCR), SUNY at Stony Brook (WUSB), Bridgeport (WPKN), Connecticut (WHUS), San

Francisco (KUSF), and Loyola Marymount (KXLU).

Besides its large audience, Fordham's 50,000-watt WFUV has another distinction: it may have the most supportive listeners in college radio. WFUV raised $300,000 in donations in one recent year, an amazing total for a college radio station fund drive.

STRONGEST SIGNAL

Most college radio stations transmit with less than 10,000 watts of power, but a few broadcast quite strong signals. WRAS-FM at Georgia State in Atlanta is a 100,000-watt station, producing the most powerful college radio signal in the nation.

Television

Iowa State started the nation's first college-owned and college-operated TV station, WOI, in 1950.

In 1953 Houston's KUHT-TV went on the air as the first public television station on a college campus.

Theater

The American College Theater Festival, founded in 1969 and located at the Kennedy Center in Washington, D.C., is the Olympic Games for college playwrights, actors, and designers. Students from colleges around the country first enter a regional competition, and the winners advance to the finals in the nation's capital.

The categories are:

Best all-around play
Best musical
Best set and costume design
Best play about the American
  experience
Best comedy
Best actor or actress
Best theatrical criticism
Best play about the black experience

Through 1987, the colleges that have won the most awards are:

	Number of awards
UCLA	9
Angelo State	5
Iowa	5
Evansville	4
Missouri	4
Alabama	3
Cal State Fullerton	3
Florida	3
Indiana	3
North Carolina A&T	3
Webster	3

The 1987 National Student Playwriting Award went to Glen Blumstein of the University of Iowa for his play *Nijinsky: God's Mad Clown.*

Among the former festival winners who have gone on to successful careers are Tom Berenger (*Platoon*), Sheryl Lee Ralph (*Dreamgirls*), Julie Campbell (*Ryan's Hope* and *Santa Barbara*), and Matt Williams (senior writer, *The Cosby Show*).

Debate

OLDEST

The oldest college debating club is the Whig-Cliosophic Society at Princeton, founded as the Plain Dealing Club and the Well Meaning Club in 1765. Literary and debating societies like Whig and Clio were the main focus of undergraduate life until Greek-letter fraternities replaced them in the late 1800s. These societies served to sharpen the skills of persuasion and exposition that were part of early American higher education. At Princeton the debating society was the training ground for two future national leaders, James Madison (Whig) and Aaron Burr (Clio).

NATIONAL TOURNAMENT

The forty-first National Debate Tournament was held at Illinois State in 1987. The winner among the sixteen finalists that qualified through regional competitions was Baylor University. The topic was:

Resolved: That present restrictions on First Amendment freedoms of speech and press be curtailed or prohibited.

The colleges with the most victories in the National Debate Tournament since its inception in 1947 are:

continued

	Number of wins
Northwestern	6
Harvard	5
Dartmouth	4
Kansas	4
Alabama	2
Baylor	2
Redlands	2

In the forty-one-year history of the championship, the list of debate topics provides a barometer of issues that were important to the American public at the time.

1923–24	Resolved: That the U.S. should enter the World Court of the League of Nations as proposed by President Harding.
1926–27	Resolved: That the Volstead Act should be modified to permit the manufacture and sale of light wines and beer.
1933–34	Resolved: That the powers of the President of the United States should be substantially increased as a settled policy.
1939–40	Resolved: That the United States should follow a policy of strict economic and military isolation towards all nations outside the Western Hemisphere engaged in armed international or civil conflict.
1947–48	Resolved: That a federal world government should be established.
1958–59	Resolved: That the further development of nuclear weapons should be prohibited by international agreement.
1974–75	Resolved: That the power of the president should be significantly curtailed.

Music

FIRST ORCHESTRA

The first formal university musical group was started at Harvard in 1808. It was known then as Pierian Sodality. Its name was changed to the Harvard University Orchestra in 1968.

LARGEST BAND

Purdue's "All-American" marching band is believed to be the nation's largest, with 400 members. Besides musicians, the group includes twirlers, flag wavers, and the Goldusters. Purdue and Illinois were the first bands to march in complicated formations and to break ranks to form letters.

BIGGEST DRUM

The marching bands of Texas, with "Big Bertha," and Purdue, featuring "Big Boomer," each claim to have the world's largest

drum. Texas has released the dimensions of "Big Bertha," a diameter of 8 feet and a width of nearly 5 feet. Purdue's "Big Boomer" measurements are classified information, but

estimates place its diameter at 10 feet. While the argument between Texas and Purdue continues, Disneyland claims its Big Bass Drum is 10½ feet high and therefore the world's largest.

ROWDY BANDS

The Rice University Marching Band is known as the MOB. Not only is MOB an acronym for Marching Owl Band, it was also inspired by the gangsterlike uniforms worn by the Rice musicians. Rather than march in formation like other college bands, the MOB straggles out during halftime to put on satirical shows that make fun of opposing teams, current events, and other bands. During the 1986 football season, the band staged one show in which all members rode bicycles. Another time the MOB wore skirts to kid the Texas A&M band about its recent decision to accept female members.

The marching bands of the Ivy League colleges often present humorous halftime shows like those of the MOB. One of the more memorable escapades happened during a Princeton appearance at Harvard in the 1960s. At halftime the Princeton band formed the letters ABC to salute the network that was televising the contest. As announcer Chris Schenkel thanked Princeton for its acknowledgment, the Tiger band changed formation to spell NBC, forcing the embarrassed ABC program director to go to an unscheduled commercial break.

Cheerleading

Two organizations sponsor national cheerleading championships—the National Cheerleading Association (NCA) in Dallas and the Universal Cheerleading Association (UCA) in Memphis. The winning colleges have been:

Year	*NCA*	*UCA*
1983	Memphis State	Ohio State
1984	Louisville	Alabama
1985	Louisville	Kentucky
1986	Louisville	North Carolina State
1987	No championship held	Kentucky

According to officials familiar with cheerleading, year in and year out the top college teams are Louisville, Kentucky, North Carolina State, and Ohio State.

The championship competition routines performed by cheerleaders consist of tumbling, pyramids, partner stunts, jumps, a dance routine, and at least one cheer. Human mascots are allowed, but live animals are not. Judges grade the teams based on choreography, difficulty, precision, projection, dance, transitions, safety, and overall execution. The winning team receives the Golden Megaphone.

There is also a yearly pom-pom dance team championship. The winner in both 1986 and 1987 was Memphis State.

Clubs and Organizations

OFFBEAT CLUBS

There are a number of colleges that have more than 500 student organizations, among them Texas, UCLA, Ohio State, Penn State, Michigan State, and Cornell. With hundreds of clubs on a single campus, some organizations are likely to be rather unusual. A sample:

The Earplug Opera Company	Michigan
No Business as Usual	NYU
Womyn's Center	NYU
Hawaiian Punch	NYU

continued

Radical Alternatives to Apathy	NYU
Stand-Up Comedy Club	NYU
Lonely Guys	U Cal Irvine
Chicanos for Creative Medicine	U Cal Irvine
Wildebeest Horse Owners Association	U Cal Irvine
Team Grunion Body Surfing	U Cal Irvine
Society for Creating Science	U Cal Irvine
Society to Oppose Pseudoscience	Texas
Shake Hands with the World	Texas
Progressive Conservatives	Texas
Armadillo Folk Dancers	Texas
Society to Stop Continental Drift	Texas
Electrical Engineers for Christ	Texas
Generic Students Association	Texas
Siamese Fighting Fish Association	Texas
Bellringing Society	Chicago

AVIATION

College students have been known to have flights of fancy, so it is only natural that there is an Intercollegiate Flying Association. The association has been in existence since 1935, and each year it sponsors a safety and flight evaluation conference. In 1988, for the third year in a row, the winning team was from the University of North Dakota.

The association also gives the Loening Award to America's premier college aviation club. Since the award was first made in 1929, the Oklahoma State Flying Aggies have dominated the competition, winning the silver cup nineteen times. Southern Illinois and Harvard are tied for second place with four awards each.

FIRE DEPARTMENT

Most departments on a college campus are staffed by faculty or administrators. In at least five colleges a very important department, the one in charge of putting out fires, is run by students. Hampden-Sydney, Maryland, Sewanee, Oklahoma, and Franklin Pierce all have fire departments with student volunteers. At Franklin Pierce the fire chief, who is a junior business major, supervises a squad of twenty-one. The students are trained at a nearby fire school. Although Franklin Pierce's fire fighters are called on often, actual fires are rare. The vast majority of alerts are false alarms.

SERIOUS ACTIVITY

Virginia Military Institute of Lexington, Virginia, is the only college whose entire student body participated as a unit in a wartime battle, the Battle of New Market, Virginia, during the Civil War on May 15, 1864. The tide of the battle was turned in

The tide of a Civil War battle was turned in the favor of the South by a charge executed by the cadets of VMI.

favor of the South by the charge of the VMI cadets after they were moved in to fill a breach in the Confederate line.

POLITICAL EXTREMES

Brandeis and Arizona State are separated by 2,500 miles, but they may be even further apart in the political attitudes of their students. At least some of the undergraduates at Arizona State are among the most conservative in the United States: Arizona State is the only college that has its own chapter of the John Birch Society. Brandeis, on the other hand, has the largest Democratic club of any college.

OUTDOORS

The University of Wisconsin Hoofers is the largest college outing club. The Dartmouth Outing Club, an organization of campers, boaters, and skiers, started in 1909, is the oldest.

Festivals and Traditions

BABY, IT'S COLD OUTSIDE

Winters can be somewhat long in Collegeville, Minnesota, the home of Saint John's University

and the College of Saint Benedict. The students imagine themselves in a warmer climate by going to a "Dive-In" movie. Each January they dig out their bathing suits, collect dozens of inner tubes, head for the swimming pool, and watch the film *Jaws*.

When the winter blues hit students at Beloit College in Wisconsin, they stage the Banana Olympics. There are a

number of events, including banana relays, slam dunking bananas, odes to bananas, and banana art.

BIG BIKE RACE

The Little 500 at Indiana University is labeled the "World's Greatest College Weekend." Although an equally strong argument might be made for the Texas-Oklahoma football game, UCLA's Mardi Gras, or Dartmouth's Winter Carnival, there is no question that the Little 500 is a major college event. A full-time staff of four

Indiana's annual Little 500 bicycle race.

and a steering committee of twenty-nine are needed to organize the weekend activities, which include a golf jamboree, the Cream and Crimson football game, the Mini 500, the Big Red Relay, a musical concert, and the Little 500 bicycle race itself. The race consists of thirty-three teams competing for 200 laps around the track in Armstrong Stadium.

In 1988 the attendance was 29,500, one of the largest crowds ever. Profits from gate receipts and donations from corporate sponsors finance Little 500 scholarships and support the public-service programs of the Indiana University Student Foundation. And it is true that life can imitate fiction. As in the exciting finish of the 1979 movie *Breaking Away*, the 1988 Little 500 champion was the Cutter team from the town of Bloomington.

MIDDLE AGES

For its main celebration Indiana's Big Ten neighbor Ohio State, turns the clock back to the Middle Ages to put on its Medieval and Renaissance Festival. After the opening

coronation of King Henry VIII and Anne Boleyn, there are a variety of activities that feature medieval theater, art, dance, and music. Also included are wandering jugglers, mimes, and mock battles between armor-clad combatants.

DRAGON DAY

One of the rites of spring at Cornell is Dragon Day. Tradition calls for freshmen in the College of Architecture to build a giant (30 feet to 40 feet high) green dragon from chicken wire, papier-mâché, and cloth.

The idea is to successfully navigate the beast across the campus through a shower of snowballs, mud clods, and rotten vegetables thrown at the dragon by rival engineering students. The day ends with the dragon makers setting the huge model on fire, followed by a picnic for all.

NEW ORLEANS WEST

The largest college festival is UCLA's Mardi Gras. This springtime carnival, started in 1941, has an annual budget of nearly $300,000 and is directed by a committee of 100, with 4,000 helpers. The three-day festival has 115 booths featuring games and food. Rides, live entertainment, and nightly fireworks are also part of the carnival. The UCLA Mardi Gras earns about $100,000, which goes to a student-run summer camp for handicapped and disadvantaged children in the Los Angeles area.

A DEVIL OF A TIME

Each year on October 31, the University of Wisconsin Student Association puts on a massive Halloween party and parade for students and the townspeople of Madison. The crowd, numbering as many as 100,000, is swelled by busloads of students who come to town from other Wisconsin campuses for the big night. The costumes range from the typical—skeletons,

pumpkins, and cartoon figures—to the outrageous—a frozen TV dinner and the Statue of Liberty in a leotard. For a reason no one seems able to explain, the two most popular costumes in a recent year were nuns and ninjas.

LARGEST STUDENT PRODUCTION

The University of Florida's Gator Growl is the largest student-produced show and pep rally. It takes place on the Friday night before the homecoming football game. The Gator Growl began as a simple pep rally and bonfire, but today it fills Florida's 73,000-seat football stadium. The show includes student skits, the university's marching band, fireworks, a homecoming queen, and a featured entertainer.

BLOWING BUBBLES

Once a year students at Northern Michigan University in Marquette sponsor National Bubble Gum Week. One reason

for the success of this jamboree of bubble-blowing contests and other games is the ready availability of gum. During the

---

During National Bubble Gum Week, the Northern Michigan bookstore puts on a special bubble gum sale: one cent apiece or two pieces for nothing.

---

week the Northern Michigan bookstore puts on a special bubble gum sale: one cent apiece or two pieces for nothing.

HOOP ROLLING

At Bryn Mawr and Wellesley, when students talk about hoopsters, they aren't referring to their basketball teams. A spring ritual at each college is hoop rolling. Wellesley's tradition began in 1885 when playful seniors, dressed in caps and gowns, rolled children's wooden hoops from the campus to the village of Wellesley. After a while the informal hoop rolling turned into an annual race, with the winner expected to be the first one in her class to marry. (As a sign of the times, today the winner is assured by many that she will be the first to become president of a Fortune 500 company.) Even during the antiwar protest years of the late sixties, the hoop rolling went on. The only noticeable difference was that the hoops were covered with crepe paper and converted into movable peace symbols.

The spring celebration at Bryn Mawr occurs on May 1 and begins with Greek songs to the

Wellesley students participate in their annual hoop rolling tradition, ca. 1913.

rising sun. There also are Maypole dances, games, and a medieval banquet. Similar to the Wellesley hoop race, tradition at Bryn Mawr says the winner will be the first in her class to get married, the runner-up the first to earn a Ph.D.

MOUNTAIN DAY

Elmira has a tradition that goes back more than 100 years, a day with no classes called Mountain Day. Each year Elmira's president chooses a day in the fall to call off classes so the college community can enjoy the last of the good weather before winter sets in. The day's name comes from the practice of hiking up East Hill with a picnic lunch to visit Mark Twain's study at Quarry Farm. Beginning on October 15, Elmira students gather nightly in front of the president's home to serenade him until he cancels classes.

FUN WITH ROCKS

At Whittier College in California, the large rock in the center of the campus is so popular that the college's alumni magazine is named after it—called simply *The Rock*. Wanting to leave behind a permanent gift to Whittier, two seniors in the class of 1912 took a horse and cart into the hills beyond the college and brought a 2-ton granite boulder back to campus. They dug a hole and partly buried the rock in the ground.

Now, over seventy-five years later, the rock is still there, having withstood many attempts by rival football fans to remove it. The rock serves as a kind of granite message board. Along with the usual collection of names and initials, well-wishers offer congratulations on birthdays, engagements, and other events and achievements.

BAD LUCK

The John C. Calhoun Mansion is located on the campus of Clemson University. Thousands of visitors tour the site annually, but Clemson students avoid the historic landmark. Tradition says it is bad luck for undergraduates to enter the house; they will not graduate if they do.

GRADUATION TRADITION

The University of Texas has the Sunflower Ceremony. This tradition dates back to 1900, when the senior class met and decided to wear caps and gowns for graduation. Somehow the class officers forgot to invite the law school representative to the meeting. To protest the oversight, law school seniors wore Prince Albert coats, silk hats, and sunflowers rather than graduation gowns. Years later, this time with all schools present, the senior class changed the graduation outfit to suits and dresses. The law students conformed to the new attire but continued to wear their sunflowers. Today the Sunflower Ceremony, at which the dean pins a flower on all law school graduates, is held after the university commencement.

THESIS PARADE

For many years Reed College has required each senior to write a thesis and hand deliver it to the Registrar's Office no later than noon on the due date. Rather than turn in the papers one by one, the class of 1961 organized a senior thesis parade featuring music and costumes. The ceremony is now one of Reed's most distinctive features. The parade starts from the library and proceeds to the Registrar's Office, which is decorated with balloons and streamers. There are a costume theme (in a recent year it was Western), a fire-breathing thesis dragon, and a makeshift band. The registrar's staff, along with the college president, greet the paraders with party horns and confetti. For the much-relieved seniors, the conclusion of the short walk is the signal for the start of a long party.

TRIVIA

The largest trivia contest in the world is sponsored by WWSP-FM, the student radio station at the University of Wisconsin at Stevens Point. The contest runs for 54 continuous hours, from 6 p.m. on Friday until midnight on

The radio station at the University of Wisconsin at Stevens Point sponsors the world's largest trivia contest.

Sunday. About 8,000 contestants on 350 different teams listen to WWSP for trivia questions broadcast throughout the weekend while the station plays "Golden Oldies" music. The teams have 5 minutes to phone in their answers. The 1987 winning team was "Hour 54 Where Are You?", a name that referred to the loss of 1 hour out of the scheduled 54 because clocks were moved forward to mark the beginning of daylight saving time during the contest.

GOWNS

The University of the South, often called Sewanee, has always had close ties to Oxford and Cambridge universities in England. An Oxford and Cambridge tradition that Sewanee continues to follow is the wearing of black academic gowns to class by students and professors. Originally worn by all students, the custom is now limited to the Order of the Gownsmen, an academic honor organization with about 250 members.

ROSE BOWL

A big event at Cal Poly, which has campuses in San Luis Obispo and Pomona, is the building of a float for the Rose Bowl parade. The work begins in the spring, nine months before the Rose Bowl football game on New Year's Day, when the float's theme is set and the seeds of the flowers to be used are planted. Construction begins in earnest over the summer, including the installation of an on-board computer that controls the movements of the hydraulic and pneumatic systems that provide animation. There is also a closed-circuit video system inside the float that permits computer technicians as well as the driver to see every part of the float during its journey. The skeleton of the float is made from steel rods, wire screening, and polyurethane foam. Just before the parade, the flowers are added and last-minute preparations completed. On the day of the Rose Parade, students from both Cal Poly campuses line the route in great numbers to cheer their entry.

COLLEGE SPIRIT

Emory University uses Eagles as the nickname for its athletic teams, but Emory's real mascot is Dooley, the skeleton. Dooley started things off in 1899 when he wrote articles for the student newspaper. Today, nearly ninety years later, he still appears on campus. The modern Dooley is dressed like the Phantom of the Opera with a skull face, top hat, black cloak, and white gloves.

A "ghost" named Dooley makes appearances each spring on the Emory University campus.

One reason the ghost is popular with students is that during Dooley's Week, Emory's spring carnival, the caped cadaver has the audacity (and the authority) to enter a classroom, shoot a water pistol at the professor, and write "Class Dismissed, Eternally Yours, James T. Dooley" on the blackboard.

STUDENT ETIQUETTE

One of the distinctive trends in the 350-year history of American education is for college authorities to exercise less control over the social behavior of their students. The idea of in loco parentis, the college acting in place of a student's parents, has gradually diminished, the greatest change having taken place since 1950.

In the current laissez-faire social environment, Hampden-Sydney, an all-male college in Virginia, stands out as a one-of-a-kind institution. Because Hampden-Sydney believes its students should learn proper social behavior, it publishes an etiquette guide, *To Manner Born, To Manners Bred*, and gives a copy to each undergraduate.

For the career-minded, the booklet describes social conventions that prospective employers will expect to be observed when they meet with candidates at luncheons, dinners, and cocktail parties.

For those interested in social graces for their own sake, the booklet provides tips on how to be a true gentleman. In only thirty pages a Hampden-Sydney student can learn about "Women and How to Treat Them" ("Whether or not you subscribe to the doctrine of women's liberation, all women should be treated with respect and courtesy."), "Dress" ("The virtues most highly prized in a man's suit are the quality of the fabric and the care in the tailoring."), "Table Manners" ("Never mix food items on your fork."), and "Events" ("Receptions are generally characterized by a surplus of people and a paucity of food and drink. They are your social cross; bear them stoically.").

Student Pranks

CALTECH

On a list of notable pranksters, Caltech clearly occupies the number one position among American colleges. At Caltech, student pranks have such a long tradition and are so elaborate that they are known as legends— a fitting label for some of the more noteworthy capers. Among Caltech's more famous legends:

Room Stacking

In almost unlimited variations, room stacking consists of making it very difficult for the occupant to get back into his or her room, and then, when reentry is finally made, having a surprise waiting. In its most benign form, the person merely finds furniture rearranged or missing. More diabolical examples of room stacking have been reported to involve a car (taken apart and reassembled, sometimes with the engine running); a weather balloon filled with water and with no drain valve; 2 tons of sand, creating a desert scene; and an operating cement mixer dumping its contents on the floor. Making reentry difficult can be accomplished by barricading the doorway with blocks of ice or concrete. Artful room stackers have been known to build a wall over the entrance and replace the molding and light fixtures so that it is virtually impossible to determine where the door originally was. The occupant has no choice but to knock holes in the wall until the door is located.

As a prank, students at Caltech move and relabel the designated parking spots of unpopular members of the faculty and staff.

Parking Space

Tech students make the designated parking spots of unpopular faculty and staff members disappear by painting over the old lines and moving and relabeling the spaces.

Modern Art

Caltech students like to hang paintings or add sculptures to exhibitions at the Baxter Art Gallery and see how long they go unnoticed. A construction called the *Three-Legged Guitar,* inserted into an exhibit of surrealism, lasted for months and even received a favorable review from a local art critic.

Big-Time Football

The Rose Bowl, known as the "Granddaddy of Bowl Games," was a fitting location for the "Granddaddy" of Caltech's legends. The 1961 game between Washington and Minnesota was the scene of perhaps the most elaborate hoax ever perpetrated by college students. The Techers arranged to replace the 2,232 flashcards in the Washington rooting section. The trick involved changing every card as well as the instructions without being discovered. After a number of close calls, the switch was successfully made. As NBC-TV cameras showed the halftime card stunts to a national audience, the first eleven displays went off normally. Stunt number twelve, intended to depict a Washington Husky, turned out to be the Caltech Beaver instead. Next the word "Washington" in script was written backward. The fourteenth card display formed "CALTECH" in block letters rather than "HUSKIES." The card section was now thoroughly confused. The stunned cheerleaders who were directing the show, afraid of what might happen next, aborted the routine. The Washington band marched off the field in bewilderment. Caltech had made the Rose Bowl.

Ice Machine

A modest but brilliant prank conceived by the Techers is to make ice coins of the proper weight and size to use in vending machines.

Going Hollywood

Caltech students described a recent trick as a birthday present to the city of Hollywood on its 100th anniversary. On May 17, 1987, a group of nine Techers mastered the slopes of Mount

Caltech students had their way with the famous Hollywood sign.

Lee, scaled the 45-foot-high letters of the famous HOLLYWOOD sign, and changed it to read CALTECH. While this prank involved a good bit of daring, for example cutting through concertina wire and climbing with the assistance of safety ropes, it was made possible by the kind of technical wizardry one expects of Caltech students. On two previous visits to the sign, the pranksters measured the letters. Computer graphics were then used to design 45-foot-long plastic drop cloths that, when unfurled from the top of each letter, made the name transformation possible.

MICKEY MOUSE

As if the California air gives rise to such antics, Stanford students also have some fun now and then. Among their escapades was a trick they pulled during the May 10, 1983, ceremony for a new clock tower. On the morning of the dedication, when Stanford trustee William Kimball looked up to what his generous gift had purchased, he saw a colorful Mickey Mouse clock with Mickey at the center and his hands pointing to the time. Displaying a sense of humor rarely seen in such circumstances, Kimball laughed at the prank and said, "Leave Mickey there."

The students at Duke have a tradition of decorating the huge clock face on Gothic Crowell Tower. A giant Mickey Mouse watch was constructed in 1979, and more recently a huge basketball appeared to honor the Blue Devils' appearance in the 1986 NCAA basketball championship.

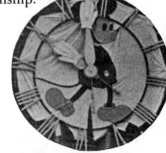

YO-YO

Maybe it's not the California life-style, but rather the somewhat offbeat nature of engineering students that creates a spawning ground for practical jokes. On the East Coast, MIT has established itself as a leader in the prank business. MIT students feel particularly proud of their record for the world's longest yo-yo drop. Easily surpassing Caltech's 6-inch yo-yo spun from a bridge in the San Gabriel Mountains was MIT's 26-inch model, connected to an electric-powered "finger," that unwound 200 feet down the side of a twenty-one-story building.

WEATHER BALLOON

Like their Caltech counterparts, MIT students can't refrain from poking fun at serious football teams. This "hack," as MIT undergrads call their pranks, involved burying a weather balloon below the surface of the Harvard football field. During a tense moment in the 1982 Harvard-Yale game, the balloon, triggered by a remote-control device, emerged from the ground and lifted into the air.

TAKING JOKES TO NEW HEIGHTS

At MIT the focal point of many jokes is the dome atop the Maclaurin Building. Items ranging from automobiles to plastic cows to a small house (complete with mailbox and welcome mat) have been hoisted to the building's 149-foot summit. One year the dome was capped with a phone booth

MIT students once hoisted a phone booth — with working phone — to the peak of a domed building on campus.

complete with a working phone. As an extra touch, the MIT gagsters arranged for the phone to ring as a maintenance crew, sent up to remove the structure, approached the booth.

MIT hackers are not satisfied merely to cause problems on the exterior of the Great Dome. One year they constructed a remote-control motor that caused 2,000 Ping-Pong balls to rain down from inside the dome.

OLIVER SMOOT

Undergraduates in an MIT physics class, given an assignment to calculate the length of the Harvard Bridge,

Undergraduates at MIT once measured the length of a bridge over the Charles River using a classmate's body as the unit of measure.

which crosses the Charles River between Boston and Cambridge, turned to a classmate, Oliver Smoot Jr., class of 1962. A dozen friends of the 5'6" Smoot spent the better part of an afternoon moving Smoot yardstick-fashion across the bridge. The next day in class the students reported that the Harvard Bridge was officially 364.4 Smoots and one ear in length.

SILENCE IS FROZEN

Students at Penn State occasionally tire of the hourly ringing of the bell in Old Main.

In the wintertime they turn the bell upside down, fill it with water, let it freeze, and restore the silent bell to its original position.

BIG FOOT

Another cold-weather prank was the work of Cornell student Hugh Troy. Troy took a wastepaper basket and modified the bottom so it left an impression that looked like a rhinoceros's foot. One day, after a fresh snowfall had blanketed Lake Cayuga, he suspended the rhino basket from a long pole and made tracks in the snow leading up to a hole he had made in the ice. Troy then called the animal science department and told them a rhino had escaped from the zoo and was seen heading for the lake.

A HOLE LOT OF TROUBLE

A similar trick was pulled off by Rutgers in the mid-1970s on a Friday night prior to the traditional football game with Princeton. For decades a Revolutionary War cannon buried barrel-first with its end exposed had been the target of red paintbrushes wielded by Rutgers students. On Saturday morning, the Princeton campus awoke to find a 6-foot-deep hole dug in the ground and the cannon missing. Search parties were sent to Rutgers but had no luck. Princeton officials phoned

their counterparts at Rutgers to complain about the serious nature of antique cannon thievery. On Monday, with relations between the two colleges still tense, a workman was sent to shovel the dirt back into the hole. As he shoveled, the workman struck the metal end of the cannon. The Rutgers pranksters hadn't stolen anything; they had simply dug a hole next to the cannon and covered its exposed end with dirt.

WHEN THE CANNONS ROAR

During a Valentine's Day concert in 1952 at the University of Rochester's Eastman School of Music, guest conductor Erich Leinsdorf was leading the Rochester Philharmonic Orchestra. At the appropriate point in a spirited performance of the 1812 Overture, a cannon was fired on stage and, "timed to the second," a cloud of feathers descended from the ceiling. Both the audience and orchestra broke out in laughter. Leinsdorf left the stage and returned with a gun with which he pretended to kill himself.

OLD TRICKS

Student pranks are not a recent phenomenon. College histories recount numerous student antics of the 1800s and even some that go back to the Colonial period. Pranks were quite prevalent before the twentieth century, when organized athletics became a way to channel the spirited behavior of students. An example of an olden-day prank occurred in the mid-1800s at the University of South Carolina. President Henry announced that there were too many dogs on campus and decreed that they must be expelled. The next day he noticed several dogs suspended by their collars from one of the horse racks. When Henry asked what was going on, the students replied that they had changed his order from expulsion to suspension.

FICTITIOUS STUDENTS

The longest-running and most widespread practical joke that college students like to put over on the administration is the creation of a fictitious student who is admitted, goes to class, takes exams, and, if the pranksters' luck holds out, graduates.

A successful case in point is George P. Burdell of Georgia Tech. Burdell originated when Ed Smith, class of 1931, received two admissions applications by mistake. On the second form Smith combined the first name and middle initial of a relative with his cat's name, Burdell, to create a fictitious student who became a Georgia Tech legend.

Smith's classmates joined in on the trick and helped write papers and take exams in Burdell's name. In fact, they worked so hard that George P. received his Bachelor of Science degree in only three years. Burdell then proceeded on to a master's degree, was appointed a Regents Professor, and eventually designated the Dean of Humanities and Fine Arts.

One advantage of inventing a fictitious student like Burdell is that his accomplishments go on and on. He is constantly recycled to enter with a new class, to enroll in different courses, to be honored with elaborate birthday celebrations, and, of course, to subscribe to an endless variety of magazines.

What Princeton lacks in attention to a single make-believe student it makes up for in numbers. During the 1900s Princeton undergraduates have created fictitious students Bert Hormone, class of 1917, Ephriam Di Kahble, class of 1939, and Joseph Oznot, class of 1968. There also is a once-a-year mythical messenger named Henry Fairfax who delivers Valentine's Day cards to Princeton coeds.

Fraternities and Sororities

THE FIRST CHAPTERS

In 1825 four students at Union College in Schenectady, New York, formed a secret society called Kappa Alpha, the first social fraternity. In 1827 Kappa

Alpha was joined by Sigma Phi and Delta Phi, and the Union Triad was formed.

Miami University in Ohio was particularly supportive and became known as the "Mother of Fraternities." Miami was the founding site of Beta Theta Pi, Phi Delta Theta, Sigma Chi, and Phi Kappa Tau.

The first collegiate social fraternity was born at Union College in 1825.

The oldest sorority is the Alpha Delta Pi chapter established (originally called the Adelphean Society) at Wesleyan Female College of Georgia in 1851. The first sorority with a Greek name, Kappa Alpha Theta, was founded at DePauw in 1870.

FRATERNITIES TODAY

In the United States there are a total of sixty-one national fraternities; they have 5,618 chapters on 720 college campuses. Of the 3.2 million total fraternity members, 400,000 are current undergraduates.

In total membership, the five largest fraternities are:

	Members
Sigma Alpha Epsilon	197,600
Sigma Chi	180,000
Lambda Chi Alpha	173,162
Phi Delta Theta	164,363
Tau Kappa Epsilon	157,850

The five with the most chapters are:

	Chapters
Omega Psi Phi	306
Kappa Alpha Psi	294
Tau Kappa Epsilon	274
Sigma Phi Epsilon	243
Lambda Chi Alpha	214

SORORITIES TODAY

There are twenty-six national sororities with 2,446 chapters. Their total membership is 2.2 million, of whom 220,000 are currently enrolled in college. Chi Omega has the largest total membership, 170,000, and also leads in undergraduate members with 15,550.

MAKING A COMEBACK

Greek-letter societies have made a strong recovery since the late 1960s and early 1970s, when they fell out of favor with many students. Since 1975 fraternity membership has more than doubled, from 182,000 to 400,000, and more than 1,000 new chapters have been formed. In the same period, many more women have joined sororities, whose membership has increased from 186,000 to 243,000. Even U Cal Berkeley, whose reputation will always be linked to the rebelliousness of the 1960s, has added nine new fraternities and three sororities in the last ten years.

SWEETHEART

The most famous song to come from the Greek societies is "The Sweetheart of Sigma Chi." In

The Albion students who wrote the song "The Sweetheart of Sigma Chi" originally expected it to be sung once and forgotten.

1911 Albion students Byron Stokes and Dudleigh Vernor were given a pledge chore to come up with a song to commemorate the twenty-fifth anniversery of the local Alpha Pi chapter. Stokes wrote the lyrics during a class and Vernor set the words to music on the organ in the college chapel. By the time "The Sweetheart of Sigma Chi" had become a standard, Stokes and Vernor couldn't even remember on what date they created the song. They had expected it to be sung once and forgotten.

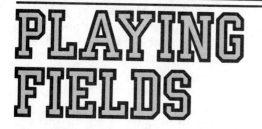

6

PLAYING FIELDS

COLLEGE NICKNAMES, NATIONAL CHAMPIONSHIPS, EXCELLENCE IN FOOTBALL AND BASKETBALL, THE ATHLETE IN THE CLASSROOM, ATHLETIC FACILITIES, COACHES, SPORTS STORIES

College Nicknames

The names of college athletic teams are an abundant source of good stories and good trivia. They range from the most common category, aggressive animals like the Screaming Eagles (Indiana State), to more gentle names like Poets (Whittier) or Angels (Meredith). Sometimes a peaceful nickname is made more ferocious by adding a combative adjective: for example, the Fighting Saints of Mount Senario or the Battling Bishops of North Carolina Wesleyan. Earlham College of Richmond, Indiana, called its teams the Fighting Quakers until the Vietnam War, when the name was changed to the Hustling Quakers.

TEN MOST COMMON NICKNAMES

Of the hundreds of college nicknames, which ones are used most often?

	Number of colleges
1. Eagles	72
2. Tigers	68
3. Cougars	50
4. Bulldogs	48
5. Warriors	43
6. Lions	41
7. Panthers	36
8. Indians	34
9. Wildcats	32
10. Bears	31

Although the Indians nickname occupies the eighth position, if all its variations— such as Braves, Redmen, and

Chiefs—were counted, the earliest Americans would be first on the list.

STORIES ABOUT NICKNAMES

Heidelberg Student Princes

Heidelberg's teams were called the Cardinals until 1926, when the director of admissions noticed an advertisement for the movie *The Student Prince of Heidelberg*. Seeing an opportunity to provide the college with a more attention-grabbing nickname and to link the Heidelberg in America to its ancestor in Germany, he waged a successful campaign to have the Cardinals changed to the Student Princes.

Trinity Christian Trolls

The name was derived from TRinity cOLLege Students. With the popularization of the childhood story "The Three Billy Goats Gruff," the troll took on physical attributes and became the college's mascot. Presumably the Trinity Troll can scare opponents the same way the fictional troll intimidated the goats as they tried to cross the bridge.

Nazareth Moles

This nickname comes not from the animal, but from the habits of Nazareth students. Since the Nazareth campus buildings are connected by tunnels, the students began to refer to themselves as "moles" because they tunneled their way to classes. Thus the nickname was born, even though the logo depicts an animal mole rather than a squinty-eyed student.

Manhattan Jaspers

This team was named in the late 1800s for Manhattan's prefect of discipline and baseball coach, Brother Jasper, whose claim to fame is that, while coaching the Manhattan baseball team during a game in 1882, he relieved the restlessness of the home crowd as the Jaspers came to bat in the late innings by calling time out to allow the fans to stand up and relax. This is the origin of the seventh inning stretch. It soon spread to professional baseball, because Manhattan often played practice games against the New York Giants of the National League.

South Florida Brahmans

When the students selected their mascot in 1962 they chose "Golden Brahmas" thinking they had picked a bull. Some months later they found out that a

Brahma is a chicken, and it took some time for them to unfowl their mistake. The teams are now known as the Golden Brahmans, or Bulls.

Knox Siwash
The athletic teams were given this name because a 1910 article in the *Saturday Evening Post* described a college named Siwash that strongly resembled Knox. There is no mascot (despite the football coach's effort to introduce the owl as a symbol of wisdom and strength) or logo because Siwash is a fictional name.

Wayland Baptist Pioneers and Hutcherson Flying Queens
The name Pioneers for the men's teams is not unusual, but what about Hutcherson Flying Queens for the women? The name comes from Claude Hutcherson, who furnished a private airplane for the Wayland women's basketball team to travel to Mexico in 1948. The name, as well as the tradition of flying to away games, has remained to this day.

Michigan State Spartans
In 1925, after Michigan Agricultural College changed its name to Michigan State, it sponsored a contest to select a nickname, and "Staters" won. When the Michigan State baseball team played in the South that year, a sportswriter for the local Lansing newspaper decided he didn't like "Staters" and substituted "Spartans" in his

Michigan State's Spartan.

stories about the team. To his amazement, no one complained, and, when the student newspaper began to use the nickname, Spartans took hold and gained acceptance.

Duke Blue Devils
In 1917 Duke student newspaper reporters polled the

The Duke Blue Devils derived their nickname from a French fighting unit of World War I.

undergraduates to choose a college mascot, but no clear favorite emerged. At the same time, sports editor Bill Lander, who had been following the progress of World War I closely, began to use the term Blue Devils as a nickname for the Duke athletic teams. The Blue Devils Lander referred to were an elite French alpine fighting unit famous for heroic feats during the war. Owing to its repetitive use during the 1920s, the name gradually caught on and the Blue Devil has been Duke's unique and popular mascot for over seventy years.

Georgetown Hoyas

This nickname comes from "Hoya saxa!" a loose Latin translation for "What rocks!" This term apparently relates to Georgetown's original nickname for its baseball team, the Stonewalls. The name Hoya stuck and was later used for all Georgetown teams.

Indiana Purdue at Fort Wayne Tuskers

This is one of the few nicknames tied to the academic side of a college. At the same time the Indiana Purdue athletic department was running a contest for a nickname, faculty members in the geology department happened to unearth mastodon bones while on a field trip. Tuskers is derived from the tusks of a mastodon.

Coastal Carolina Chanticleers

In 1965 a Coastal Carolina English professor and his class decided it was time to come up with a mascot for the college. While reading Chaucer's *Canterbury Tales,* they came across the chanticleer, a proud

and fierce rooster about which Chaucer wrote, "For crowing there was not his equal in all the land. His voice was merrier than the merry organ that plays in church, and his crowing from his resting place was more trustworthy than a clock." The Chanticleer caught on immediately with the students. Since Coastal is a branch campus of the University of South Carolina, an added advantage of the Chanticleer is its similarity to SC's Fighting Gamecock.

Southern Illinois Salukis

This college's mascot was named after an Egyptian hunting dog reputed to be the oldest pure breed in the world. Besides having mascotlike characteristics of speed and endurance, the Saluki's origins are appropriate to the area in which Southern Illinois is located, known as "Little Egypt."

Texas A&I Javelinas

Javelina is the Spanish name for a species of wild dog. Fighting spirit is a desirable trait in a mascot, and javelinas are known as intrepid and relentless fighters. Once attacked, they never have been known to retreat.

Pacific University Boxers

This nickname does not come from the college's prizefighting team but from one of Pacific's valuable possessions, a rare statue of a Boxer, a member of the Chinese secret society that attempted to drive foreigners out of the country in 1900. Pacific's logo is a dragonlike dog with flames emerging from its tail.

St. Louis Billikens
A billiken is an Alaskan good-luck piece; the word means "god of things as they should be."

Oglethorpe Stormy Petrels
A small sea bird, a petrel, supposedly guided General James Oglethorpe's ship safely to shore in 1733. After landing, Oglethorpe went on to establish the colony of Georgia.

Tufts Jumbos
The Tufts nickname is the Jumbos, but its athletes get their

The ashes of Jumbo the Elephant provide inspiration to the Tufts University teams named after him.

inspiration from a peanut butter jar. Tufts players became the Jumbos when Phineas T. Barnum gave the college a stuffed mount of the famous circus elephant after it was killed by a train in 1885. (Legend has it that Jumbo died saving the life of a baby elephant and his trainer by pushing them out of the path of an onrushing train.) After a 1975 fire destroyed the museum where Jumbo was kept

on display, Jumbo's ashes were saved in a peanut butter jar, which is now kept in the athletic department. Before a big game, Tufts captains show younger players the jar and tell of Jumbo's heroics as a way of getting the team psyched for the contest.

IF THE MEN'S TEAM IS THE RAMS, WHAT DO YOU CALL THE WOMEN?

The rapid growth of intercollegiate athletics for women has led to some interesting nicknames. In most cases the college nickname was established for the men's teams. With genderless names like the Kutztown Owls or the Defiance Yellow Jackets, it was simply a matter of using the same name for both teams. But it wasn't always easy to feminize the mascot. When the men's nickname didn't quite fit, "Lady" was usually added, like the Delta State Lady Statesmen or the Cincinnati Lady Bearcats. Beyond such straightforward examples of sexual adaptation, other variations—some creative and some rather strange—abound.

	Men	*Women*
Albany State	Rams	Rammettes
Angelo State	Rams	Rambelles
Tarleton State	Texans	Texanns
Mercer	Bears	Teddy Bears
North Arizona	Lumberjacks	Lumberjills
Washington and Jefferson	Presidents	First Ladies
Fort Valley State	Wildcats	Wildkittens
Kentucky	Wildcats	Lady Kats
Salisbury State	Sea Gulls	She Gulls
St. Peter's (New Jersey)	Peacocks	Peahens
New Orleans	Privateers	Buc-ettes
Massachusetts	Minutemen	Minutewomen
St. Mary's (Minnesota)	Redmen	Cardinals
St. John's (New York)	Redmen	Basketball Express
Alcorn	Braves	Bravettes
Albany College of Pharmacy	Panthers	Pink Panthers
Montclair State	Indians ⸱	Tomahawks

To prove that turnabout is fair play, perhaps the University of Delaware Blue Hens should rename their men's teams the Blue Roosters. On the other hand, the Lane College Dragons shouldn't pass up the opportunity to call their women's teams the Dragon Ladies.

TEAMS WITH MORE THAN ONE NICKNAME

There are a number of colleges that have two nicknames for their teams. For example, MIT has Engineers and Beavers, Yale Bulldogs and Elis, Virginia Cavaliers and Wahoos, and Virginia Tech Gobblers and Hokies. But Auburn University is the only college that tries to keep three going at once: War Eagles, Tigers, and Plainsmen.

Auburn University is the only college that currently has three distinct names — War Eagles, Tigers, and Plainsmen.

WHEN THE NICKNAME IS NOT THE MASCOT

In most cases, the college nickname comes first and both the mascot and logo are derived from the name. Occasionally a nickname is hard enough to pin down so that the college comes up with a different symbol.

	Nickname	*Mascot*
Akron	Zips	Kangaroo
Alabama	Crimson Tide	Elephant
Cornell	Big Red	Bear
Georgetown	Hoyas	Bulldog
Indiana State	Sycamores	Indian

CATEGORIES OF NICKNAMES

It's possible to group college nicknames according to various classifications, for example:

Military

Christopher Newport	Captains
Vanderbilt	Generals
St. Louis Christian	Soldiers
West Illinois	Leathernecks
Eastern Kentucky	Colonels

Occupations

Davis and Elkins	Senators
Franklin and Marshall	Diplomats
Washington and Jefferson	Presidents
Lincoln	Railsplitters
Whittier	Poets
Brandeis	Judges
William Penn	Statesmen
Colorado School of Mines	Orediggers

Religious

Bloomfield	Deacons
Concordia Seminary	Preachers
Elon	Fighting Christians
Flagler	Saints
North Carolina Wesleyan	Battling Bishops
Nyack	Fighting Parsons
Oklahoma Baptist	Prophets

MTV

South Dakota State	Hardrockers

First Names

St. John's (Minnesota)	Johnnies
St. Thomas (Minnesota)	Tommies
Jamestown (North Dakota)	Jimmies
St. Lawrence (New York)	Larries

Years

Cal State Long Beach	49ers
Viterbo	76ers

WORST NICKNAME

Barat College in Lake Forest, Illinois, stands out. Their nickname is the Barat-cudas.

BEST NICKNAME

For a combination of appropriateness, a likable animal, and an appealing logo, the John Jay College of Criminal Justice Bloodhound takes the prize.

NICKNAMES TOO GOOD TO BE LEFT OUT

Scottsdale Community College Artichokes

Colby White Mules

Campbell (North Carolina) Fighting Camels

Bethany (Kansas) Terrible Swedes

U Cal Irvine Anteaters

MOST UNUSUAL LOGO

Washington College in Chestertown, Maryland, on the shore of the Chesapeake Bay, is the only college with written permission from George himself to use his name and likeness. The result, however, is a rather strange mixture of politics and sport.

INSECTS AND WEEDS

The University of Rochester has an insect, the yellow jacket, for its mascot and a weed, the dandelion, for its flower.

MOST PROPHETIC NICKNAME

Pepperdine originally was named the Waves in 1937 when it was located in south central Los Angeles, a good distance from the ocean. In 1972 Pepperdine's main campus was moved to Malibu, a stone's throw from the Pacific and an appropriate location for the Wave nickname.

MOST COLORFUL NICKNAME

There is the Big Red of Cornell, Big Green of Dartmouth, and Big Blue of Millikin, but the most colorful college nickname is the University of Hawaii Rainbows.

THREE CARDINALS

The Ball State Cardinals have a nickname and a logo patterned after the bird, an exact copy of the mascot of the St. Louis Cardinal baseball team.

Catholic University's teams are called the Cardinal's (possessive, not plural) because an early baseball squad took on the name of Catholic's first chancellor, Cardinal James Gibbons.

Then there is the Stanford Cardinal (singular, not plural). Stanford's nickname comes neither from the bird nor from a religious rank, but from the color, cardinal red.

COMMERCIAL CONNECTIONS

At least three colleges have nicknames derived from commercial products. The Akron Zips are named after the Zippers, which were overshoes manufactured by B. F. Goodrich

Converse College chose to name its teams after the All-Star basketball sneaker.

in 1925. Converse College, a women's school in Spartanburg, South Carolina, chose to name its teams after the All-Star basketball sneaker. Stetson, of DeLand, Florida, was named for John Stetson, the hat manufacturer, who was chairman of the board of trustees and a major benefactor. In honor of Mr. Stetson's source of income, the Hatter nickname seemed a natural. The mascot is a student dressed in a giant hat.

UNIVERSITY OF MIAMI

In recent years, the University of Miami has made the sports headlines because of its successful football teams. Nearly every football fan knows that Miami's nickname is the Hurricanes, commonly shortened to Canes. But how many know Miami's mascot? It's not a human version of a hurricane that blows away the opposition, but a peaceful, white-feathered, long-billed wading bird, the ibis.

National Championships

Colleges educate some 12 million students each year. Professors conduct research of great importance in science, agriculture, and medicine. But, more often than not, colleges are better known for the success of their athletic teams than they are for the accomplishments of their students or faculty. What colleges have produced the best

teams? One measure of achievement is the number of national championships won.

NCAA

The American public is most familiar with the championships sponsored by the National Collegiate Athletic Association (NCAA). For both men and women, the NCAA is the largest sports organization. It divides its teams into three levels— Divisions I, II, and III. In football only, there is a further split in Division I between I-A and I-AA.

Men's NCAA Division I— Team Championships in Eighteen Sports (1921 to 1987)

	Titles
1. USC	63
2. UCLA	51
3. Oklahoma State	37
4. Stanford	29
5. Michigan	25
Yale	25
7. Texas at El Paso	21
8. Denver	19
9. Indiana	18
Ohio State	18

Not only does USC have a substantial lead in the number of championships won, but its consistency has been impressive.

In 1985, Southern Cal failed to win a single NCAA team championship for the first time in twenty-seven years.

The year 1985 marked the first time in twenty-seven years the Trojans failed to win a national title.

While USC saw its consecutive streak end, PAC 10 rivals UCLA and Stanford have enjoyed a great deal of success in recent years. During the 1985–86 and 1986–87 academic years, Stanford won six national championships and UCLA four.

At the other end of the big-time sports scale from the PAC 10 powerhouses is the University of Chicago. A dominant football team in the 1920s and 1930s, Chicago began to deemphasize athletics in 1939 and now competes in Division III. Before turning away from major competition, the Maroons won their only national title, the NCAA gymnastics championship, in 1938.

Even though Duke has a rich athletic tradition with a good overall record in many Division I sports, its 1986 men's soccer title was the Blue Devils' first national championship.

Women's NCAA Division I— Team Championships in Sixteen Sports (1981 to 1987)

	Titles
1. Texas	8
2. UCLA	6
3. Stanford	5
USC	5
Utah	5
6. North Carolina	4
Old Dominion	4

Like Stanford in the men's competition, Texas has done very well in women's sports since 1985, with three national championships in 1985–86 (basketball, swimming, and outdoor track) and two in 1986–87 (cross-country and swimming).

Men's NCAA Division II— Team Championships in Fourteen Sports (1957 to 1987)

	Titles
1. Cal Poly San Luis Obispo	18
Cal State Northridge	18
3. U Cal Irvine	15
4. Florida Southern	11
Southern Illinois at Edwardsville	11

Women's NCAA Division II—Team Championships in Ten Sports (1981 to 1987)

	Titles
1. Cal State Northridge	9
2. Cal Poly San Luis Obispo	8
3. Abilene Christian	3
Cal Poly Pomona	3
Clarion	3
Tennessee at Chattanooga	3

In Division II Cal State Northridge and Cal Poly San Luis Obispo have the best teams for both men and women, and the two colleges have nearly identical overall records. They are tied for first in the men's division with eighteen titles each, while Northridge inched ahead of Cal Poly in women's sports, nine championships to eight, on the strength of a spring 1987 softball title.

Men's NCAA Division III— Team Championships in Thirteen Sports (1973 to 1987)

	Titles
1. Cal State Stanislaus	12
2. Glassboro State	8
Hobart	8
Kenyon	8
5. North Central	6

Men's Division III is dominated by teams that are very successful in one sport. Cal State Stanislaus has won ten golf titles, Kenyon eight in swimming, and Hobart eight in lacrosse.

Although it has captured only four Division III national tennis titles, Kalamazoo has an amazing overall record. The Hornets have won fifty consecutive Michigan Intercollegiate Athletic Association championships while compiling a dual meet record of 317-1.

Women's NCAA Division III—Team Championships in Ten Sports (1981 to 1987)

	College	Titles
1.	Trenton State	8
2.	U Cal San Diego	5
3.	Kenyon	4
	U Mass Boston	4
5.	Eastern Connecticut State	3
	St. Thomas (Minnesota)	3
	Wisconsin at La Crosse	3

With five national championships in the last two years, Trenton State in New Jersey has become the most successful college in women's NCAA Division III sports.

In the number of NCAA championships across all divisions, including both men's and women's sports, the accomplishments of the California colleges are remarkable. Of the six divisions, a California college is the leader in five. The only college to break the California lock on first place is Trenton State in women's Division III.

MEN'S NCAA DIVISION I—CHAMPIONS BY SPORT (to 1986–87)

In the eighteen sports in which the NCAA sponsors championships, the following colleges are the leaders:

Sport	College	Titles
Baseball	USC	11
Basketball	UCLA	10
Cross-country	Michigan State	8
Fencing	NYU	12
Golf	Yale	21
Gymnastics	Penn State	9
Ice hockey	Michigan	7
Lacrosse	Johns Hopkins	6
Rifle*	Tennessee Tech, West Virginia	3
Skiing*	Denver	14

continued

Soccer	Saint Louis	10
Swimming	Ohio State	11
Tennis	UCLA	14
Indoor track	Texas at El Paso	7
Outdoor track	USC	26
Volleyball	UCLA	11
Water polo	U Cal Berkeley	6
Wrestling	Oklahoma State	27

*Rifle and skiing championships combine both men's and women's competition.

The teams that have been most impressive in a particular sport are USC in outdoor track and Oklahoma State in wrestling. In track, USC's twenty-six titles are twenty ahead of UCLA and Texas at El Paso, which have six each. Oklahoma's twenty-seven wrestling championships are sixteen more than the eleven titles won by runner-up Iowa.

MOST CONSECUTIVE NCAA CHAMPIONSHIPS

The record of nine in a row is shared by three colleges—Yale, USC, and Iowa.

Sport	College	Championship years
Golf	Yale	1905–1913
Track	USC	1935–1943
Wrestling	Iowa	1978–1986

COACH WITH MOST NCAA CHAMPIONSHIPS

Dave Williams, golf coach at the University of Houston, is the all-time leader, having guided the Cougars to sixteen national titles between 1956 and 1985.

NAIA AND NJCAA

The NCAA is not the only college athletic association to sponsor national championships. The National Association of Intercollegiate Athletics (NAIA) and the National Junior College Athletic Association (NJCAA) also conduct play-offs to determine champions.

Men's NAIA—Team Championships in Eleven Sports (1937 to 1987)

	Titles
1. Adams State	16
2. Simon Fraser	14
3. Eastern Michigan	13
Lamar	13
5. Quincy	11
Redlands	11

Women's NAIA—Team Championships in Eight Sports (1980 to 1987)

	Titles
1. Prairie View A&M	7
2. Hawaii at Hilo	4
Simon Fraser	4
Southwestern Oklahoma	4
5. Texas Southern	3
Wisconsin at Eau Claire	3

Men's NJCAA—Team Championships in Eighteen Sports (1937 to 1987)

	Titles
1. Odessa	31
2. Nassau	19
3. Mesa	14
4. Indian River	13
5. Vermont Technical	12
6. Brevard	11
7. Miami-Dade North	10
SUNY A&T Canton	10

Women's NJCAA—Team Championships in Fifteen Sports (1975 to 1987)

	Titles
1. Erie North	10
Indian River	10
3. Eastern Oklahoma	8
4. Champlain	7
5. Odessa	6
6. Adirondack	5
Barton County	5

Excellence in Football and Basketball

Among the many sports in which colleges compete, the major revenue sports—football and basketball—receive the most publicity. Looking at both team and individual accomplishments in football and basketball, which colleges have done best?

FOOTBALL DIVISION I ALL-TIME WINNING TEAMS (to 1987)

	Winning percentage
1. Notre Dame	.754
2. Michigan	.741
3. Alabama	.728
4. Texas	.722
Oklahoma	.722
6. USC	.707
7. Ohio State	.705
8. Penn State	.690
9. Nebraska	.683
10. Tennessee	.682

FOOTBALL DIVISION I NATIONAL CHAMPIONSHIPS

NCAA Division I-A football does not have an official national champion. Because there is no arrangement for a play-off, the number one team is decided by a vote among coaches and sportswriters. Based on the Associated Press poll, these colleges won the most football championships from 1936 to 1987:

	Titles
1. Notre Dame	7
2. Oklahoma	6
3. Alabama	5
4. Minnesota	4
5. Ohio State	3
USC	3
7. Nebraska	2
Penn State	2
Pittsburgh	2
Texas	2
West Point	2

Although Notre Dame holds the number one position, the Fighting Irish have not won a national championship since 1977.

In Division I-A football more than in other NCAA sports, it has proved increasingly difficult to build a dynasty. There hasn't been a repeat national champion since Alabama won consecutive titles in 1978 and 1979.

Nevertheless, the consistency of the top football teams across three measures of excellence—national championships, consensus All-Americans, and best winning percentage—is remarkable. Of the ten winningest teams, nine are in the top ten in the number of All-Americans produced and eight are in the top eleven in national championships won. Only Michigan is an exception. The Wolverines are second in all-time winning percentage and fourth in All-Americans, but they have won only one national championship, the 1948 title.

In Division I-AA football, which began in 1978, the only colleges that have won more than one championship are Eastern Kentucky and Georgia Southern, with two each. Georgia Southern, in capturing the title for the second year in a row in 1986, made an amazing turnaround. After giving up football in 1939, Georgia Southern started up again with a club team in 1982, and in 1984 they played their first game against college competition. The Eagles then proceeded to win the Division I-AA championship the next two years.

In Division II, North Dakota State leads the way with three championships. Southwest Texas State and Troy State, the 1987 national champion, are second with two apiece.

Today's dominant college football team plays in Division III. Tiny Augustana College (enrollment 2,200) of Rock Island, Illinois, had won four consecutive national championships before they lost in the 1987 quarterfinals to Dayton. The Wagner Seahawks of Staten Island, New York, were the eventual champions. No other college football team can match Augustana's record.

MEN'S BASKETBALL DIVISION I ALL-TIME WINNING TEAMS (to 1987)

	Winning percentage
1. Kentucky	.760
2. North Carolina	.733
3. St. John's (New York)	.705
4. UCLA	.693
5. Western Kentucky	.691
6. Kansas	.679
Weber State	.679
8. DePaul	.675
9. Notre Dame	.674
Syracuse	.674

This list of the top basketball teams contains one college that is relatively unknown, Weber (pronounced Wee-ber) State of Ogden, Utah. The Weber State Wildcats are a perennial power in the Big Sky Conference.

MEN'S BASKETBALL DIVISION I NATIONAL CHAMPIONSHIPS (to 1987)

	Titles
1. UCLA	10
2. Indiana	5
Kentucky	5

4. Cincinnati	2
Louisville	2
North Carolina	2
North Carolina State	2
Oklahoma State	2
San Francisco	2

In men's Division I basketball, UCLA leads by a comfortable margin with ten titles. The Bruins' ten championships came in a span of twelve years from 1964 to 1975 under the coaching of John Wooden and the playing of All-Americans like Lew Alcindor (Kareem Abdul-Jabbar), Sidney Wicks, and Bill Walton.

In Division II, Evansville, Indiana, and Kentucky Wesleyan are the leaders with five championships each. The five titles won by North Park, Illinois, puts it at the top of Division III.

WOMEN'S BASKETBALL NATIONAL CHAMPIONSHIPS

Since the NCAA began to offer women's basketball championships in 1982, USC and Louisiana Tech (Division I) and Cal Poly Pomona (Division II) are the only multiple winners, each college having won twice. For the eleven years the Association of Intercollegiate Athletics for Women (AIAW) sponsored women's play-offs before the NCAA took over, Delta State and Immaculata won three titles and Old Dominion two.

ALL-AMERICANS

Another indication of a college's athletic success is the number of players named to All-American teams. Looking at NCAA consensus All-Americans in football and basketball, which colleges are at the top of the list?

Football Division I Consensus All-Americans (1889 to 1986)

Number of selections

1. Yale		100
2. Harvard		89
3. Notre Dame		79
4. Princeton		65
5. Michigan		58
6. USC		54
7. Ohio State		51
8. Oklahoma		47
9. Penn		46
10. Pittsburgh		43

Yale, Harvard, Princeton, and Penn are among the leaders because they dominated the All-American teams from 1889 through the 1920s. In fact, the first nine All-American teams consisted entirely of Ivy League players. If one starts counting in 1924 (the year of Red Grange and Notre Dame's Four Horsemen) rather than 1889, the results are quite different. Yale, Harvard, Princeton, and Penn are reduced to about ten All-Americans each and are replaced by Texas, Nebraska, Alabama, and Tennessee. The list from 1924 on looks like this:

Football Division I Consensus All-Americans (1924 to 1986)

Number of selections

1. Notre Dame		75
2. USC		54

3. Oklahoma	47
4. Michigan	45
Ohio State	45
6. Pittsburgh	33
7. Texas	32
8. Nebraska	31
9. Alabama	30
10. Tennessee	25

Football Divisions II and III Consensus All-Americans (1924 to 1986)

Number of selections

1. Texas A&I	32
2. Grambling	25
3. Delaware	23
4. Nevada Reno	19
North Dakota State	19
6. Tennessee Chattanooga	17
7. Boise State	16
Massachusetts	16
South Carolina State	16
10. Arkansas State	15
Lehigh	15
Tennessee State	15

Men's Basketball Division I Consensus All-Americans (1929 to 1987)

Number of selections

1. Kentucky	17
Notre Dame	17
UCLA	17
4. Purdue	15
5. North Carolina	13
6. Indiana	12
7. Kansas	8
Ohio State	8
9. Oklahoma	7
10. DePaul	6
Duke	6
Pittsburgh	6

It is not surprising that UCLA and Kentucky head this list, because they hold down the number one and two positions in national championships won.

Although Notre Dame has never won a national basketball championship, it has an outstanding record producing All-Americans.

Notre Dame's appearance, though, is more of a surprise. Although the Fighting Irish have never won a national title, they have an outstanding record in producing All-Americans.

Looking at Divisions II and III in men's basketball, Potsdam State leads with eight consensus All-Americans. Tied for second place with six are Assumption, Kentucky Wesleyan, Otterbein, Roanoke, and Sacred Heart.

Women's Basketball Division I Consensus All-Americans (1975 to 1986)

Number of selections

1. Louisiana Tech	9
Old Dominion	9
Tennessee	9
4. Georgia	7
UCLA	7
USC	7
7. Long Beach State	6
8. Texas	5
Wayland Baptist	5

In women's basketball in Divisions II and III, Cal Poly Pomona leads with seven All-Americans, followed by Scranton with four and seven colleges with three each: Abilene Christian, Buena Vista, Central Missouri State, Elizabethtown, Hampton, New Rochelle, and Salem State.

RHODES SCHOLARS

There have been three All-American football players and two All-American basketball players who were Rhodes Scholars:

Football

	College	Class
Byron "Whizzer" White	Colorado	1938
Pete Dawkins	West Point	1958
Joe Romig	Colorado	1961

Basketball

	College	Class
Bill Bradley	Princeton	1965
Tom McMillen	Maryland	1974

Pat Haden, USC class of 1974, was also a Rhodes Scholar. Although Haden was not a first team All-American, he did quarterback a national championship team, lead USC to a Rose Bowl victory, and play professional football for the Los Angeles Rams.

Athletic Facilities

LARGEST CROWD

The University of Michigan football team plays its home games in Michigan Stadium, which has a seating capacity of 101,701. The largest crowd was 106,155 for a November 17, 1979, game against Ohio State. Each football season Michigan

draws more fans than any other college in the country. As of the end of the 1987 season, the Wolverines had played seventy-nine straight games before crowds in excess of 100,000.

The largest crowd to watch a college football game was 106,869 for the 1973 Rose Bowl game in which USC defeated Ohio State 42-17.

LARGEST ARENA

The Carrier Dome (capacity 33,000), located on the Syracuse campus, is the largest college indoor stadium. Along with other events that take place there, the Orangemen play their home football and basketball games in the Dome. The biggest

basketball crowd was 32,602 for the February 22, 1987, game between Syracuse and Georgetown, which Georgetown won 72-71.

The largest crowd ever to watch a college basketball game was 64,959 at the New Orleans Superdome on March 30, 1987. Indiana beat Syracuse 74-73 for the NCAA championship.

SMALLEST CROWD

On January 9, 1985, the Northeastern Huskies women's basketball team played before a crowd of zero. Due to an outbreak of measles on the campus of their opponent, Boston University, no spectators were permitted at the game. The handful of media people who were allowed to attend were required to show inoculation records before gaining entrance. Some of the seats, however, were occupied. The players created their own crowd with cardboard cutouts of their favorite basketball team, the Boston Celtics. The Huskies, however, didn't do as well as their idols usually do, losing to Boston University 58-34.

On the subject of large stadiums and small crowds, Caltech's home football field is the Rose Bowl, located a few blocks from its campus in

Northeastern's passive crowd.

Pasadena. While the Rose Bowl has a capacity of 102,000, the attendance at a Beaver football game (one rival is the Tijuana Institute of Technology) rarely exceeds 1,000. It is likely that Caltech plays before more empty seats than any other college team.

LARGEST BY SPORT

The largest college-owned athletic facilities are:

	Sport	College	Capacity
Michigan Stadium	Football	Michigan	101,701
Carrier Dome	Basketball	Syracuse	33,000
Edwards Track Stadium	Track	U Cal Berkeley	22,000
Armstrong Stadium	Soccer	Indiana	9,000
Yost Ice Arena	Hockey	Michigan	8,100
Disch-Falk Field	Baseball	Texas	8,000
Indiana Natatorium	Swimming	Indiana at Indianapolis	4,500

Although the indoor pool on the Indianapolis campus of Indiana University has the largest seating capacity, Texas has a comparable facility. Both colleges have two separate eight-lane pools, one for competition and one for warm-up, along with a diving tank that has both a platform and springboards.

The capacity of Armstrong Stadium, the home of Indiana University's soccer team, can be expanded from 9,000 to 30,000 for the annual Little 500 bicycle race.

IT'S NOT MY FAULT

U Cal Berkeley's football team is known as the Golden Bears, but a more appropriate nickname might be the Earthquakes. Berkeley's California Memorial Stadium has the only college football field with an active earthquake fault running through the middle of it. Although there hasn't been a major earthquake along the Hayward fault in 100 years, there is constant creep movement. The result is two long cracks in each end wall of Memorial Stadium that mark the fault line. Because the stadium is occupied for only six Saturdays a year, it is not designated a

Burying Bully I at Mississippi State.

hazardous structure. Nevertheless, U Cal Berkeley officials half jokingly recommend that earthquake-shy visitors choose a seat in the east stands. If a tremor should occur during a game, the spectators in the west stands will end up with a more distant view of the playing field than they had when they entered.

FOOTBALL CAN BE A GRAVE UNDERTAKING

The Mississippi State Bulldogs have a long football tradition dating back to the turn of the century, but they didn't have a mascot to go with their nickname until 1935, when Bully I was given to the university. In 1939 Bully I died and the students put on an elaborate funeral, attended by thousands. The bulldog was buried on the 50-yard line of Scott Field, near the home team's bench. The grave is still there, honored yearly by players and fans alike.

LARGEST ATHLETIC EVENT

A sport that confines itself to two teams playing within an enclosed playing field is unlikely to qualify for the record. What type of competition stages multiple events before crowds that spread out over a large area? Crew is one such sport, and two East Coast regattas are the largest. For the number of participants, the Dad Vail regatta on the Schuylkill River in Philadelphia heads the list, with seventy-three colleges and 3,500 rowers. For the most spectators, Harvard's Head of the Charles crew races take place before crowds estimated as high as 125,000.

OLYMPIC TRAINING

The U.S. Olympic Committee has designated three Olympic Training Centers. The only one located on a college campus is at Northern Michigan University in Marquette. Northern Michigan has a speed-skating oval, a luge run, a cross-country skiing course, a number of indoor facilities, and a modern sports medicine center for rehabilitation and research. In the planning stages are a bobsled run, 40-meter and 60-meter ski jumps, and a biathlon range. Altogether the Northern Michigan Olympic Training Center has the capability to train athletes for competition in twenty-five Olympic sports.

OLYMPIC BUILDING

On the subject of the Olympics, in 1904 Washington University in St. Louis hosted the first Olympic Games on American soil. St. Louis was chosen as the Olympic site because it was the location of the 1904 World's Fair. A member of the Washington University board of trustees, Robert Brookings, saw an opportunity for the university to move from its cramped and dingy downtown location to a newer and more spacious campus. On behalf of the college, Brookings erected a number of buildings and athletic facilities in the Forest Park area

west of the city and leased them to the World's Fair group. He used the rental income to put up more buildings. In 1905, when the fair ended, Washington had a beautiful new campus at very little cost. Today the World's Fair buildings remain as the architectural theme of the college. One change, however, eventually had to be made. For eighty years Washington's track team competed on an odd-size running track that had three laps to the mile, the Olympic standard in 1904. Finally, in 1985, the university rebuilt the track and made it the standard four laps.

Coaches

LONGEST COACHING TENURE

The record is held by Amos Alonzo Stagg, who coached at the college level for seventy years, from 1890 to 1960. Before

Amos Alonzo Stagg coached at the college level for seventy years.

retiring at age 98, Stagg coached at Springfield, the College of the Pacific, Susquehanna, and Stockton Junior College in California. As a head coach, Stagg won 314 games. He died in 1965 at age 102.

CRADLE OF COACHES

Miami of Ohio has a remarkable record for producing football coaches. Among college coaches who either played or coached at Miami are Earl Blaik (Army), Woody Hayes (Ohio State), Paul Dietzel (LSU), Ara Parseghian (Notre Dame), John Pont (Indiana), Bo Schembechler (Michigan), Carmen Cozza (Yale), and Dick Crum (North Carolina). Miamians who coached professional teams include Paul Brown (Cleveland), Weeb Eubank (New York Jets), and Sid Gillman (San Diego). Miami's cradle is not limited to football coaches. Walter Alston (baseball) and Wayne Embry (basketball) also are graduates.

HIGHEST-PAID COACH

In the modern-day world of college sports, the direction of a team is no longer left to the players as it once was, but is in the hands of a collection of head and assistant coaches. With the amount of money a college earns from ticket sales, television rights, and concessions, it is not surprising that top-level coaches are paid handsomely for winning games. Records of coaches' salaries are only occasionally available and there is little information about income earned from endorsements, television and radio shows, and summer camps. Even so, it is likely that Jim Valvano, the basketball coach at North Carolina State, is the highest paid, with an estimated annual income of $600,000. Although Valvano's base pay is only $85,000, he has a number

of very lucrative endorsements and is a tireless and popular speaker at $5,000 per appearance.

One of the first coaches to earn a large salary was Jackie Sherrill, the football coach at Texas A&M, who signed a $1.6-million six-year contract ($267,000 per year) in 1982. The arrangement included a $114,000 annual salary, $142,000 a year for media shows, and other benefits like a free car and country club membership. He also receives an additional $10,000 each time Texas A&M appears in a bowl game. Should Texas A&M decide to fire Sherrill before his contract expires, it will cost the university a lump-sum payment of $1.3-million.

MONEY FOR MUSCLES

The company that makes Arm and Hammer Baking Soda paid the Brown University wrestling coach of the early 1900s, Frank Herrick, to be the arm model for its trademark. Herrick, who at the time was described as having the perfect body, bared more than his arm. He was also the model for the six male figures that adorn the frieze on the portico of the New York Stock Exchange.

THE PULITZER PRIZE FOR X'S AND O'S

Coaches are more likely to be adept at histrionics than history. An exception to this rule is

Vernon Parrington, Oklahoma's second football coach. After he was fired in 1907 for refusing to give up smoking, Parrington moved to Washington University, became a history professor, and won the 1928 Pulitzer Prize in history for his book *Main Currents in American Thought.*

Sports Stories

SENIOR ATHLETES

It isn't often that a college athlete is twenty-six years older than his coach, but not that many players are 71 years old. Joe Sweeney, a tennis player for the Salem State Vikings, is a sophomore majoring in physical education. In the matches he played during the 1986–87 season, his record was 0-3 in singles and 2-1 in doubles. Joe is the oldest athlete ever to play a varsity sport.

In women's sports, 46-year-old Thomasina Robinson plays basketball for Hunter College in New York City. A 5'2" playmaker for the Lady Hawks' junior varsity, Robinson is believed to be the oldest woman playing on an intercollegiate team.

Georgia State's 39-year-old cross-country runner, Nora Weed, is seven years younger than Thomasina Robinson but nevertheless holds a college sport distinction. Both Nora and her daughter Theresa ran for the Panthers during the 1987–88 season, the first mother-daughter combination to perform for the same college team.

THE SHORTEST SEASON

St. John's College of Annapolis, Maryland, does not field intercollegiate teams, preferring an intramural sports program. Once a year, however, St. John's makes an exception to its insular sports philosophy and plays a game against its neighbor, the U.S. Naval Academy. The sport is croquet. Even though they had

The only intercollegiate sport at St. John's College is croquet.

the home lawn advantage, the Johnnies dropped the 1987 match. Through the end of 1987 the series record stands at 3-2 in favor of St. John's.

Hunter's Thomasina Robinson.

DR. J'S OTHER BROTHER

Yeshiva in New York City, a college that combines a rigorous program of Hebrew studies with a liberal arts education, is not known for its basketball teams. In fact, in 1984–85 the Maccabees finished 11-8 to complete their first winning season in twenty-four years. Yeshiva had somewhat of an excuse for its long stretch of nonwinning basketball seasons. Since 1935, when their first game took place, the Maccabees did not have a home court. After a half century of traveling by subway, bus, and car to home games on its opponents' courts, Yeshiva finally played before its own fans at the new Max Stern Center on November 19, 1985, scoring a victory over Bard College.

One of the reasons for Yeshiva's newfound success on the court was the dazzling play of 5'9" guard Joey Eaves from Roxbury, Massachusetts. Joey lead the team in both scoring and assists. Joey, besides being a Jewish basketball player, also happens to be black. Thus his nickname, "Rabbi J."

Yeshiva's "Rabbi J."

HORSE SENSE

It is not uncommon for athletes to face handicaps of various kinds. Some play injured, while others have to deal with hostile crowds or bad officiating. It is rare, however, for an athlete with a serious physical handicap to compete in an intercollegiate sport. But her handicap did not stop Kristen Knouse of Rutgers, who is blind, from riding for her college's equestrian team. After winning the eastern regional title, Kristen finished in fourth place in the walk-trot event at the 1988 Intercollegiate Horse Show Association's national riding championship competition.

SIGNALS

Gallaudet, a Washington, D.C., private college for the hearing impaired, fields teams in fourteen Division III sports. Although Gallaudet players usually compete on even terms with nonhandicapped teams, occasionally special techniques are called for. For example, in football many of the players are unable to hear the quarterback's snap signal. To overcome this problem, the coach coordinates the snap of the ball with the pounding of a bass drum on the sidelines. Those who can't hear are able to sense the drum's vibrations and thus begin the play on the same count as their teammates.

Gallaudet is credited with another innovation in college football—the huddle. Nearly a century ago, under the leadership of quarterback Paul Hubbard, class of 1896, the Gallaudet players came up with a way to gather around Hubbard so they could read his hand signals while shielding the play from their opponents. This was the forerunner of the modern-day football huddle.

THE ORIGIN OF THE WAVE

The spectacle of crowds at baseball and football games standing and raising their arms in a ripplelike motion around the stadium has become a common sight in American sports. The wave originated at a University of Washington football game against Stanford on October 31, 1981. After he graduated, a former Husky cheerleader, Rob Wellor, came back to Seattle for home games and led cheers in one section of the stands. Part of the ritual was for his group to do a "vertical wave," beginning in the first row and proceeding up to the last row. Rob had the idea of making the wave horizontal by running around the track that encircled the football field and encouraging the fans to stand as he passed in front of them. After a number of efforts, the ripple went all the way around the stadium and the wave was born.

LONGEST ROAD TRIP

It is likely that Willamette University of Salem, Oregon, holds the record for the longest away trip. It was the Willamette Bearcats' tough luck to schedule a football game on December 6, 1941, at the University of Hawaii. Since the bombing of Pearl Harbor occurred the next morning, the team was stranded on the island. The majority of players finally returned to the mainland early in 1942, serving as aides on a hospital ship bound for San Francisco. Some of them, however, didn't conclude their road trip until 1945, since they immediately enlisted in the military and were shipped to the South Pacific.

DURABILITY RECORDS

During Thanksgiving week in 1892, the University of North Carolina team played four football games in five days. Not

The University of North Carolina once won four football games in five days — by a combined score of 138-0!

only did the Tarheels win every game, they did so by a combined score of 138-0, and all without making a single substitution. On November 22 North Carolina defeated Duke 24-0 in Chapel Hill. They then took to the road and beat Auburn 64-0 and Vanderbilt 24-0 on consecutive days. They took Thanksgiving Day off before defeating

Virginia 26-0 the next day in Atlanta. The Tarheels kept their spirits up by taking an occasional drink of North Carolina moonshine before the games and during halftime.

A similar feat was accomplished by the Sewanee football team in 1899. On their way to a 12-0 season, Sewanee played and won five games in six days, beating Texas, Texas A&M, Tulane, LSU, and Mississippi. On the seventh day they rested.

BIGGEST UPSET

Tiny Centre College of Danville, Kentucky, known as the Prayin' Colonels, played a football game against Harvard on October 29, 1921. Harvard, the defending national champion and unbeaten in five seasons, was expected to win the game by four or five touchdowns. Centre, however, was not without talent. Among its sixteen players was Bo McMillian, an All-American running back. After a scoreless first half, McMillian scored on a 32-yard run. In the last few minutes of the game Harvard moved to Centre's 3-yard line but was stopped by a penalty. Centre held on to win 6-0. The Colonels' prayers had been answered. A small, almost unknown Kentucky college with an enrollment of 200 had conquered mighty Harvard and, for a moment, stood at the top of the football world.

COOKING UP A NEW SHOE

A kitchen served as the laboratory for an invention that launched the jogging craze and helped found the Nike sportswear company. In 1972 Bill Bowerman, the track coach at the University of Oregon, was looking for an all-purpose running shoe that could be used on the track, for cross-country races, and on paved roads. The only options available at the time were spiked running shoes, sneakers, or European warm-up shoes. Bowerman tried drilling holes in the bottom of a pair of sneakers, but the holes filled with dirt. Then, one morning, he noticed the pattern of the family's waffle iron. He took urethane, spread it on the iron, and let it bake. Since he forgot to grease the waffle iron, Bowerman could only pry enough urethane loose to see that the waffle pattern was what he was looking for. The waffle iron went into the garbage, but the idea was passed along to Nike, a small company that had just been started by Phil Knight, a former Oregon runner. Before long Nike's waffle-sole jogging shoe became the standard for the industry, eventually selling more than a million pairs. In over fifteen years of research since Bowerman's discovery, shoe designers have been unable to come up with a better sole. As it turns out, the waffle design provides the ideal combination of shock absorbency and traction in a running shoe.

BAG OF WIND

In the late 1800s, when football was just beginning to gain acceptance on college campuses, not everyone enthusiastically welcomed the opportunity for young men to block and tackle each other. It was during this time that Michigan invited Cornell to play a game on a neutral field in Cleveland. Declining the invitation, Cornell's president, Andrew Dickson White, replied to Michigan's president, James Angell, "I will not permit thirty men to travel 400 miles merely to agitate a bag of wind."

ATHLETIC FIRSTS

The first college athletic contest was a crew race between Harvard and Yale in 1852.

In what is now described as the first football game (it was actually a combination of rugby and soccer with twenty-five players on a side), Rutgers defeated Princeton six goals to four goals on November 6, 1869.

Fordham participated in the first college baseball game played according to Abner Doubleday's rules (nine men on a side, three outs to an inning) on November 3, 1859, against St. Francis Xavier College of New York. The Rose Hills, as Fordham was called then, won 33-11 in a six-inning game.

There was a college baseball game that preceded the Fordham–St. Francis contest. On July 1, 1859, Amherst defeated Williams 73-32 in round, or town, ball, which featured as many as twenty players on a team. Depending on one's definition of baseball, either the New Yorkers or the New Englanders played the first game.

Homecoming is a tradition that started at the University of Illinois in 1910. The idea soon caught on at other colleges, especially UCLA, which organized elaborate parades like the 1933 spectacular with fifty-two floats of varied theme and design.

In 1973 the University of Miami was the first college to give athletic scholarships to women. First to accept one of the fifteen tuition grants was Terry Williams of Homestead, Florida.

The University of Chicago started the first lettermen's club on January 29, 1904. The club was known as "Order of the C" and was founded by Amos Alonzo Stagg.

The first coed to participate in an intercollegiate contest against men was Sally Stearns of Rollins College in Winter Park, Florida, a coxswain for the heavyweight crew in 1936. Under her direction the crew's record was 1-1.

In 1985–86 Brenda Maxey of Northern Illinois was the only female college wrestler in the country and the first woman ever to win an NCAA wrestling match. Wrestling in the 118-pound class, she finished with a record of 3-7. The males Brenda defeated should not feel too bad about the outcome. She is a two-time world champion in judo wrestling.

Northern Illinois's Brenda Maxey.

The University of Pittsburgh Panthers were the first football team to wear numbers on their jerseys.

SWIMMING

Pablo Morales of Stanford holds the record for winning the most individual events at the NCAA swimming championships. On April 4, 1987, at Austin, Texas, Morales won the 200-yard butterfly final for his eleventh title, breaking the previous record of ten held by John Nabers of USC.

For overall excellence by both men's and women's swimming teams, no college can match Kenyon, a Division III powerhouse. In 1987 the men captured their eighth consecutive NCAA championship, while the women won their fourth in a row. Kenyon also does a good job of combining swimming and classroom excellence. In recent years more than a dozen Kenyon swimmers have won NCAA postgraduate scholarships.

PARACHUTING

Since 1969 the U.S. Parachuting Association has sponsored the National Collegiate Parachuting championships. In nineteen years the Air Force Academy has won the team title fifteen times, including their victory at the 1987 championship held in Tucson, Arizona. On its way to winning the 1987 team competition, the Air Force

Academy placed first in each of the four classes—novice, intermediate, advanced, and master. Cadet Jim Joyce of Madison, Connecticut, was the overall master champion.

SAILING

If Air Force Academy cadets can do well at falling out of airplanes, it's not suprising that midshipmen at Annapolis are proficient at steering boats through the water. The Intercollegiate Sailing Champion is the college that accumulates the most points in five different events: single-handed sailing, sloop sailing, team racing, women's competition, and two-person sailing. In fourteen years of championships, since 1973, the leading college sailing teams have been Annapolis, with seven victories, and Tufts, with four.

MONEY AND SPORTS

The Fiesta Bowl football game on January 2, 1987, between Penn State and Miami provided each college with $2.4-million, a record for bowl payments. Twenty-two million viewers watched the game on television, the most ever to see a college sports event.

Each of the Final Four—Providence, Nevada Las Vegas, Indiana, and Syracuse—at the 1987 NCAA men's basketball tournament earned $1,050,000. After expenses, the NCAA made a total of $41,473,000. The NCAA kept $16,590,000 and distributed $24,883,000 to the sixty-four colleges that participated in the tournament.

The Big East basketball conference was quite successful in 1986–87, both on the court and financially. In the NCAA play-offs alone, the Big East teams earned $3.8-million: $2.1-million earned by Providence and Syracuse and another $1.7-million by Georgetown, Pittsburgh, and St. John's. The $3.8-million figure does not include revenue from regular season gate receipts and television contracts, which added millions of dollars more to the Big East coffers.

INTRAMURALS

According to officials in the national association, Ohio State, Texas, U Cal Berkeley, Illinois, and Michigan have the most extensive recreational sports programs in the country. For example, Texas reports 1.25 million student-hours of

---

The University of Texas fields over 1,600 intramural teams a year in softball, football, and basketball alone.

---

participation each year. In intramural sports, UT fields 589 softball teams, 477 football teams, and 600 basketball teams.

One of the largest recreational sports buildings on a college campus is the Intramural–Physical Education Building at the University of Illinois. Opened in 1971, the facility houses eight basketball courts, thirty-one badminton courts, thirteen volleyball courts, twenty-three handball-racquetball courts, seven squash courts, an indoor pool 50 meters by 25 meters, an outdoor Olympic-size pool, a twelve-lap indoor running track, two exercise rooms, an outdoor ice rink that converts to four tennis courts during warm weather, and karate, golf, and archery rooms. The locker rooms contain 22,347 lockers. It is estimated that more than a million people enter the complex each academic year.

Although not quite as large as the Illinois intramural building, the new sports facility at U Cal Berkeley is a state-of-the-art multipurpose gym. Completed in 1984, the Berkeley athletic facility includes three connecting buildings: a field house, a large gym, and a swimming pool–locker room building. Beautiful as well as functional, Berkeley's sports center has been featured in architectural magazines.

EXTRAMURALS

Even normally low-key intramural sports directors have recently been bitten by the big-time sports bug. There is now a national flag football play-off that features intramural teams from colleges around the country. The U.S. flag football champion emerges from the tournament, which is held as part of the festivities that lead up to the Sugar Bowl football game. In 1986 the University of New Orleans won the men's title, while Georgia Tech captured the women's crown.

7

DOLLARS AND DONORS

BENEFACTORS, INCOME AND EXPENSE, STATE AND FEDERAL AID, VOLUNTARY GIVING, BUILDING AN ENDOWMENT, CAPITAL CAMPAIGNS, MONEY TO GET STARTED, COLLEGE COSTS, STUDENT AID

Benefactors

Money, or sometimes the lack of it, often has played a critical role in the early days of a college. The initial bank accounts of colleges have ranged from 37 cents to millions of dollars.

KEEP THE CHANGE

A college doesn't usually open its doors until it has enough money to survive for a year or two while tuition income builds up. An exception was Florida Institute of Technology, called "Countdown College" because of its location next to Cape Canaveral in Melbourne, Florida. Jerome Keuper, an MIT physicist, arrived in Melbourne in 1957 as NASA was gearing up for the space program. Dr. Keuper saw the need for a technical college to attract people to the area and provide training in space-related fields like physics, computer science, and aircraft systems. In 1958 Keuper founded the Florida Institute of Technology, not with a healthy bankroll, but with "a lot of vision, a lot of determination, and 37 cents." The 37 cents was change from a long-distance phone call, donated to the school by a friend of Keuper's. It was carefully entered in FIT's ledger as the college's first receipt. Later that year a dance was held to raise money to pay for the course catalog. FIT did not have enough money to cover a second shipment of catalogs until it sold the first truckload. Today FIT, with an enrollment of more than 7,000, is the Southeast's only independent technological university.

DO IT YOURSELF

At Tuskegee Institute the students built their own school. Started in 1881 with a $2,000 appropriation from the Alabama legislature, Tuskegee had no money for land or buildings. Its founder and first president, Booker T. Washington, borrowed $500 to purchase 100 acres of farmland and received a $500 donation to construct a school building. The lack of money proved to be a blessing in disguise since it allowed Washington to practice his educational philosophy— learning through labor—by using Tuskegee students to construct the main campus building. After two years and many man-hours of student labor, Porter Hall, containing all of the college's facilities— classrooms, dining hall, and dormitories—was completed. As Tuskegee survived and grew, northern philanthropists, impressed by Booker T. Washington's innovative educational methods, made numerous gifts to the college, the largest being Andrew Carnegie's $600,000 donation in 1903.

CLASSIFIED AD GETS RESULTS

In 1840, in response to a classified advertisement placed in the *Providence Journal* by a poor Rhode Island college, Nicholas Brown gave $5,000 for the honor of having the college named after him. Not only did Mr. Brown acquire a niche in history as a result of his donation, he also was a shrewd bargainer. The ad had specified $6,000, but Brown lowered the asking price by $1,000 before agreeing to the terms.

GOODS AND SERVICES

In 1823 Trinity College was looking for a home in Connecticut. The college trustees needed $20,000 and asked New Haven, Middletown, and Hartford to bid for the college. Hartford immediately expressed interest and began to raise money. Seven individuals and two businesses came up with $11,000 and the town gave $5,000, leaving Hartford $4,000 short. At this point dozens of local workers and shopkeepers pledged labor and materials worth $4,000. Some of the items donated were stonework, blacksmithing, hay, timber, fifty sealskins, boots, shoes, groceries, dry goods, window sashes, books, and tailor's work. The trustees, impressed with the community spirit that accompanied the $20,000, decided to locate Trinity in Hartford.

DOOR-TO-DOOR SALESMAN

Of the many colleges named after the first president of the United States, Washington College in Chestertown, Maryland, is the oldest. In fact, since it was founded in 1782, seven years before Washington became president, it actually was named after the commander in chief of the Continental Army. The original college charter required the school to raise £5000 before it could open its doors to students. In 1782 £5000 was an enormous amount of money; it was estimated that there was only £100,000 in circulation in the entire state of Maryland. The college's

founder, the Reverend William Smith, undaunted by the magnitude of his fund-raising task, set out on horseback to visit every county in eastern Maryland until he came up with the money. Within a period of six months, he convinced 294 donors to give £10,000, a truly impressive total. Of this amount, George Washington himself contributed 50 guineas.

FUEL INJECTION

Large sums of money can turn a modest college into a major university in a short period of time. In 1888, John D. Rockefeller, after earning millions in the oil business, wanted to make a donation to a

The Reverend William Smith of Washington College.

college. The University of Chicago's president, William Rainey Harper, befriended Rockefeller and convinced him that Chicago deserved his support. Although Rockefeller initially planned to give only

Chicago's William Rainey Harper.

$600,000, by the time Harper was finished, Chicago had acquired $35-million in endowment and operating funds.

Harper, well armed with money, undertook a mass raid on professors at other colleges. Within a year Harper collected 8 former college presidents, 5 Yale professors, 15 of Clark's faculty, and numerous others for a total of 120 additional staff members. When Chicago opened in 1892, a new style of university awaited the students. It had an academic year with four quarters, a system

of major and minor studies, and upper and lower divisions. The academic college for freshmen and sophomores offered a foundation in language, writing, social sciences, and physical sciences. Juniors and seniors enrolled in a university college that emphasized independent work and research.

Although both Cornell and Johns Hopkins had previously taken major steps in the development of the American university, Harper's Chicago, known as "Standard Oil College," was the first university structured along modern lines.

MONUMENTAL UNDERTAKING

The idea for the University of Chicago worked because Harper was strong and innovative and Rockefeller provided the money and stayed clear of day-to-day operations. Stanford, in contrast, was both helped and hindered by the $5-million gift of Mr. and Mrs. Leland Stanford in honor of their son, Leland Jr., who died at age 15 of typhoid fever. From the outset, Leland Stanford exercised hands-on control over how his money would be spent. He designed a beautiful campus on the Palo Alto farm he gave to the university. He drafted the charter that specified in great detail how Stanford would be organized and operated.

The problems arose after Mr. Stanford's death, when his wife decided that educational goals would be secondary to erecting a monument to her son. To the exclusion of other important needs, building after building was constructed. Two examples stand out. One was a 90-foot-high stone arch entrance

to the campus ambitiously titled "The Progress of Civilization in America." The second was an art museum (copied from the National Museum in Athens, which Leland Jr. had admired) with enough floor space to house seven football fields, although at the time Stanford's art collection filled only a few end zones. Unfortunately neither the faculty nor the buildings stayed for long. Faculty salaries were so low that many professors, with the encouragement of the university's president, took jobs elsewhere. The buildings took their leave courtesy of the 1906 San Francisco earthquake. While parts of Stanford's campus escaped destruction, many structures, including both the arch and the museum, were damaged beyond repair. Eventually Leland Stanford Junior University overcame its early setbacks. As the joke goes,

among the nation's many junior colleges, Stanford stands out as the best and only junior university.

PUT UP YOUR DUKES

Surpassing the $35-million that Chicago received from John D. Rockefeller in the late 1800s was the $107-million that James B. Duke used to establish the Duke Endowment in 1924 and 1925. The Duke family fortune came from tobacco, textiles, and the development of hydroelectric power in the Carolinas. The main beneficiary of the endowment was tiny Trinity College in Durham, North Carolina. In return for an initial payment of $17-million, Trinity's name was changed to Duke University.

Today the Duke Endowment is worth about $800-million and produces $16-million in yearly income for Duke and about $1.5-million for Furman, Davidson, and Johnson C. Smith, three other southern colleges that share in the proceeds. Since 1925 Duke has received hundreds of millions of dollars from the endowment.

An often-repeated college myth is the story that James B. Duke first offered his money to Princeton if it would change its name to Duke. As the tale goes, when Princeton refused, Duke made the same proposal to Trinity where it was gratefully accepted. Although the story seemed plausible because the

Duke estate was located in Somerville, New Jersey, only a few miles from Princeton, there is no truth to it. The Duke family, native North Carolinians, had supported Trinity in their hometown of Durham since 1892, as well as other charities in both North Carolina and South Carolina.

THE PAID PIPERS

Colleges have not always relied on highly structured capital campaigns to meet their financial needs. A far different approach was taken in 1871 by a black college, Fisk, of Nashville, Tennessee. Facing a severe financial crisis that threatened the college's very existence, Fisk music professor George White came up with the idea of using students to raise money. Professor White formed the students into a choral ensemble, the Jubilee Singers, and took them on the road.

After a slow start, the singers shifted to a more upbeat gospel-style musical performance. Indifferent responses soon changed to standing ovations as the Jubilee Singers became a big hit all over the country. They concluded their tour with an appearance at the White House before President Ulysses S. Grant, earned thousands of dollars, and spread the name of Fisk across the nation. With the help of the Jubilee Singers, Fisk's early financial troubles were overcome and the college went on to become one of the nation's

foremost black institutions of higher learning. After more than a century, the Fisk Jubilee Singers are still actively performing and are credited with introducing the spiritual as a unique form of American music.

A century later, in the late 1970s, Fisk again ran into serious financial problems and found itself on the edge of bankruptcy. This time it wasn't a singing group but a comedian who pulled Fisk out of trouble. A $1.3-million gift from Bill Cosby has provided breathing room while Fisk works to get its financial affairs in order.

WORTHLESS LAND?

Colleges have been astute fund-raisers and managers of the money at their disposal. For years colleges have traded in real estate, usually for their own use but sometimes for speculation. In 1814, when Union College of Schenectady petitioned the New York State legislature for money to construct new buildings, Columbia was asked to throw its weight behind the proposal. Naturally, Columbia wanted something in return for its efforts. The Union president, Eliphalet Nott, worked out a compromise. Union would receive $200,000, with Columbia acquiring 12 acres of land in New York City. President Moon of Columbia was publicly scolded for accepting a worthless tract whose value had fallen from

$80,000 to a mere $6,000 during the past five years. As it turned out, Columbia's midtown Manhattan land was the acreage on which Rockefeller Center was built. In 1985, Columbia sold the land to the Rockefeller family for $400-million, a return of about $34-million an acre.

GENEROUS PROFESSORS

The normal arrangement is for the college to pay the professor. But some professors have earned a great deal of money for their colleges. This can happen when faculty members discover new products for which they are paid royalty or patent income, and the university receives a share of the profit.

At the University of Wisconsin, biochemistry professor Harry Steenbock produced vitamin D by ultraviolet irradiation of foods. His colleague, Paul Link, discovered an anticoagulant that is used for preventing thrombosis and heart disease. These two inventions, along with other discoveries by Wisconsin biochemists, have earned the university $113-million since 1925.

The University of Florida has done quite well from Professor Robert Cade's invention of a sport drink that replaces fluids lost during exercise. Florida receives 20 percent of the profits from Gatorade.

COLLEGE SPECULATORS

Colleges, with endowments worth about $38-billion, are always looking for profitable ways to invest their money. In the past decade endowment managers have become more speculative in using the funds at their disposal.

Stanford was the first to actively seek land development income, and its current real estate investments are the largest of any college's. Stanford manages a shopping center and research park that brings in a yearly income of about $11-million.

Princeton's Forrestal Center is another extensive college development project. Located in the fast-growing Route 1 corridor between New York and Philadelphia, this complex includes nearly 2,000 acres of land on which are located over fifty businesses, along with foundations, research institutions, hotel facilities, shopping centers, and clusters of town houses and apartments.

A high-risk but potentially lucrative form of investment is to back companies that are just starting. In 1961, Princeton lent an entrepreneur $1-million to buy hamburger franchises from the McDonald brothers. In exchange, Princeton received a fraction of a cent for each McDonald's hamburger sold. In ten years, Princeton earned $5.4-million on its $1-million investment.

Stanford and Carnegie Mellon each have invested $660,000 in Steven Jobs's new corporation, NeXT. Jobs, who started Apple computers, founded NeXT to manufacture a powerful new microcomputer and compatible software for higher education.

COLLEGE BUSINESSES

While it isn't unusual for colleges to invest in businesses run by other people, it is rare for a college to be both the owner and the operator of a profit-making company. Even so, there have been some notable examples of this arrangement.

New York University

In 1947, New York University Law School purchased the C. F. Mueller Company for $3.5-million. Besides making macaroni, spaghetti, vermicelli, and other pastas, the Mueller Company made money. From 1947 to 1975, the NYU Law School received $17-million in profits. While the spaghetti money put the law school on a solid financial footing, the rest of NYU was in trouble. By the early 1970s, NYU was running deficits of about $4-million each year, and its ability to survive was in jeopardy. Something clearly had to be done to spread the Mueller money around. After a year of negotiations, the law school and the university agreed to sell Mueller and divide the profits. In 1976, the company was sold for $115-million, thirty-three

A macaroni company purchased by NYU Law School in 1948 was sold twenty-eight years later for thirty-three times the original purchase price.

times its original cost. The law school received $67.5-million and the university $47.5-million. The law school continued to grow and prosper, while NYU retired its debt and established a secure financial base. The noodle factory had come to NYU's rescue. In 1984, NYU completed a fund drive that raised $100-million, and in 1987 it announced a new campaign with a goal of $1-billion by the year 2000.

Loyola

Loyola of New Orleans owns and operates a commercial TV station as well as AM and FM radio stations. Loyola's yearly income from its broadcasting business is enough to reduce each student's tuition by $2,000.

Augustana

During its 1983 fund-raising campaign, Augustana College of Sioux Falls, South Dakota, was given the State Bank of Hendricks, Minnesota. Although some members of Augustana's board of trustees recommended that the bank be sold immediately, the college administration decided to keep the bank and operate it. The Augustana vice president of finance has turned out to be an able financier. The Hendricks bank, now worth millions, brings in a yearly income of $200,000.

Wesleyan

After acquiring American Education Publications (noted for *My Weekly Reader*) in 1949, Wesleyan operated the business for sixteen years before selling the company. Wesleyan's total profits during its period of ownership were more than $100-million.

Washington State

Washington State University in Pullman is in the cheese business. The WSU creamery produces its best-selling "Cougar Gold" along with American Cheddar, Hot Pepper, and Smoky Cheddar. Annual production is about 100,000 thirty-ounce tins, and total sales are nearly $1-million. A national

magazine recently rated Cougar Gold one of the ten best cheeses in the world.

COLLEGE STORES

In order of 1986 sales, the largest college bookstores are:

	Amount
1. Harvard	$60,000,000
2. UCLA	38,000,000
3. Washington (Seattle)	29,000,000
4. Minnesota	26,000,000
5. Brigham Young	24,000,000

Of the five biggest stores, UCLA, Brigham Young, and Minnesota are owned and operated by the colleges themselves, while the bookstores at Harvard and Washington are independent enterprises located on university property. The term bookstore is somewhat of a misnomer, as the larger college stores are actually diverse retail

Washington State's creamery in action.

establishments. The most popular line at UCLA is the Bearwear brand of sports apparel, bringing in $5-million per year.

THE NAME SOUNDS FAMILIAR

One of the first employees at the Harvard bookstore was a 16-year-old named John Bartlett, who worked there partly to earn money but mostly to satisfy his appetite for reading. In 1849, after thirteen years of labor, Bartlett had saved enough money to buy the store. Because of his vast knowledge of literature, Bartlett was often called on to answer questions about the origins of quotations. As a service to his friends and customers, in 1855 Bartlett on his own published 1,000 copies of a book listing citations from famous literary works. The name of the book was *Bartlett's Familiar Quotations*. It is now in its fifteenth printing and has sold millions of copies.

Income and Expense

Colleges are in the business of educating students. But when taken together, the approximately 3,100 colleges that comprise U.S. higher education make up a vast financial enterprise. In 1985–86 colleges earned $100-billion in revenues and spent $97-billion, with the surplus going to reserves. If higher education were considered a single business, it would rank second on the Fortune 500 list after General Motors' $108-billion in sales. The $100-billion in higher education revenue does not include the value of physical-plant assets, in excess of $100-billion, or endowments that total $48-billion. Colleges are not only big business, they also are a growth industry. Total revenues increased by 7 percent in the last year.

Where does the money come from and where does it go? The largest source of income is state appropriations for public colleges, $28-billion. Next are tuition charges, $23-billion; sales and services, $21-billion; federal support, $15-billion; and voluntary giving.

This income is spent primarily on instruction, $31-billion, and auxiliary enterprises such as dining halls, athletics, and hospitals, $19-billion. Other large expenses are research, institutional support, and plant operation and maintenance.

State Aid

MONEY FOR COLLEGE OPERATIONS

Since state governments provide more money to colleges than any other source, it is worthwhile to look at the ten states that received the largest appropriations for 1986–87.

	Amount
1. California	$4,562,651,000
2. New York	2,720,779,000
3. Texas	2,141,392,000
4. Illinois	1,390,614,000
5. Florida	1,277,704,000
6. Michigan	1,228,559,000
7. Ohio	1,208,210,000
8. North Carolina	1,172,120,000
9. Pennsylvania	1,108,982,000
10. Virginia	901,452,000

As might be expected, the two states with the most extensive systems of higher education, California and New York, rank first and second. California supports 9 universities, 19 state universities, and over 100 community colleges. The State University of New York consists of 4 university centers, 26 four-year colleges, and an assortment of two-year colleges. Among individual campuses, the University of Illinois at Urbana-Champaign received the most state money, $485.5-million. Next were UCLA, $403.9-million; Minnesota, $364.5-million; Louisiana State, $309.6-million; and Florida, $302.2-million.

At the other extreme, the University of Vermont is the college easiest on its state's pocketbook, receiving only $28-million in public funds.

MONEY FOR STUDENTS

In addition to giving money directly to colleges, virtually every state provides scholarships to residents who attend college in their home state. The most generous states in awarding undergraduate student aid in 1986–87 were:

	Amount
1. New York	$442,627,000
2. Illinois	143,079,000
3. California	131,146,000
4. Pennsylvania	104,148,000
5. Michigan	68,015,000
6. New Jersey	67,678,000
7. Ohio	67,239,000
8. Minnesota	59,706,000
9. Massachusetts	59,032,000
10. Indiana	40,902,000

Total student aid given by the fifty states, the District of Columbia, and Puerto Rico was $1.5-billion to about 1.5-million students.

Federal Aid

In 1986 the federal government spent more than $15-billion on colleges and universities. The two largest items were research, $6.5-billion, and student aid, $8-billion.

RESEARCH GRANTS

The leading sponsors of the $6.5-billion in federal research grants were the Department of Health and Human Services and the Department of Defense. In fiscal 1986, which colleges fared the best in the competition for the federal research dollar?

	Amount
1. Johns Hopkins	$445,718,000
2. MIT	188,120,000
3. Stanford	180,186,000
4. Washington (Seattle)	146,718,000
5. U Cal San Diego	133,243,000

6. Columbia	127,131,000
7. UCLA	125,483,000
8. Wisconsin	120,626,000
9. Cornell	112,707,000
10. Yale	111,687,000

Johns Hopkins occupies first place primarily on the strength of a $313-million grant to its applied physics laboratory. Stanford, Cornell, and MIT also have federally funded research laboratories whose grants are counted separately and not listed above.

OPERATING EXPENSES

Two colleges in Washington, D.C., Howard and Gallaudet, are the beneficiaries of substantial yearly appropriations for day-to-day expenses. For fiscal year 1986 Howard received $160-million and Gallaudet $58-million. When the $9-million that Howard received in federal research funds is combined with the direct grant, Howard ranks fifth in total federal aid.

AID TO STUDENTS

Beginning with the G.I. bill in 1944, the federal government has become more and more involved in providing money to college students. After Russia launched its grapefruit-sized satellite, Sputnik I, on October 4, 1957, Congress passed the National Defense Education Act to provide loans to students. Starting with a 1958 appropriation of $200-million, by 1986–87 the federal government was spending upwards of $8-billion a year in direct student aid and guaranteeing another $8-billion in loans.

Today the federal government's largest financial aid program is the Pell Grant for low-income students. The Department of Education also gives money to colleges, so-called campus-based aid. In 1985–86 total federal expenditures for Pell Grants were $3.7-billion, and for campus-based aid, $1.9-billion. Which colleges received the largest share of this largesse?

	Amount
1. City University of New York System	$104,444,000
2. Inter American University of Puerto Rico	65,875,000
3. State University of New York System*	53,923,000
4. University of Puerto Rico System	51,548,000
5. Ana G. Mendez Foundation, Puerto Rico	34,167,000
6. Pennsylvania State University System	20,930,000
7. Catholic University of Puerto Rico	20,318,000
8. City Colleges of Chicago	20,251,000
9. National Education Center†	19,774,000
10. Adelphi Business College†	15,991,000

*Additional campus-based money not included
†Commercial trade school

Voluntary Giving

Besides the money that flows into a college from state and federal appropriations, virtually every college has a fund-raising office to solicit donations from corporations, foundations, and individuals. In 1986–87 colleges received $8.5-billion from these sources, a 15 percent increase over the 1985–86 total of $7.4-billion.

Here is a breakdown of where the $8.5-billion came from:

	Amount
Foundations	$1,513,000,000
Corporations	1,819,000,000
Individuals	4,412,000,000
Others	756,000,000
Total	$8,500,000,000

THE LEADING MONEY GATHERERS

For many years large and well-organized campaigns were mounted mainly by private colleges. This is no longer true. Of the $8.5-billion, about $2.8-billion was raised by public institutions or statewide systems.

Looking at total voluntary support for 1986–87, the top ten colleges were:

	Amount
1. Stanford	$198,535,000
2. Harvard	177,976,000
3. Cornell	149,702,000
4. Yale	120,064,000
5. Minnesota	116,328,000
6. Washington (Missouri)	110,427,000
7. Columbia	104,646,000
8. MIT	101,422,000
9. Johns Hopkins	92,467,000
10. USC	91,204,000

Besides Minnesota, which ranks fifth, four of the second ten are public institutions. In addition, the University of California System raised $229,667,000 and the University of Texas System $139,114,000.

Stanford's total of $198-million is the most money ever raised by a single university in one year. Stanford was the leader in both 1986 and 1987, dethroning Harvard from the number-one position it had occupied for many years.

FOUNDATION GIFTS

Foundations are institutions organized to distribute money for public purposes. There are about 4,000 foundations in the United States that have assets in excess of $1-million. The two most common forms of foundations are independent (assets come from an individual or family) and company sponsored.

The world's richest foundation is the Howard Hughes Medical Institute, with assets of $5-billion. The Hughes foundation normally gives about $200-million each year to university medical centers. Based on a recent agreement between the institute and the Internal Revenue Service, the amount donated will increase to $700-million per year over the next ten years. Other foundations whose annual gifts to colleges total more than $30-million are Kellogg, Pew, Mellon, Ford, and MacArthur.

The Largest Foundation Gifts Ever Made

Foundation	Year	College	Amount
Norton Simon	1987	UCLA	$730,000,000
Danforth	1986	Washington (Missouri)	100,000,000
Danforth	1986	Washington (Missouri)	55,000,000
Lilly	1987	Indiana colleges	50,000,000
Beckman	1986	Caltech	50,000,000
Danforth	1979	Washington (Missouri)	45,000,000
Beckman	1988	Caltech	40,000,000
Olin	1986	Washington (Missouri)	30,000,000
Sylvester	1986	Minnesota	27,500,000
Conrad Hilton	1983	Houston	21,400,000

The Simon Foundation's $730-million gift is the estimated value of the art collection promised to UCLA. There is now a possibility that the gift will be reduced or withdrawn.

The $100-million Danforth donation in 1986 is to be used for new capital projects at Washington University in St. Louis, whose total endowment is now nearly $1-billion, one of the ten largest. This $100-million is in addition to other Danforth gifts of $55-million in 1986 and $45-million in 1979. Beyond these major contributions to Washington's capital campaign, the Danforth Foundation has made other large donations to the university in the last decade. The Danforth Foundation is funded by the Ralston Purina Company, a business owned and operated by the Danforth family. The chancellor of Washington, William H. Danforth, is also the chairman of the board of trustees of the Danforth Foundation.

Colleges That Received the Most Money from Foundations (1986–87)

	Amount			Amount
1. Washington (Missouri)	$69,100,000		6. Yale	26,944,000
2. Caltech	42,651,000		7. Texas Medical School (Galveston)	23,763,000
3. Harvard	41,743,000		8. NYU	22,779,000
4. Minnesota	36,763,000		9. Columbia	22,178,000
5. Stanford	32,952,000		10. Duke	21,299,000

CORPORATE GIFTS

Although individual gifts remain the largest single source, donations by private companies have grown very rapidly in the past few years, more than doubling: from $778-million in 1981 to $1.8-billion in 1987.

The Largest Corporate Gifts Ever Made

Company	Year	College	Amount
Gulf Oil	1985	Pittsburgh	$100,000,000
Hearst	1981	UCLA	62,000,000
Digital Equipment	1982	MIT	52,000,000

continued

R. J. Reynolds	1987	Wake Forest	40,000,000
IBM	1983	20 universities	40,000,000
IBM	1986	Cornell	30,000,000
IBM	1985	13 universities	27,000,000
Systems Development	1983	Stanford	21,000,000
Standard Oil	1987	Mississippi	20,000,000
IBM	1984	Illinois	12,500,000

Colleges That Received the Most Money from Corporations (1986–87)

	Amount		Amount
1. Wake Forest	$51,183,000	6. Minnesota	30,904,000
2. MIT	49,754,000	7. Washington (Seattle)	29,360,000
3. Harvard	33,954,000	8. U Cal Berkeley	28,257,000
4. Cornell	33,658,000	9. UCLA	23,117,000
5. Stanford	33,572,000	10. Ohio State	22,418,000

More than 20 percent of the $1.8-billion given by corporations was in the form of company products, for example, research equipment and computers.

Wake Forest heads the list due to the donation by R. J. Reynolds of its corporate headquarters, valued at $40-million.

INDIVIDUAL GIFTS

Early Gifts

For 350 years colleges have relied on the generosity of individuals to pay for specific projects or add to their endowments. The first gift made to a college was the £800 John Harvard left in 1638 to a small struggling college that took his name in gratitude.

The largest gift made to a college before 1800 was George Washington's 1796 donation of $50,000 worth of James River Canal stock to Liberty Hall Academy in Lexington, Kentucky. In his honor, the academy was renamed Washington College; then, in 1870, after its president Robert E. Lee died, to Washington and Lee.

The Largest Individual Gifts Ever Made

Donor	Year	College	Amount
Liliore Green Rains	1986	Caltech, Pomona, Loyola Marymount, Stanford	$160,000,000
C. B. Pennington	1983	LSU	125,000,000
Robert E. Woodruff	1980	Emory	105,000,000
Edwin Land	1983	MIT	100,000,000
Edward Mallinckrodt	1982	Harvard	77,000,000
W. M. Keck	1984	Caltech	70,000,000
David Packard	1986	Stanford	70,000,000
James L. Knight	1986	Miami (Florida)	56,000,000
William Hewlett	1986	Stanford	50,000,000

continued

| Claiborne Robins | 1969 | Richmond | 50,000,000 |
| Anonymous | 1984 | Cornell | 50,000,000 |

The $160-million from the estate of Liliore Green Rains is the largest individual gift to higher education. Each of the four colleges received $40-million, the same amount designated for the other two recipients, the Good Samaritan Hospital in Los Angeles and the Menninger Clinic in Topeka, Kansas. The Green family members were the major stockholders in the Bell Ridge Oil Company.

The C. B. Pennington gift of $125-million (estimated value of oil-well production) to LSU is the largest by an individual to a single university. The money is being used for the construction of a nutrition research center.

By the end of 1986, the Woodruff family, the major stockholders in Coca-Cola, had given a total of $230-million to Emory. For this kind of money, a donor can have the family name liberally spread around campus. Emory is overflowing with Woodruffs—Woodruff Physical Education Center, Woodruff Nursing School, Woodruff Library, Woodruff Health Science Center, Woodruff Endowed Professors, and Woodruff Scholars.

Robert Woodruff and his brother George are not the only Coca-Cola connection to Emory. In 1914 Asa Candler, the Atlanta pharmacist who founded the company, gave Emory $1-million in cash and 75 acres of land in Atlanta on which to build a new campus. The person who convinced Asa Candler to give the money was his brother Warren, a former president of Emory.

Emory is known as the Coca-Cola School for good reason. Because so much of Emory's endowment is tied to Coca-Cola stock, each time a share of Coke goes up $1, the value of Emory's holdings increases by $5-million.

A chorus from a school song pays proper respect for the hundreds of millions of dollars that have made Emory financially secure:

Em'ry, Em'ry,
The future we foretell.
We were raised on Coca-Cola,
So no wonder we raise Hell.
And when we meet Tech's engineers,
We'll drink them off their stool.
So lift your cup,
Here's to the luck
Of the Coca-Cola School.

The $120-million given by William Hewlett and David Packard was part of $307-million in pledges and gifts that Stanford raised

continued

before announcing its $1.1-billion campaign in February 1987. Hewlett and Packard were classmates at Stanford, graduating in 1939 before going on to start a small company that later grew into one of the world's largest manufacturers of electronic measurement and computing products.

Based on the number of students enrolled, the largest gift to a college was the $18-million that Buena Vista College of Storm Lake, Iowa, received in May 1980. This anonymous gift amounted to $14,000 per student.

Colleges That Received the Most Money from Individuals (1986–87)

		Amount
1.	Stanford	$126,261,000
2.	Cornell	96,457,000
3.	Harvard	93,623,000
4.	Yale	61,166,000
5.	Princeton	60,283,000
6.	Johns Hopkins	58,366,000
7.	Columbia	56,337,000
8.	USC	50,645,000
9.	Penn	44,238,000
10.	Chicago	41,650,000

Strings Attached

In 1939 Alfred Shriver left $800,000 to Johns Hopkins with the stipulation that the money be used to build a lecture hall decorated with murals depicting Baltimore clipper ships, members of the Shriver family, ten local philanthropists, and ten beautiful women of the city of Baltimore.

Pet Giving Plans

More complicated than most fund-raising efforts are elaborate deferred-giving plans. An unusual arrangement for a charitable trust has been developed by Texas A&M. A trust fund can be established by animal owners who want to provide care for their pets while supporting research at Texas A&M. After the owner dies, the

yearly interest from the trust pays for Fido's room and board. When the pet dies, the entire trust goes to Texas A&M to pay for programs in veterinary medicine.

ALUMNI DONATIONS

Over the years, the most common form of individual support to colleges has been gifts from alumni. Some colleges have been very successful in convincing graduates to empty their pockets to help keep the alma mater in good financial shape. The three primary measures of successful alumni fund drives are total dollars, number of donors, and rate of participation.

Most Money Received from Alumni (1986–87)

		Amount
1.	Stanford	$79,238,000
2.	Harvard	71,238,000

3. Cornell	65,657,000
4. Yale	51,905,000
5. Princeton	48,496,000
6. Illinois	36,801,000
7. MIT	29,700,000
8. Dartmouth	29,200,000
9. Brown	29,183,000
10. Columbia	28,454,000

Nine of the top ten colleges are private institutions that have operated alumni funds for many years. Recently, public universities have begun to organize annual campaigns like those of private colleges. Besides Illinois, the public colleges most successful in collecting money from their alumni in 1986–87 were North Carolina ($26,597,000), Michigan ($20,562,000), Virginia Tech ($19,092,000), and Cal Berkeley ($18,582,000).

Most Donors to the Annual Fund (1986–87)

	Number of donors
1. Harvard	64,016
2. Michigan	56,872
3. Penn	54,594
4. Ohio State	51,015
5. Penn State	45,897
6. Columbia	45,541
7. Tennessee	43,995
8. Indiana	43,373
9. NYU	38,474
10. Northwestern	37,418

Highest Percentage of Alumni Contributing to the Annual Fund (1986–87)

	Percent
1. Centre	77
2. Williams	75
3. Hampden-Sydney	70
4. Dartmouth	65
Hamilton	65
6. Swarthmore	64
7. Amherst	63
Lehigh	63
9. Gustavus Adolphus	62
Mount Holyoke	62

In this category, as in other areas of alumni giving, the private colleges occupy most of the top positions, but public institutions have been gaining ground. Among public colleges, those with the highest level of participation are Washburn (52 percent), VMI (49 percent), Southern Mississippi (37 percent), and Fitchburg State (36 percent).

On an honor roll of outstanding performances by colleges in raising money from alumni, Centre College of Danville, Kentucky, would occupy the number one position. In 1986–87, Centre set an all-time record, with 77 percent of its alumni contributing. Centre has won eight straight CASE/U.S. Steel awards for distinguished achievement in alumni giving, the most of any college.

Building an Endowment

A college can establish a strong financial base by building an endowment. Colleges do not spend endowed money, but invest the principal and use the yearly interest to pay expenses. Endowment income can be used indefinitely, although only a small portion, usually between 5 percent and 10 percent, is available in any one year. As an example of how an endowment works, a college establishes a faculty chair with an initial investment of $500,000. Assuming an 8 percent return, $40,000 would be available to pay for the professor's salary and benefits.

The managers of endowment funds are able and experienced investors. From 1985–86 to 1986–87, the value of college endowments increased by 14 percent.

LARGEST ENDOWMENTS (as of June 30, 1987)

	Amount
1. Harvard	$4,018,270,000
2. U of Texas System	2,829,000,000
3. Princeton	2,291,110,000
4. Yale	2,098,400,000
5. Stanford	1,676,950,000
6. Columbia	1,387,060,000
7. Texas A&M System	1,214,220,000
8. Washington (Missouri)	1,199,930,000
9. MIT	1,169,740,000
10. U Cal System	1,122,160,000

During the last decade the University of Texas and Harvard have been locked in a struggle for the distinction of having the largest college endowment. But in 1986 administrators of the Texas endowment split it into two separate funds, one for the University of Texas System and one for the Texas A&M System. Although this division leaves Harvard alone in first place, Texas remains in the second position, and Texas A&M's $1.2-billion places it seventh.

For the most part, black colleges have had less financial backing than predominantly white institutions. Two historically black colleges,

however, have built substantial reserves. Spelman in Georgia and Tuskegee in Alabama have endowments of $33-million and $28-million, respectively.

For a prestigious college, Bennington has one of the smallest endowments, some $4-million. With relatively little income from investments, Bennington must rely heavily on tuition revenue. The result is a 1987–88 tuition of $14,850, the highest in the nation.

LARGEST ENDOWMENTS PER STUDENT

Because colleges vary greatly in size, total endowment is not always the best indicator of an institution's overall financial strength. A more accurate measure is endowment per student. As of 1987, the leaders in this category were:

	Amount
1. Princeton	$365,800
2. Harvard	247,500
3. Caltech	221,100
4. Rice	215,000
5. Swarthmore	210,400
6. Yale	199,800
7. Grinnell	181,000

Among public colleges the largest per capita endowments are Virginia Military Institute, $49,400; University of Texas System, $31,400; Virginia Commonwealth, $27,700; Virginia, $23,700; Delaware, $18,400; Cincinnati, $10,200; and Pittsburgh, $8,200.

If special-purpose institutions are considered, Rockefeller University in New York, a graduate medical school, is the overwhelming leader in endowment per student. Each of Rockefeller's 119 students is backed by $4.5-million of endowment. Rockefeller's solid financial base enables it to offer free tuition to every one of its students.

Capital Campaigns

Once every ten years or so, a college will conduct a special fund-raising drive, called a capital campaign, to increase the size of its endowment or to pay for special projects. The major development campaigns of the 1980s are of a size and scope that far exceed any previous fund-raising records. Colleges have become aggressive, sophisticated, and immensely successful at fund-raising. The largest campaigns currently in progress are:

	Goal	Start	Finish	Total as of 1987
Stanford	$1,100,000,000	1987	1991	$304,000,000
NYU	1,000,000,000	1986	2000	200,000,000
USC	557,000,000	1984	1990	249,000,000
Columbia	500,000,000	1982	1987	602,000,000
Johns Hopkins	450,000,000	1984	1990	333,000,000
Miami (Florida)	400,000,000	1984	1989	304,000,000
Ohio State	350,000,000	1985	1990	186,000,000
Washington (Missouri)	300,000,000	1979	1987	607,000,000

Stanford's $1.1-billion total consists of $567-million for additions and improvements and $533-million to support current programs. This record-breaking campaign goal continues Stanford's tradition of setting new standards in college fund-raising. In 1962 Stanford announced a campaign for $100-million and in 1972 one for $300-million, each one the largest ever at the time.

The "money race" among colleges has accelerated so rapidly that new campaign records are set every year. In the fall of 1985, Harvard was the first college to pass the $300-million level, raising $360-million. By the spring of 1986, Princeton had raised $410-million. Princeton's impressive record lasted for only six months until Washington U passed $410-million on the way to its final total of $607-million. In a concurrent campaign, Columbia fell just short of Washington, coming up with a total of $602-million in five years. By the end of 1988, it is likely that Stanford will have exceeded Columbia's total.

Among smaller colleges, DePauw of Greencastle, Indiana, began a $100-million campaign in 1983, the most ambitious target ever for a college of its size. Since DePauw announced its goal (so far it has raised $114-million), Pomona College in Claremont, California, embarked on a $130-million campaign. Pomona

continued

recently passed the $115-million mark and hoped to have collected $130-million by the spring of 1988.

For years the University of Michigan has been the leading fund-raiser among public colleges. In 1948 Michigan was the first state university to stage a major capital gifts campaign; it continued to hold the public-college record of $175-million until Minnesota reached $306-million in 1988.

College Costs

Tuition, the price colleges charge for instruction, varies greatly among different institutions. In 1987–88 the range was $0 to $14,850. Although actual teaching costs are not very dissimilar from one college to the next, the state subsidies that public institutions receive permit them to charge much lower tuitions than private colleges. For the (1988–89) academic year, which colleges charged the highest and lowest tuitions?

TWO-YEAR COLLEGES

Lowest 1988–89 Tuition and Fees

Community College of the Air Force	$ 0
Deep Springs	0
Williamson Free School of Mechanical Trades	0
75 California Community Colleges	99–120

Highest 1988–89 Tuition and Fees

Sterling	$8,900
New England Institute of Applied Arts and Sciences	8,442
Suomi	8,300
Art Institute of Houston	8,235
Mitchell	8,160

FOUR-YEAR PUBLIC COLLEGES

The most inexpensive four-year public colleges, all with free tuition, are the Air Force Academy, the Coast Guard Academy, the Merchant Marine Academy, West Point, and Annapolis. Other than service academies, the least expensive are:

Lowest 1988–89 In-State Tuition and Fees

Hawaii at Hilo	$ 450
Texas Southwestern Medical Center at Dallas	570
Texas Health Science Center at San Antonio	580
Texas Health Science Center at Houston	645
East Central	746 (est.)
Cal State, Los Angeles	786 (est.)

continued

Highest 1988–89 In-State Tuition and Fees

Temple	$ 3,894
Vermont	3,714
VMI	3,355 (est.)
Miami	3,036
Rutgers, College of Engineering	2,978
William and Mary	2,966
Old Dominion	2,940

Lowest 1988–89 Out-of-State Tuition and Fees

Oglala Lakota	$ 920
Troy State	1,125
Jacksonville State	1,400
Eastern Oregon State	1,500 (est.)
Missouri Western	2,070 (est.)
East Central	2,075 (est.)

Highest 1988–89 Out-of-State Tuition and Fees

Vermont	$10,764
Colorado	7,812
William and Mary	7,812
Temple	6,802
Miami	6,600
Virginia	6,362

FOUR-YEAR PRIVATE COLLEGES

Lowest 1988–89 Tuition and Fees

Webb Institute of Naval Architecture	$ 0
Berea	141 (est.)
Atlanta Christian	277 (est.)
Cooper Union	300
Moody Bible Institute	465
Mid-Continent Baptist Bible	1,280
Brigham Young–Hawaii	1,350

Highest 1988–89 Tuition and Fees

Bennington	$15,670
Brown	13,759
Hampshire	13,743 (est.)
Harvard	13,665
MIT	13,400
Princeton	13,380
Dartmouth	13,360
Wesleyan	13,325
Sarah Lawrence	13,280

Two Bargains

Much attention has recently been focused on rapidly increasing college costs, but there are at least two colleges that are working hard, literally, to remain affordable—Berea and Blackburn.

Which U.S. college charges no tuition, admits only low-income students, requires all students to work, and is committed to serving the people of Appalachia? It is Berea, in Berea, Kentucky, a truly unique college. Berea, with 1,500 undergraduates, may be the only U.S. college that turns down students for admission if their parents earn too much money. Berea takes pains to make itself accessible for poor students. Besides its free tuition (there is a yearly fee of $141) and its student aid program, Berea has a labor arrangement by which every student works 10 to 15 hours per week to earn money for books and personal expenses. Besides offering jobs in the dining hall, library, and computer center, Berea encourages students to work in its Appalachian craft center making furniture, brooms, blankets, and a variety of ceramic products.

Blackburn College of Carlinville, Illinois, has a work setup much like Berea's. In place since 1913, Blackburn's work program requires students to contribute 15 hours of work a week, for which they receive a $2,000 credit toward tuition. Blackburn's arrangement is different from the usual work-study program because every student must be employed, the jobs are central to the operation of the college (for example, maintaining the buildings and grounds), and the work is managed by the students themselves. The efficient and widespread use of student labor enables Blackburn to charge a tuition that is considerably lower than tuition at comparable colleges.

THREE CENTURIES OF COLLEGE COSTS

How have costs changed from the 1700s to the present day? Using Princeton as an example, here is a look at the pattern over a 300-year period.

Academic Year 1799–1800

"Necessary expenses of Education in the College, excluding those of Clothing and Chamber Furniture. Tuition, Chamber Rent, Board, Books, Wood, Lights, the Use of the Library, Servant's Wages, and Washerwoman's bills: $180.00.

"Beyond this sum, except for clothing and travelling expenses, parents are earnestly requested to be very frugal in the allowances of money granted to their sons, and to refuse the payment of all debts contracted on credit. Instructors of the College have found that nothing is more pernicious to the morals and the studious habits of the youth committed to their care than an unrestricted credit, or excessive remittances of money. Fines can be levied for tardiness at prayers, profanity, lying, rudeness, loud noises, fighting and refusing to give evidence."

Academic Year 1899–1900

"Estimate of Annual Expenses. Attention is called to the following approximate estimate of necessary annual expenses for a student occupying an unfurnished room in one of the colleges, without including clothes, travelling or vacation expenses:

	Minimum	Medium	Maximum
Board, 36 weeks at $3 to $7 per week	$108	$180	$252
Washing, 36 weeks at $.50 per week	18	18	18
Tuition and Public Room Fees	150	150	150
Infirmary Fee	6	6	6
Building Fee	4	4	4
Matriculation Fee	5	5	5
Room Rent	30	60	175
Fuel	10	20	30
Gas	0	10	25
	$331	$453	$665

"Students are required to call at the Treasurer's office in the course of the first ten days of each term, and give information about their place of boarding so that their bills can be made out. All bills must be paid within the first four weeks of the term."

Academic Year 1987–88

"Fees and other charges for the 1987–88 academic year:

Comprehensive fee (tuition, matriculation, graduation, medical insurance, and use of library, infirmary, and laboratories):	$12,550
Board rate	2,397
Room charge	1,971
	$16,918

"Current fees and expenses cover approximately one-half of the University's educational costs for a student. Since experience has shown that steadily increasing costs must be expected, students should plan on regular annual increases in student charges for the foreseeable future."

Student Aid

Because of the widespread availability of student aid funds, which totaled about $21-billion in 1986–87, less than one half of all undergraduates pay the full cost of their education. In addition to the state and federal aid already mentioned, private donors, corporations, and colleges themselves award money to students or arrange for loans and jobs.

EARLY STUDENT AID

The first scholarship at an American university was established at Harvard in 1643 with a gift from Lady Ann Radcliffe Mowlson.

The first student to work his way through college was Zechariah Brigden, who graduated from Harvard in 1657. Brigden earned his tuition and expense money by "ringing the bell and waytinge."

DOLLARS FOR SCHOLARS

With a drop in the number of high school graduates in the 1980s, the competition among colleges for good students has become intense. One way to attract students is to offer academic scholarships. In a state where colleges have been known to spend a dollar or two on football recruiting, Trinity University of San Antonio has gone after top scholars. Trinity offers 100 annual scholarships worth $5,000 each to National Merit Finalists who apply for admission. So far the results have been impressive. With 80 merit scholars in a class of 650, the average combined math and verbal SAT score of Trinity's freshman class has risen from 1095 to 1200 in the past five years.

"I HAVE A DREAM" SCHOLARSHIPS

The "I Have a Dream" program was started in 1981 by Eugene Lang, a New York City businessman, when he gave a commencement address to sixty-one sixth graders at his former grammar school in East Harlem. To encourage young minority students to complete high school and go on to college, Mr. Lang guaranteed to pay their tuition. In June 1987, twenty-seven members of the class to which Lang made his promise graduated from high school and twenty-five were admitted to college, including one student who received his diploma while he was in jail. The other twenty-four students (ten moved out of the district) are graduating in 1988, and most of them are expected to go to college. The anticipated college attendance rate of over 90 percent is about three times higher than the average for inner-city students. Besides the tuition bills Mr. Lang is facing, he has already spent $125,000 on counseling and tutors.

Mr. Lang is expanding his "I Have a Dream" concept beyond New York. Currently there are similar efforts in fifteen other cities, helping about 4,000 underprivileged students. One variation is Jerome Holmes's Reward-for-Success Program in Cleveland, which establishes a scholarship bank account based on grades. A sixth grader who maintains an A average through high school will earn about $5,500 for college expenses. Students who receive B's and C's accumulate lesser amounts.

MORAL OBLIGATION SCHOLARSHIPS

Students at Beloit in Wisconsin who receive grants from the college sign an agreement to repay the scholarship after they graduate. Beloit has a tradition of taking a different approach to student aid. In 1972 it was the first college to adjust tuition charges according to family income. At the time, families who earned less than $7,000 had their tuition reduced from $1,650 to $500.

ODD SCHOLARSHIPS

Some scholarship donors are very particular about how they want their money spent. Here is a sample of restrictive scholarships at various colleges.

To a girl from Iowa who was raised on a farm of less than 350 acres, whose parents are tenant farmers, who attended a high school with fewer than 300 students, and who played in the Iowa girls' basketball tournament.

To a student who was born in a hospital in Matapan, Massachusetts.

To an Eagle Scout from St. Louis.

To a boy named Murphy. (To give Murphy families the opportunity to apply for the scholarships, the college was required to place ads in the Boston and New York newspapers.)

To a student who is skilled at the art of reading the English language aloud.

To a girl who has never been married, whose studies have been continuous, and who is not in the top 10 percent of her class.

To a student who does not smoke cigarettes.

To a student from Wheelock, Vermont. (This fund has gone unused for many years, since the town of Wheelock consists of one gas station, twenty-eight residents, and no school.)

For a student enrolled in horticulture or agricultural engineering. Recipients should be persons of honesty and integrity; have a zest for living, a sense of humor, and a friendly personality; be nonpolitical and noncontroversial; be serious when necessary and adjustable to change; exhibit self-control and not overreact; be tolerant of others and loyal to commitments; be patient and show perseverance; and have visions of grandeur. (In order to make it easier for students who receive the scholarship to have a "zest for living" and "visions of grandeur," there is another provision—recipients will have grade point averages of not less than 2.0 or greater than 3.0. In other words, if students get better than a B average, they lose the scholarship.)

8

ALMA MATER

GOVERNMENT LEADERS, THE RICH AND FAMOUS, OTHER GRADUATES OF NOTE

Whatever their profession, the vast majority of famous people attended college. Except for those born before 1800 when college opportunities were rare, a college degree is important in most career fields. Where did well-known people go to college as undergraduates? This chapter shows various categories of individuals who have made their marks on American society along with facts and stories about their college attendance.

Government Leaders

PRESIDENTS OF THE UNITED STATES

Of the thirty-nine U.S. presidents, thirty attended college and all but five graduated. Harvard has produced the most presidents, with five (John Adams, John Quincy Adams, Teddy Roosevelt, Franklin Roosevelt, and John Kennedy). William and Mary, which calls itself the "Alma Mater of the Nation," is second with three (Thomas Jefferson, James Monroe, and John Tyler). If William and Mary wants to stretch a point, it can add George Washington, who received his surveyor's license from the college. The only other colleges to produce more than one president are Princeton and West Point, with two each: Princeton—James Madison and Woodrow Wilson; West Point—Ulysses Grant and Dwight Eisenhower.

	College	Graduating class or years attended
George Washington	No college	
John Adams	Harvard	1775
Thomas Jefferson	William and Mary	att 1760–62
James Madison	Princeton	1771
James Monroe	William and Mary	att 1776
John Quincy Adams	Harvard	1787

continued

Andrew Jackson	No college	
Martin Van Buren	No college	
William Henry Harrison	Hampden-Sydney	att 1787–90
John Tyler	William and Mary	1807
James Polk	North Carolina	1818
Zachary Taylor	No college	
Millard Fillmore	No college	
Franklin Pierce	Bowdoin	1824
James Buchanan	Dickinson	1809
Abraham Lincoln	No college	
Andrew Johnson	No college	
Ulysses Grant	West Point	1843
Rutherford Hayes	Kenyon	1842
James Garfield	Williams	1856
Chester Arthur	Union	1848
Grover Cleveland	No college	
Benjamin Harrison	Miami (Ohio)	1852
William McKinley	Allegheny	att 1860
Theodore Roosevelt	Harvard	1880
William Taft	Yale	1878
Woodrow Wilson	Princeton	1879
Warren Harding	Ohio Central	1882
Calvin Coolidge	Amherst	1895
Herbert Hoover	Stanford	1895
Franklin Roosevelt	Harvard	1904
Harry Truman	No college	
Dwight Eisenhower	West Point	1915
John Kennedy	Harvard	1940
Lyndon Johnson	Southwest Texas State	1930
Richard Nixon	Whittier	1934
Gerald Ford	Michigan	1935
Jimmy Carter	Annapolis	1946
Ronald Reagan	Eureka	1932

On the gridiron:
Ford (left)
and Reagan.

continued

Of the twenty-five presidents who received degrees, only two were members of the same class. Both Coolidge (Amherst) and Hoover (Stanford) graduated in the class of 1895.

There is a striking similarity in the college activities of two recent Republican presidents—Ford and Reagan. Both went to college on partial athletic scholarships, were linemen on their football teams, and washed dishes in fraternity houses to help pay for college. Ford worked in the Delta Kappa Epsilon house at Michigan and Reagan at Eureka's Tau Kappa Epsilon.

The list of presidential alma maters would be somewhat different if Woodrow Wilson and John Kennedy had remained at the colleges where they first enrolled. Wilson spent one year at Davidson, withdrew because of ill health, and transferred to Princeton. Kennedy attended Princeton for less than a semester, dropped out because of a recurrence of jaundice he had contracted over the summer, and switched to Harvard.

The twenty-fifth president, William McKinley, cannot be faulted for taking a casual approach to learning. He attended Allegheny College in Meadville, Pennsylvania, but dropped out due to physical exhaustion brought on by studying too hard.

Jimmy Carter spent a year at Georgia Tech in 1942–43 to brush up on his math skills before going to the Naval Academy.

Of the nine presidents who didn't go to college, some were taught at home and some learned by on-the-job training. Zachary Taylor was taught by tutors, and Abraham Lincoln's self-education is well known. Harry Truman first worked in the mailroom of the *Kansas City Star* and then as a bookkeeper for a bank. Grover Cleveland was a grocery clerk.

Andrew Johnson became educated at the oldest age of any president. He was illiterate until age 19, when his wife taught him to read and write.

There is an unfortunate connection between James Garfield and his alma mater, Williams. While on his way to his twenty-fifth reunion in 1881, Garfield was assassinated by Charles Guiteau in a Washington, D.C., railroad station.

Warren Harding received his diploma at age 18 after three years at Ohio Central College, a small rural academy that no longer exists.

Of the three presidents who graduated from military academies, Jimmy Carter had the highest class rank, finishing in the top 7 percent (59th of 820). Next was Eisenhower, 27 percent (61st of 168), and then Grant, 54 percent (21st of 39).

continued

Spurned but not forgotten: Bowdoin's Franklin Pierce.

PRESIDENTS WHO WERE PRESIDENTS

Three U.S. presidents were also college presidents, and two became chancellors.

James Garfield was president of Hiram College in Ohio from 1859 to 1861, twenty years before he was inaugurated. Wilson headed Princeton from 1902 to 1910 and was elected president in 1912. Dwight Eisenhower became Columbia's president in 1948 and held the job until 1951, when he ran for the nation's highest office.

From 1788 to 1799 George Washington served as chancellor of William and Mary. Since the post was largely ceremonial, Washington was rarely called on to preside at college functions. Another former president, John Tyler, held the same position from 1859 to 1862.

THE RODNEY DANGERFIELD OF PRESIDENTS

There are only twenty-two colleges that can claim a U.S. president, and Bowdoin is one of them because of its 1824 graduate Franklin Pierce. But Bowdoin hasn't so much as a building named after the fourteenth president, seeing fit to honor Pierce only with a reading room on the second floor of the library. This lack of recognition is not unusual for a president whose wife refused to attend his inauguration, whose party denied him a second term, and whose most distinguished cabinet member was Jefferson Davis.

VICE PRESIDENTS

There have been twenty-nine vice presidents who never assumed the presidency. Six did not attend college. Of the other twenty-three, all had some college education and twenty received degrees. Three colleges can claim two vice presidents each: Princeton (Aaron Burr and George Dallas), Yale (John Calhoun and George Bush), and Centre College (John Breckinridge and Adlai Stevenson Sr.).

Aaron Burr, vice president under Jefferson, enrolled at Princeton (then called the College of New Jersey) in 1769 as a 13-year-old sophomore. He graduated three years later at age 16. Burr's father served as Princeton's president from 1747 to 1757.

Two vice presidents were early advocates of the current "stop-out" practice. Henry Wallace, one of Franklin Roosevelt's three vice presidents, enrolled at Iowa State in 1884, withdrew to work for four years, and returned to graduate in 1892. Hubert Humphrey, vice president under Lyndon Johnson, started at the University of Minnesota in 1929 and finally graduated in 1939. Humphrey spent 1932 to 1937 working as a pharmacist.

The 1892 election, in which Benjamin Harrison and Whitelaw Reid were elected on the Republican ticket, was the

---

Benjamin Harrison and his vice president, Whitelaw Reid, graduated from the same college — Miami of Ohio.

---

only time in U.S. history that both the president and vice president were from the same college, in this case Miami of Ohio. Harrison was in the class of 1852, Reid the class of 1856.

Of the six vice presidents who never attended college, Charles Curtis served the most unusual apprenticeship. He was a jockey at a racetrack in Topeka, Kansas.

CABINET MEMBERS

Many important figures in American history have served in the president's cabinet. Here are some of the most notable:

Cabinet member/position	College	Graduating class or years attended
Alexander Hamilton		
Secretary of the Treasury	Columbia	att 1773–76
Henry Knox		
Secretary of War	No college	
Edmund Randolph		
Attorney General	William and Mary	att 1773–75
Albert Gallatin		
Secretary of the Treasury	No U.S. college	
William Seward		
Secretary of State	Union	1820
Hamilton Fish		
Secretary of State	Columbia	1827
Edward Stanton		
Secretary of War	Kenyon	att 1831
Elihu Root		
Secretary of State	Hamilton	1864
Andrew Mellon		
Secretary of the Treasury	Pittsburgh	1873
William Jennings Bryan		
Secretary of State	Illinois College	1881

continued

Henry Stimson		
Secretary of State	Yale	1888
Cordell Hull		
Secretary of State	Montvale	att 1886–88
John Foster Dulles		
Secretary of State	Princeton	1900
George Marshall		
Secretary of State	Virginia Military Institute	1901
Frances Perkins		
Secretary of Labor	Mount Holyoke	1902
James Forrestal		
Secretary of Defense	Princeton	1915
Robert McNamara		
Secretary of Defense	U Cal Berkeley	1937
Robert Kennedy		
Attorney General	Harvard	1948
Henry Kissinger		
Secretary of State	Harvard	1950

At the time when the United States had two secretaries of state, both were graduates of the same college. During the Civil War, Union graduate William Seward (remembered for "Seward's Folly," the purchase of Alaska) was secretary of state under Lincoln. The secretary of state for the Confederacy was Robert Toombs, Union class of 1828.

Elihu Root's connection with Hamilton College was one of the closest anyone has ever had with a college. Since his father was on the faculty at Hamilton, Root was born on the campus in 1845. He grew up across the street from the college and enrolled there in 1860. Root's father and brother were both math professors. His father, F. Oren, was known as "Cube" Root, and his brother, B. Oren, was nicknamed "Square" Root. After decades of public service (he also was a senator, secretary of war, and Nobel Peace Prize winner), Root returned to Hamilton and served on the board of trustees until he died at age 92.

Son of "Cube,"
brother of "Square":
Hamilton's Elihu Root.

Cordell Hull, distinguished secretary of state under Franklin Roosevelt, was raised in a log cabin in the northern Tennessee town of Star Point. In 1886, when Hull was 15, he went away to college, sort of. Montvale College in Celina, Tennessee, had only a handful of students, and half the faculty was Joe McMillin, professor of surveying, geometry, anatomy, and Greek. In 1889 Hull

continued

transferred to National Normal University in Lebanon, Ohio, and went on to receive his law degree from Cumberland in 1891.

George Marshall, the architect of the Marshall Plan after World War II and a Nobel recipient, had an outstanding college career. At Virginia Military Institute he was senior first captain of the corps of cadets and a tackle on the football team. He is the only professional military officer to have won the Nobel Peace Prize.

George C. Marshall at VMI.

Mount Holyoke's Frances Perkins.

Frances Perkins's experience at Mount Holyoke directly influenced her later position as secretary of labor under Franklin Roosevelt. As part of an economics course, Perkins's class toured a paper mill in the town of Holyoke. During the visit Perkins was struck by the terrible working conditions and the lack of safety precautions. From that time on, her career goal was to improve the plight of laborers.

Albert Gallatin, secretary of the treasury under Jefferson, went to college in Geneva, Switzerland, where he was born. Although Gallatin never attended school in the United States, he had a very close connection with an American college. In 1832 he organized the group that founded New York University and he served as the first president of its board of trustees.

CONGRESSMEN

Following are some notable members of the U.S. Congress.

	College	Graduating class or years attended
Daniel Webster	Dartmouth	1801
Jefferson Davis	West Point	1828

continued

Henry Clay	No college	
Stephen Douglas	No college	
Robert La Follette	Wisconsin	1879
Sam Rayburn	East Texas State	1903
Huey Long	Tulane	1915
Everett Dirksen	Minnesota	att 1913–17
Sam Ervin	North Carolina	1917
Strom Thurmond	Clemson	1925
Jacob Javits	NYU School of Law	1927
Carl Albert	Oklahoma	1931
Eugene McCarthy	St. John's (Minnesota)	1935
Tip O'Neill	Boston College	1936
James Wright	Texas	att 1941–42

In 1917, one semester short of receiving his degree from the University of Minnesota, Everett Dirksen was drafted into the Army. He was sent overseas and served as a balloon observer during the final stages of World War I. After the service, he became interested in politics and never returned to college.

After Jacob Javits graduated from George Washington High School on the Lower East Side in Manhattan, he had a number of part-time jobs, including helping his mother sell dry goods from a pushcart. In the evenings Javits enrolled in classes at NYU but couldn't put together enough credits to graduate. By 1926, however, he did well enough in his law courses to be awarded an LL.B. degree from NYU's law school.

William Fulbright, a Rhodes Scholar, was president of the University of Arkansas before he went to Congress in 1945. In the thirty years he served in the Senate, he founded the Fulbright Scholars program and was chairman of the Senate Foreign Relations Committee for more than a decade.

SUPREME COURT JUSTICES

Following are lists of some notable chief and associate justices of the U.S. Supreme Court.

	College	Graduating class or years attended
Chief justices		
John Jay	Columbia	1764
John Marshall	William and Mary	att 1780
Roger Taney	Dickinson	1795
Salmon Chase	Dartmouth	1826
Charles Hughes	Brown	1881
Harlan Stone	Amherst	1894
Earl Warren	U Cal Berkeley	1912
Warren Burger	Minnesota	att 1925
William Rehnquist	Stanford	1948

continued

Associate justices

Louis Brandeis	No U.S. college	
Felix Frankfurter	CUNY	1902
Hugo Black	Alabama	1906
William Douglas	Whitman	1920
Thurgood Marshall	Lincoln	1930
Sandra O'Connor	Stanford	1950

William and Mary's claim to John Marshall, chief justice of the Supreme Court from 1801 to 1835, is rather thin. While serving as a captain in the Continental Army during the Revolutionary War, Marshall returned home in June 1780, to await orders. While he was on leave, Marshall attended a two-month course of lectures at William and Mary given by Chancellor George Wythe.

Salmon Chase, chief justice of the Supreme Court from 1864 to 1873, was one of the most versatile politicians of all time. Besides sitting on the Supreme Court, he was a governor, senator, and candidate for the presidential nomination of both the Republican and Democratic parties. Today his likeness can be seen on a $10,000 bill.

Although born in Louisville, Kentucky, Louis Brandeis was educated in Germany at the Annen Realschule in Dresden from 1873 to 1875. Brandeis then went to Harvard Law School, where he earned his LL.B.

The Rich and Famous

HISTORIC FIGURES

Name/occupation	College	Graduating class or years attended
Alexander Graham Bell		
Inventor	No U.S. college	
Alexander Calder	(	
Sculptor	Stevens Tech	1919
Andrew Carnegie		
Industrialist	No college	
Stephen Crane		
Author	Lafayette	att 1890
John Dewey		
Educator	Vermont	1879
Walt Disney		
Filmmaker	No college	
Thomas Edison		
Inventor	No college	
Henry Ford		
Automobile manufacturer	No college	
Benjamin Franklin		
Educator, inventor	No college	

continued

Buckminster Fuller		
Architect	Harvard	att 1913–15
George Gershwin		
Songwriter	No college	
Jean Paul Getty		
Oil executive	USC	att 1910–11
	U Cal Berkeley	att 1910–12
Nathaniel Hawthorne		
Author	Bowdoin	1825
William Randolph Hearst		
Publisher	Harvard	att 1882–85
Patrick Henry		
Revolutionary statesman	No college	
Howard Hughes		
Industrialist, movie producer	Rice	att 1924
Ray Kroc		
Restaurant executive	No college	
Robert E. Lee		
Confederate general	West Point	1829
Charles Lindbergh		
Aviator	Wisconsin	att 1921–22
Henry Wadsworth Longfellow		
Author	Bowdoin	1825
Douglas MacArthur		
Army officer	West Point	1903
J. P. Morgan		
Banker	No U.S. college	
Edward R. Murrow		
Broadcast journalist	Washington State	1930
Edgar Allan Poe		
Author	Virginia	att 1826–27
	West Point	att 1830–31
John D. Rockefeller		
Oil executive	No college	
Adlai Stevenson III		
Governor, presidential candidate	Princeton	1922
Mark Twain		
Author	No college	
Frank Lloyd Wright		
Architect	Wisconsin	att 1884–87
Brigham Young		
Religious leader	No college	

Stephen Crane, author of *The Red Badge of Courage*, dropped out of Lafayette after failing freshman English. He later commented, "Lafayette has turned out some good men. They turned me out."

Mark Twain was fond of saying he went to Mississippi University. By that Twain did not mean he attended the University of Mississippi, but rather that he was schooled on the Mississippi River. While serving as an apprentice river pilot, Twain studied the course and behavior of the river, observed everyday events, and

continued

took responsibility for the safe passage of the ship, all the education Twain said he would ever need.

Edgar Allan Poe attended the University of Virginia in the 1826–27 academic year but left because he had no money. In 1830 his guardian, John Allan, arranged for Poe to receive an appointment to West Point. At the time, Poe was a 21-year-old Army veteran and had published his first book. He had no appetite for the strict rules of the military academy and was soon dismissed for neglect of duty.

Brigham Young never attended college. It is not known how many of his fifty-six children went to college, but presumably he spent a good part of his income on tuition payments.

Alexander Graham Bell went to college at Edinburgh in Scotland and the University of London before coming to the United States in 1870.

J. P. Morgan, although born in Hartford, Connecticut, attended the University of Göttingen in Germany for two years while his father worked as a London banker.

Thomas Edison was taken out of school and educated by his mother because his teachers thought he was inept in mathematics and a slow learner overall.

William Randolph Hearst was expelled from Harvard in 1885 for giving his professors chamber pots with their names engraved on them. This wasn't Hearst's first prank. The year before, he managed to get a jackass into a professor's office. Around its neck Hearst had attached a note that said, "Now there are two of you."

Andrew Carnegie came to the United States from Scotland in 1848 when he was 13 years old and never went to college. While working as a bobbin boy in a cotton factory, Carnegie acquired an insatiable appetite for reading. A family friend, James Anderson, opened his personal library of 400 volumes to young Andrew, who educated himself by reading virtually every book in Anderson's collection. After Carnegie became a successful businessman, his memory of the great benefits he received from Anderson's books caused him to donate millions of dollars to found public libraries throughout the country.

Henry Wadsworth Longfellow and Nathaniel Hawthorne were both members of the class of 1825 at Bowdoin. Longfellow was a

Bowdoin classmates
Longfellow (left) and Hawthorne.

popular undergraduate, a strong student who delivered the oration at commencement. Hawthorne, on the other hand, was shy and sensitive and often failed his recitations. But he was a brilliant writer, and his themes won the admiration of his classmates. Hawthorne had few friends, but one of them was Franklin Pierce, later the fourteenth president of the United States.

Frank Lloyd Wright enrolled at the University of Wisconsin as a civil engineer, since Wisconsin didn't have an architecture program. After a part-time job with a local architectural firm convinced Wright that he wanted to be an architect, he left Wisconsin before graduation to work in Chicago as a draftsman.

Buckminster Fuller was expelled from Harvard not once, but twice. He was first asked to leave in 1913 for "irresponsible conduct" after he went to New York City and spent his tuition money on a lavish party for the cast of the Ziegfeld Follies. His second expulsion, in 1915, occurred because of his "lack of sustained interest in the processes within the university."

Howard Hughes dropped out of Rice Institute in 1924 to take over the family oil well drilling machinery company after his father died during Hughes's freshman year. By the time he was 20, Hughes was earning $2-million a year, already on his way to becoming the richest man in the world fifty years later.

PULITZER PRIZE WINNERS

Following are some winners of Pulitzer Prizes in several categories.

	Year of Pulitzer	College	Graduating class or years attended
Editorial Cartooning			
Herbert Block	1942, 1954, 1979	Lake Forest	att 1927–29
Paul Conrad	1964, 1971	Iowa	1950
Jeffrey MacNelly	1972, 1978, 1985	North Carolina	att 1965–69
Fiction			
Booth Tarkington	1919, 1922	Purdue	att 1889–90
		Princeton	att 1890–93
John Steinbeck	1940	Stanford	att 1919
Robert Penn Warren	1947	Vanderbilt	1925
Ernest Hemingway	1953	No college	
William Faulkner	1955, 1963	Mississippi	att 1919–21
Drama			
Eugene O'Neill	1920, 1922, 1928, 1957	Princeton	att 1906
Tennessee Williams	1948, 1955	Iowa	1938

continued

| Edward Albee | 1967, 1975 | Trinity (Connecticut) | att 1946–48 |
| Sam Shepard | 1979 | San Antonio Junior College | att 1961 |

History/Biography

Carl Sandburg	1940	Lombard (Iowa)	att 1898–1902
Samuel E. Morrison	1943, 1960	Harvard	1908
Arthur Schlesinger	1946, 1966	Harvard	1938

Poetry

| Robert Frost | 1924, 1931, 1937, 1943 | Dartmouth | att 1892 |
| Marianne Moore | 1952 | Bryn Mawr | 1909 |

Among the group of Pulitzer Prize winners, Robert Penn Warren deserves special mention. Besides the fiction award, he won in the poetry category twice. He also received a National Book Award and the Bollingen Prize in Poetry. At Vanderbilt, Warren edited the literary magazine, graduated summa cum laude, and was chosen to be a Rhodes Scholar. In 1985 he was named the nation's first Poet Laureate.

After spending a year at Purdue, Booth Tarkington attended Princeton for three years but failed to graduate because he hadn't included Greek in his studies. Tarkington was at Princeton long enough to found the Triangle Club, which has been performing humorous musical reviews for nearly 100 years.

Another Princeton undergraduate who didn't receive his degree was Eugene O'Neill, who spent only one year, 1906–07, at Old Nassau. Unlike Tarkington's academic oversight, O'Neill's reason for not graduating was quite serious. O'Neill was expelled for throwing a beer can through a window, and his departure was expedited by the fact that the window belonged to the home of Princeton's president, Woodrow Wilson.

Robert Frost dropped out of Dartmouth after less than a year. While teaching at a private school in Lawrence, Massachusetts, Frost enrolled as a special student at Harvard in 1897. He took courses off and on for a year and a half before he withdrew.

In 1899 Carl Sandburg left Lombard for West Point, but he returned two weeks later after failing tests in arithmetic and grammar. Lombard closed and merged with Knox College in 1930.

Sam Shepard, having worked on an avocado farm as a teenager, studied agriculture for one year at San Antonio Junior College before taking a job with an acting company.

ACADEMY AWARDS—BEST ACTOR AND ACTRESS

The Academy Awards have been in existence for sixty years. During that time 120 Oscars have been presented in the best actor

continued

and actress categories. Leaving out repeat winners, citizens of foreign countries, and Americans who didn't go to college, there have been thirty-three Oscar recipients with a college background.

	Year of Oscar	College	Graduating class or years attended
Fredric March	1932, 1946	Wisconsin	1920
Katharine Hepburn	1933, 1967, 1968, 1981	Bryn Mawr	1928
Clark Gable	1934	Akron	att 1919
Spencer Tracy	1937, 1938	Ripon	1924
James Stewart	1940	Princeton	1932
Gary Cooper	1941, 1952	Grinnell	att 1922–24
Jennifer Jones	1943	Northwestern	att 1936–37
Bing Crosby	1944	Gonzaga	att 1923–24
Joan Crawford	1945	Stephens (Missouri)	att 1926
Jane Wyman	1948	Missouri	att 1935
José Ferrer	1950	Princeton	1933
Joanne Woodward	1957	LSU	att 1947–49
Charlton Heston	1959	Northwestern	att 1941–43
Burt Lancaster	1960	NYU	1931
Gregory Peck	1962	U Cal Berkeley	1939
Patricia Neal	1963	Northwestern	att 1943–45
John Wayne	1969	USC	att 1925–27
George C. Scott	1970	Missouri	att 1950
Jane Fonda	1971, 1978	Vassar	att 1955–57
Jack Lemmon	1973	Harvard	1947
Louise Fletcher	1975	North Carolina State	1958
Faye Dunaway	1976	Boston University	1962
Richard Dreyfuss	1977	San Fernando State	att 1966–67
Jon Voight	1978	Catholic	1960
Dustin Hoffman	1979	Santa Monica City College	att 1955–56
Henry Fonda	1981	Minnesota	att 1923–25
Meryl Streep	1982	Vassar	1971
Robert Duvall	1983	Principia	1953
F. Murray Abraham	1984	Texas at El Paso	att 1959–61
William Hurt	1985	Tufts	1972
Paul Newman	1986	Kenyon	1949
Marlee Matlin	1986	William Rainey Harper	1985
Michael Douglas	1987	U Cal Santa Barbara	1968

Northwestern leads in Oscar honors with three recipients (Jennifer Jones, Charlton Heston, and Patricia Neal). Tied for second with two each are Princeton (James Stewart and José Ferrer), Missouri (Jane Wyman and George C. Scott), and Vassar (Jane Fonda and Meryl Streep). Actually Bryn Mawr can claim the most Oscars, four, all won by their 1928 graduate, Katharine Hepburn.

Gary Cooper attended Grinnell for two years. He tried on three occasions to make the drama club but failed each time. One of the

continued

reasons Cooper was interested in drama was the crush he had on fellow student and aspiring actress Doris Virden. Cooper dropped out of Grinnell in 1923 to follow Virden to Hollywood, where he first worked as a commercial artist. Doris Virden's acting career never panned out, but Cooper went on to win Oscars for his roles in *Sergeant York* and *High Noon.*

In contrast to Gary Cooper, another two-time winner, Spencer Tracy, was a successful actor during his college days at Ripon. He played the lead in many student productions including *The Valiant* and *Sintram of Skaggerack,* before leaving Wisconsin for Hollywood, where he starred in seventy-four films.

Paul Newman played the lead role in ten undergraduate productions at Kenyon. Not intending to be an actor, he tried the stage to fill his spare time after he was kicked off the football team.

continued

Hepburn offstage at Bryn Mawr.
Bryn Mawr College

Streep onstage at Vassar.
Vassar College

Stewart in costume at Princeton.

Newman expressed his gratitude to Kenyon by returning in 1978 to direct the student production of *C. C. Pyle and the Bunion Derby*.

Richard Dreyfuss left San Fernando State College in California in 1967, when he was drafted and declared himself a conscientious objector. Dreyfuss did two years of alternative service as a file clerk on the midnight-to-morning shift at Los Angeles County General Hospital. Upon completion of his C.O. obligation he went into acting and never returned to college.

Kenyon's Paul Newman as Charley's Aunt.

The 1986 Academy Awards for best actor and actress, won by Paul Newman and Marlee Matlin, marked the first time that both recipients were graduates of American colleges. Newman, an English major, received his B.A. from Kenyon in 1949. Matlin received an associate degree in 1985 from William Rainey Harper, a two-year college in Palatine, Illinois. Matlin, who suffered a severe hearing loss at age 2 as a result of a measles infection, was a criminal justice major.

There are a number of stories about the circumstances of Jane Fonda's departure from Vassar after two years. Official records merely state that Fonda decided not to return for her junior year. Unofficial stories say she was asked to leave for a discipline violation that involved riding a bicycle, motorcycle, or snowmobile (take your pick) in a reckless manner.

In the history of the Best Actor and Best Actress awards, there have been relatively few college graduates. Of the seventy-seven American Oscar winners, only seventeen (22 percent) received their degrees.

ENTERTAINERS

	College	Graduating class or years attended
Alan Alda	Fordham	1956

continued

Woody Allen	NYU	att 1953
	CUNY	att 1954
Carol Burnett	UCLA	att 1952–54
Johnny Carson	Nebraska	1949
Bill Cosby	Temple	att 1961–62
Howard Cosell	NYU	1940
Bob Dylan	Minnesota	att 1960
Clint Eastwood	Los Angeles City College	att 1949
Harrison Ford	Ripon	att 1960–64
Jim Henson	Maryland	1959
Eddie Murphy	Nassau Community College	att 1979–80
Robert Redford	Colorado	att 1954–56
Burt Reynolds	Florida State	att 1954–56
Cybill Shepherd	Hunter, New Rochelle, NYU	att 1969–70
Sylvester Stallone	Miami (Florida)	att 1967–69

Robert Redford received his doctorate without having earned a bachelor's degree. When Redford first attended Colorado in the

Honoring Redford at Colorado.

1950s, he flunked out after two years. His dismal academic record did not prevent the university from granting Redford an honorary doctorate during its May 1987 commencement.

At Miami, Sylvester Stallone dropped out of the drama department when the faculty judged him "too aggressive and too physical to act." He then formed his own acting group in the basement of a local church.

Woody Allen was expelled from both NYU and CUNY for poor attendance and low grades.

Cybill Shepherd was earning $500 a day as a New York fashion model when she decided to obtain an education in art history and literature. She enrolled as a part-time student at Hunter, New Rochelle, and NYU until she met Peter Bogdanovich and turned her attention to starring in *The Last Picture Show*.

ASTRONAUTS

	College	Graduating class or years attended
Project Mercury		
Scott Carpenter	Colorado	1962
Gordon Cooper	Air Force Institute of Technology	1956
John Glenn	Muskingum	att 1939–42
Virgil Grissom	Purdue	1950
Walter Schirra	Annapolis	1945
Alan Shepard	Annapolis	1944
Deke Slayton	Minnesota	1949
Apollo Moon Shot		
Edwin Aldrin	West Point	1951
Neil Armstrong	Purdue	1955
Michael Collins	West Point	1952
First Woman Astronaut		
Sally Ride	Stanford	1973
First Black Astronaut		
Guion Bluford	Penn State	1964
First Space Shuttle—Columbia		
Robert Crippen	Texas	1960
John Young	Georgia Tech	1952

Neil Armstrong, in taking a four-year leave from Purdue after completing his sophomore year in 1949, experienced a little more excitement than the typical college "stop-out." Between 1949 and 1953 Armstrong received his wings as a naval pilot, was sent to Korea, flew seventy-eight combat missions, was shot down, and won three Air Medals. After the Korean conflict ended, he returned to the more peaceful atmosphere of West Lafayette, Indiana, and picked up his studies where he had left off.

For a long time, America's most appropriately named astronaut, Sally Ride, couldn't decide whether she wanted to be a professional tennis player, a Shakespearean scholar, or an astrophysicist. She actually tried all three. Ride was an accomplished junior tennis player who eventually gave up thoughts of a professional career despite the encouragement of Billie Jean King, a one-time doubles partner. When Ride attended Stanford from 1970 to 1973 she took a double major in English literature and physics. She did well in both subjects and earned B.A. and

continued

Stanford's multitalented Sally Ride.

B.S. degrees upon graduation. She had the opportunity to go to
graduate school to study Shakespeare but she decided instead to try
for a doctorate in astrophysics. Ride had not thought about working
in the space program until she noticed a NASA ad in the student
newspaper. She eventually was selected as the nation's first woman
astronaut from more than 1,000 applicants.

The last Columbia space shuttle experimental flight, on June
27, 1982, had two Auburn graduates—Ken Mattingly, class of 1958,
and Henry Hartsfield, class of 1954—at the controls. Purdue claims
the first and last astronauts on the moon: Neil Armstrong in 1969
and Eugene Cernan in 1972.

The Naval Academy is the leading producer of astronauts.
Besides Shepard and Schirra on the original Mercury Project,
Annapolis has prepared twenty-six others for space shots as either
astronauts or mission specialists. Other colleges that have produced
a large number of astronauts are Purdue (sixteen), the Air Force
Academy (fifteen), and Colorado (ten). It is not surprising that
Purdue is the leader among civilian institutions; it was the first
college to give credit for flight courses, offer a degree in pilot
technology, and own and operate its own airport.

BUSINESS LEADERS
Chief Executive Officers
Where did the leaders of the largest U.S. corporations attend
college? Here is a list of the chief executive officers of fifty major
businesses.

Company/CEO	College	Graduating class or years attended
Aetna Life and Casualty		
James Lynn	Western Reserve	1948
American Express		
James D. Robinson	Georgia Tech	1957
AT&T		
Robert E. Allen	Wabash	1957
Atlantic Richfield		
Lowdrick Cook	LSU	1950
BankAmerica		
A. W. Clausen	Carthage	1944
Beatrice		
Donald Kelly	DePaul	1955
Bell South		
John Clendenin	Northwestern	1955
Boeing		
Frank Shrontz	Idaho	1954

continued

CBS		
Lawrence Tisch	NYU	1942
Chase Manhattan		
Willard Butcher	Brown	1947
Chemical NY		
Walter Shipley	NYU	1947
Chevron		
George Keller	MIT	1948
CIGNA		
Robert Kilpatrick	Richmond	1948
Citicorp		
John Reed	Washington and Jefferson	1959
	MIT	1961
Dart and Kraft		
John Richman	Yale	1949
Dow Chemical		
Paul Oreffice	Purdue	1949
Dupont		
Richard Heckert	Miami (Ohio)	1944
Eastman Kodak		
Colby Chandler	Maine	1950
Exxon		
Lawrence Rawl	Oklahoma	1952
Federated Department Stores		
Howard Goldfeder	Tufts	1947
Ford		
Donald Petersen	Washington (Seattle)	1946
General Electric		
John Welch	Massachusetts	1957
General Motors		
Roger Smith	Michigan	1948
Goodyear		
Robert Mercer	Yale	1946
GTE		
Theodore Brophy	Yale	1944
IBM		
John Akers	Yale	1956
ITT		
Rand Araskog	West Point	1953
K Mart		
Joseph Antonini	West Virginia	1963
Manufacturers Hanover		
John McGillicuddy	Princeton	1952
McDonnell Douglas		
Sanford McDonnell	Princeton	1945
Merrill Lynch		
William Schreyer	Penn State	1948
Mobil		
Allen Murray	NYU	1956
J. P. Morgan		
Lewis Preston	Harvard	1956
NYNEX		
Delbert Staley	Rose Poly	att 1943–44

continued

J. C. Penney		
William Howell	Oklahoma	1958
Phillips Petroleum		
C. J. Silas	Georgia Tech	1954
Procter and Gamble		
John Smale	Miami (Ohio)	1949
Rockwell		
Robert Anderson	Colorado State	1943
Safeway Stores		
Peter Magowan	Harvard	1927
Sante Fe Southern Pacific		
John Reed	Yale	1939
Sears, Roebuck		
Edward Brennan	Marquette	1955
Shell Oil		
John Bookout	Texas	1949
Sun Company		
Robert McClements	Drexel	1952
Tenneco		
James Ketelsen	Northwestern	1952
Texaco		
James Kinnear	Annapolis	1950
Travelers		
Edward Budd	Tufts	1955
Union Pacific		
William Cook	Minnesota	1948
United Technologies		
Robert Daniell	Boston University	1954
Westinghouse		
Douglas Danforth	Syracuse	1947
Xerox		
David Kearns	Rochester	1952

There is a wide variety of college backgrounds among this group of leading businessmen. The fifty CEOs attended a total of thirty-seven different institutions as undergraduates. Yale has produced the most chief executive officers with five, followed by New York University with three and Princeton, Tufts, Harvard, Georgia Tech, Northwestern, Oklahoma, and Miami of Ohio with two each.

John Reed, the chairman of Citicorp, the world's largest bank, majored in American literature at Washington and Jefferson and graduated in three years. He then went on to MIT and two years later, in 1961, he received a B.S. degree in metallurgy.

The recently appointed head of CBS, Lawrence Tisch, a self-made billionaire, has always moved quickly, in both business and education. Growing up in Brooklyn, Tisch went through high school and college in five years, graduating cum laude from NYU at age 18. By his nineteenth birthday Tisch had obtained a master's degree in business from the Wharton School at the University of Pennsylvania.

BUSINESS EXECUTIVES

Looking beyond chief executive officers at some top corporations to business leaders in general, Standard and Poor's conducts an Executive/College Survey. The latest edition of the survey, published in 1985, covers about 80,000 high-level managers. The colleges attended as undergraduates by the largest numbers of these executives were:

	Number of executives
1. Yale	1,542
2. Harvard	1,289
3. CUNY	1,277
4. Princeton	1,113
5. NYU	1,057
6. Wisconsin	1,047
7. Penn	1,039
8. Michigan	1,035
9. University of California System	1,019
10. Illinois	966
11. Minnesota	830
12. Northwestern	801

The above list consists of major universities with large enrollments. Since these colleges can be expected to graduate more business leaders than smaller institutions, it is worthwhile to look at liberal arts colleges as a separate category.

	Number of executives
1. Williams	377
2. Amherst	239
3. Colgate	193
4. Holy Cross	178
5. Washington and Lee	169
6. Lafayette	150
7. Manhattan	148
8. Trinity	145
9. Bentley	141
10. Lasalle	138
11. Bucknell	133
12. DePauw	131

Billionaires

Based on listings of net worth from *Forbes Magazine* and *U.S. News and World Report,* here are the college backgrounds of the most wealthy Americans.

	Business	Net worth	College	Graduating class or years attended
Samuel Walton	Wal-Mart Stores	$6.3B	Missouri	1940
John Dorrance	Campbell's Soup	2.6B	Princeton	1941
Leslie Wexner	The Limited	2.6B	Ohio State	1959
John Kluge	Metromedia	2.5B	Columbia	1937
Ross Perot	Electronic data management	2.5B	Annapolis	1953
David Packard	Hewlett-Packard	2.5B	Stanford	1934
Otis Chandler	L.A. Times-Mirror	1.9B	Stanford	1950
Warren Buffett	Berkshire Hathaway	1.7B	Nebraska	1950
Forrest Mars Sr.	Mars Candy	4.0B	Yale	1928
Forrest Mars Jr.		together	Yale	1953
John Mars	Mars Candy		Yale	1957
Lester Crown	Industrialist	1.3B	Northwestern	1947
August Busch	Budweiser	1.2B	No college	
Gordon Getty	Getty Oil	1.2B	San Francisco	1956
William Hewlett	Hewlett-Packard	1.2B	Stanford	1934

continued

Ewing Kauffman	Marion Labs	1.2B	Kansas City Junior Coll	1936
⎰ Samuel Newhouse	Publishing	2.3B	Syracuse	att 1947–49
⎱ Donald Newhouse	Publishing	together	Syracuse	att 1949–51
⎰ Jay Pritzker	Financier	2.3B	Northwestern	1941
⎱ Robert Pritzker	Financier	together	Illinois Tech	1946
William Gates	Microsoft	1.1B	Harvard	att 1974–75
Henry Hillman	Industrialist	1.1B	Princeton	1941
Walter Annenberg	Publishing	1.0B	Penn	att 1927–28
Phillip Anschutz	Oil, investments	1.0B	Kansas	1961
Marvin Davis	Oil, entertainment	1.0B	NYU	1954
Harry Helmsley	Real estate	1.0B	No college	
Margaret Hunt Hill	Inheritance, oil	1.0B	Mary Baldwin	1937
J. Willard Marriott	Marriott Hotels	1.0B	Utah	1954
David Rockefeller	Banking	1.0B	Harvard	1936
⎰ Laurence Tisch	Loews Corp.	2.0B	NYU	1942
⎱ Preston Tisch	Loews Corp.	together	Michigan	1948

Yale and Stanford can claim the most graduates in the billionaires' club, with three each. Colleges with two alumni on the list are Princeton, Northwestern, Syracuse, Harvard, and NYU.

Although Ross Perot graduated 454th in a class of 925 from the Naval Academy, he was voted best all-around midshipman and lifetime president of his class. Since *Fortune* magazine estimated Perot's net worth in 1986, he earned a profit of $400-million on a stock buyout by General Motors, an asset increase that could move Perot into the second position behind Samuel Walton.

David Packard, class of 1934 at Stanford (where he was a classmate of William Hewlett) was elected to Phi Beta Kappa and lettered in football and basketball. John Kluge was a four-year honors scholar at Columbia. He recently gave $25-million to his alma mater to establish scholarships for minority students.

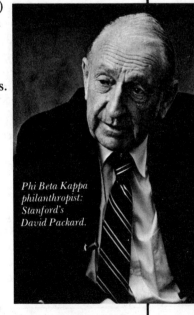

Warren Buffett spent two years at Penn, from 1947 to 1949, before graduating from Nebraska in 1950. Gordon Getty lived with his mother when he attended the University of San Francisco. He was given a strictly limited allowance, and it wasn't until after he graduated that Getty realized his father was the richest person in the United States.

Phi Beta Kappa philanthropist: Stanford's David Packard.

Otis Chandler of the *Los Angeles Times* was a star athlete at Stanford. While he was captain of the 1950 track team, Chandler missed setting a new world record in the shot put by less than a foot.

Foreign Heads of State

There are a number of foreign heads of state who attended college in the United States.

	Country	College	Class
Corazón Aquino	Philippines	Mount St. Vincent	1953
Canaan Banana	Zimbabwe	Wesley Seminary	1975
Hastings Banda	Malawi	Chicago	1931
Ingvar Carlsson	Sweden	Northwestern	1958
Leon Febres Cordero	Ecuador	Stevens Tech	1953
José Duarte	El Salvador	Notre Dame	1948
Manual Esquivel	Belize	Loyola (Louisiana)	1962
Steingrimur Hermannsson	Iceland	Illinois Tech	1951
Miguel de la Madrid	Mexico	Harvard	1965
Andreas Papandreou	Greece	Harvard	1942
Edward Seaga	Jamaica	Harvard	1952

José Duarte, president of El Salvador, arrived at Notre Dame in 1944 barely able to speak English. He supplemented his small scholarship by working 40 hours a week as a dishwasher and laundryman. One of Duarte's freshman instructors, who encouraged him to continue his studies, was Reverend Theodore Hesburgh, who later became Notre Dame's president. Duarte received his degree in civil engineering.

Duarte at Notre Dame.

Andreas Papandreou, the prime minister of Greece, lived in the United States from 1940 to 1959. In 1944 he gained American citizenship, which he renounced in 1961 when he was elected to the Greek parliament. Papandreou received both a master's and a doctorate in economics from Harvard. He was a faculty member at Harvard, Minnesota, Northwestern, and U Cal Berkeley before he returned to his home country.

Among former presidents and prime ministers of foreign countries who went to college in the United States were Olof Palme of Sweden (Kenyon, class of 1948) and Syngman Rhee of Korea (George Washington, class of 1908). In his six-year stay in the United States, from 1904 to 1910, Syngman Rhee received degrees from George Washington, Harvard, and Princeton. At Princeton, Rhee's adviser for his doctoral thesis, *Neutrality as Influenced by the United States,* was Woodrow Wilson. A few years later Wilson's scholarly viewpoint became the basis for national policy when, as president of the United States, he tried to keep America out of World War I.

Notable Blacks

Name/occupation	College	Graduating class or years attended
Marian Anderson		
Opera singer	No college	
James Baldwin		
Author	No college	
Julian Bond		
Civil rights leader	Morehouse	1961
Thomas Bradley		
Mayor of Los Angeles	UCLA	att 1937–40
Edward Brooke		
Senator	Howard	1940
Ralph Bunche		
U.N. representative	UCLA	1927
George Washington Carver		
Botanist	Iowa State	1894
Shirley Chisholm		
Congresswoman	Brooklyn	1946
Frederick Douglass		
Journalist	No college	
William Du Bois		
Author, educator	Fisk	1888
	Harvard	1890
Marian Wright Edelman		
Children's Defense Fund	Spelman	1960
Alex Haley		
Author	Elizabeth City	att 1937–39
Jesse Jackson		
Minister, civil rights leader	North Carolina A&T	1964
Martin Luther King		
Minister, civil rights leader	Morehouse	1948
Alice Walker		
Author	Sarah Lawrence	1966
Booker T. Washington		
Educator	Hampton	1875
Roy Wilkins		
Civil rights leader	Minnesota	1923
Malcolm X		
Civil rights leader	No college	
Andrew Young		
Mayor of Atlanta	Howard	1951

William Du Bois received a B.A. from Fisk in 1888 before gaining a second bachelor's degree cum laude from Harvard in 1890. He stayed on at Harvard and acquired both an M.A. and a Ph.D.; he was the first black to receive a doctorate from Harvard. At his graduation in 1890, Du Bois was chosen as one of five commencement speakers. His controversial topic, "Jefferson Davis

continued

and Slavery," won high praise, including a favorable editorial in *The Nation* magazine.

Jesse Jackson was a star football player at all-black Sterling High School in Greenville, South Carolina. In 1959 he won a scholarship to the University of Illinois, hoping to become the starting quarterback. When he was told by the coaching staff that blacks didn't play quarterback, he transferred to North Carolina A&T, where he played football, made the honor roll, and was student body president. While he was an undergraduate Jackson became involved in civil rights issues. He organized sit-ins and picket lines at Greensboro restaurants and hotels that refused to serve blacks.

Having lost sight in one eye due to a childhood accident, in 1961 Alice Walker won a scholarship for handicapped students to Spelman College in Atlanta. Actively engaged in the civil rights movement at the time, Walker found the rules at Spelman too restrictive, so she transferred to Sarah Lawrence in Bronxville, New York. Walker wrote her first volume of poems, *Once,* in 1964 during her senior year in college. Eighteen years later her highly acclaimed novel *The Color Purple* was published.

Famous Women

Name/occupation	College	Graduating class or years attended
Jane Addams		
Social worker	Rockford	1881
Susan B. Anthony		
Suffragette	No college	
Mary Calderone		
Physician	Vassar	1925
Joan Ganz Cooney		
Public television executive	Arizona	1951
Agnes de Mille		
Choreographer	UCLA	1956
Emily Dickinson		
Poet	Mount Holyoke	att 1847–48
Elizabeth Dole		
Cabinet officer	Duke	1958
Amelia Earhart		
Aviator	Columbia	att 1919–20
Geraldine Ferraro		
Congresswoman	Marymount Manhattan	1956
Katharine Graham		
Newspaper executive	Chicago	1938
Hannah Gray		
College president	Bryn Mawr	1950

continued

Grace Hopper			
Naval officer	Vassar	1928	
Nancy Kassebaum			
Senator	Kansas	1954	
Helen Keller			
Author, social worker	Radcliffe	1904	
Jeane Kirkpatrick			
U.N. representative	Barnard	1948	
Anne Morrow Lindbergh			
Author	Smith	1927	
Margaret Mead			
Anthropologist	Barnard	1923	
Jacqueline Onassis			
First Lady	George Washington	1951	
Nancy Reagan			
First Lady	Smith	1943	
Margaret Chase Smith			
Senator	No college		
Gloria Steinem			
Feminist leader	Smith	1956	
Barbara Walters			
Television journalist	Sarah Lawrence	1953	
Rosalyn Yalow			
Physicist	Hunter	1941	

Smith College

Nancy Reagan at Smith.

Helen Keller, who was deaf and blind from age 2 because of brain fever, graduated cum laude from Radcliffe. Her teacher, Anne Sullivan, communicated the lectures and reading assignments to Keller by writing the words with her finger in the palm of Keller's hand.

Susan B. Anthony did not attend public high school or college. She was educated in a school run by her father for his family and neighborhood children. Even without a formal education, Anthony taught school herself, starting at age 15, until she was 30.

Until her retirement a few years ago, Grace Hopper was a commodore in the U.S. Navy and is credited with developing the COBOL computer language.

Katharine Graham, chief executive officer of the Washington Post Company, including *Newsweek* magazine and radio and TV stations, is perhaps the nation's most prominent female business executive. In 1935 she entered Vassar, but she left after one year because she considered the atmosphere too conventional.

The Navy's Hopper at Vassar.

Graham transferred to the University of Chicago, where she became an active liberal as a result of a course she took in the history of ideas.

continued

The political perspective she formed in college can be seen today in the editorial policy of the *Washington Post* and Graham's risky but successful decision to publish the *Pentagon Papers*.

Steinem. Smith College *Dickinson.* *Lindbergh.* Smith College

Gloria Steinem, a government major, was elected to Phi Beta Kappa at Smith.

Emily Dickinson attended Mount Holyoke when it was a female seminary. Dickinson, a recluse from age 30 until she died at 56, published only two poems during her lifetime.

Not only did Anne Morrow Lindbergh graduate from Smith in 1927, but she returned there in 1940 to serve as temporary president of the college.

When Rosalyn Yalow attended Hunter College in New York City, from 1937 to 1941, she majored in physics and chemistry but also took shorthand and typing because she wasn't sure she could find a job in a scientific field. After becoming a member of Phi Beta Kappa and graduating, she was able to put her secretarial skills aside when she was offered a teaching position in the College of Engineering at Illinois. Initially the only female among 400 faculty members, in 1977 Yalow became the second woman to win the Nobel Prize in medicine.

Amelia Earhart attended Columbia in 1919 to take premedical studies, dropped out, and reenrolled in 1925–26. By the summer of 1926 flying had become Earhart's consuming passion and she stopped pursuing a college education. In 1935, after her solo flight across the Atlantic, Earhart was appointed a visiting faculty member at Purdue, where she was a flight instructor and career counselor for women. Purdue established a research fund for Earhart, and she used some of the money to purchase a twin-engine Lockheed Electra, the aircraft she was flying when she crashed in the South Pacific on July 2, 1937.

More Famous Men

Name/occupation	College	Graduating class or years attended
Leonard Bernstein		
Conductor	Harvard	1939
Frank Borman		
Airline executive	West Point	1950
George Bush		
Vice president	Yale	1948
Cesar Chavez		
Labor union organizer	No college	
Walter Cronkite		
Broadcast journalist	Texas	att 1933–35
Mario Cuomo		
Governor	St. John's (New York)	1953
Michael Dukakis		
Governor	Swarthmore	1955
Theodore Geisel (Dr. Seuss)		
Author	Dartmouth	1925
Bernhard Goetz		
Electronics engineer	NYU	1969
Billy Graham		
Evangelist	Wheaton (Illinois)	1943
Gary Hart		
Senator	Southern Nazarene	1958
Henry Heimlich		
Professor	Cornell	1941
Lee Iacocca		
Automobile executive	Lehigh	1945
Steven Jobs		
Computer executive	Reed	att 1972
Stephen King		
Author	Maine	1970
Ed Koch		
Mayor	CUNY	att 1941–43
James Michener		
Author	Swarthmore	1929
Ralph Nader		
Consumer advocate	Princeton	1955
Norman Vincent Peale		
Author, minister	Ohio Wesleyan	1920
Dan Rather		
Broadcast journalist	Sam Houston	1953
Albert Sabin		
Medical researcher	NYU	1928
Carl Sagan		
Professor, author	Chicago	1954
Jonas Salk		
Medical researcher	CUNY	1934

continued

Charles Schulz		
Cartoonist	No college	
Benjamin Spock		
Author, pediatrician	Yale	1925
George Steinbrenner		
Sports executive	Williams	1952
Donald Trump		
Real estate executive	Penn	1968
Peter Ueberroth		
Baseball commissioner	San Jose State	1959
Mike Wallace		
Broadcast journalist	Michigan	1939
Thomas Watson		
IBM founder	Brown	1937

Henry Heimlich, currently professor of clinical science at Xavier in Cincinnati, is the inventor of the Heimlich maneuver.

Carl Sagan doesn't have billions and billions of degrees, but he has quite a few: a B.A. in general education, a B.S. in physics, an M.S. in physics, and a Ph.D. in astronomy and astrophysics, all from the University of Chicago and all by the time he was 25 years old.

Upon graduation from high school in 1941, George Bush entered naval flight training on his eighteenth birthday. A year later, when he received his pilot's wings, he was the youngest aviator in the Navy. After serving in the Pacific during World War II, he entered Yale in 1945. At Yale, Bush was elected to Phi Beta Kappa and was captain of Yale's eastern championship baseball team.

Peter Ueberroth, who gained fame as president of the organizing committee for the 1984 Los Angeles Olympic Games, went to San Jose State on a water polo scholarship. Although he led the conference in scoring for two years, when he tried out for the 1956 U.S. Olympic team he was named an alternate and never participated in the games.

Ueberroth at San Jose State.

Mario Cuomo paid for his college education at St. John's by playing semipro basketball.

Cesar Chavez was educated only through the seventh grade. He attended more than thirty different schools while he traveled with his parents, who were migrant farm workers.

Steven Jobs, the cofounder of Apple Computers, didn't show signs of becoming a successful young entrepreneur when he attended Reed in 1972. On the contrary, Jobs dropped out after one semester and stayed around Reed for the next year, immersing

continued

himself in the counterculture: meditation, the I Ching, psychedelic drugs, and the Hare Krishna religion. For a while Jobs earned money by selling the "blue box," a device that allows a person to make free long distance phone calls by duplicating the dial tone.

MISS AMERICAS

The Miss America beauty pageant has been part of the nation's culture since 1921 and virtually every winner has been a college graduate. Here is a look at the colleges of Miss Americas from 1960 on.

	Year crowned	College
Lynda Lee Mead	1960	Mississippi
Nancy Fleming	1961	Michigan State/U Cal Berkeley
Maria Fletcher	1962	Vanderbilt
Jackie Mayer	1963	Northwestern/Pittsburgh
Donna Axum	1964	Arkansas
Vonda Kay Van Dyke	1965	Arizona
Deborah Bryant	1966	Kansas
Jane Jayroe	1967	Oklahoma City
Debra Barnes	1968	Pittsburg State
Judi Ford	1969	Illinois
Pam Eldred	1970	Mercy (Michigan)
Phyllis George	1971	Texas Christian
Laurie Lea Schaefer	1972	Ohio
Terry Meeuwsen	1973	St. Norbert
Becky King	1974	Colorado Women's College
Shirley Cothran	1975	North Texas State
Tawney Godin	1976	Skidmore
Dorothy Benham	1977	Macalester
Susan Perkins	1978	Miami (Ohio)
Kylene Baker	1979	Virginia Tech
Cheryl Prewitt	1980	Mississippi State
Susan Powell	1981	Oklahoma City
Elizabeth Ward	1982	Arkansas/Arkansas Tech
Debra Maffett	1983	Lamar
Suzette Charles	1984	Temple
Sharlene Wells	1985	Brigham Young
Susan Akin	1986	Mississippi
Kellye Cash	1987	Memphis State
Kaye Lani Rafko	1988	St. Vincent Medical Center
Gretchen Carlson	1989	Stanford

The University of Mississippi has produced the most Miss Americas, with three: Mary Ann Mobley (1959), Lynda Lee Mead (1960), and Susan Akin (1986). Arkansas, Oklahoma City, Colorado Women's College, Arizona, and Memphis State are runners-up with two each.

continued

Memphis State has not been reticent to use the name of the 1987 winner, Kellye Cash, in promoting the college. Cash's photograph appears on the college directory and in the alumni magazine. University mail is stamped with "Memphis State— Campus of Miss America by Choice."

Other Graduates of Note

U.S. POETS LAUREATE

The naming of a distinguished American poet to this position by the Librarian of Congress started in 1985. There have been two Poets Laureate, each of whom had previously won a Pulitzer Prize for his work.

	Term	*College*	*Class*
Robert Penn Warren	1985–87	Vanderbilt	1925
Richard Wilbur	1987 to present	Amherst	1942

BROADWAY TRIO FROM COLUMBIA

Oscar Hammerstein, Richard Rodgers, and Lorenz Hart all attended Columbia between 1916 and 1920. Although Hammerstein and Hart graduated, Rodgers completed only his freshman year. In 1919 Rodgers collaborated with Hart to write the music and lyrics for the Columbia Varsity Show, *Fly with Me.* The show was such a success that Rodgers dropped out of school and became a professional songwriter at age 17.

RADIO AND TELEVISION ANNOUNCERS FROM SYRACUSE

The Newhouse School of Public Communications and the Syracuse student radio station, WAER-FM, have an excellent record in producing radio and television personalities.

	Class
Marv Albert	1963
Len Berman	1968
Dick Clark	1951
Bob Costas	1974
Marty Glickman	1939
Ted Koppel	1960
Andy Musser	1959
Dick Stockton	1964
William B. Williams	1944

THE U.S. CONSTITUTION

Thirty-nine delegates signed their names to the U.S. Constitution on May 25, 1787. Nearly 25 percent of the representatives came from one college, Princeton University. Among Princeton's nine members of the Constitutional Convention was James Madison, class of 1771, a proponent of the Virginia plan that called for two legislative houses with delegates elected on the basis of a state's population.

FOUNDING FOURSOME FROM COLUMBIA

Four of the most prominent individuals in the early days of the nation graduated from Columbia, or King's College as it was called until 1784.

	Role	Class
John Jay	First chief justice	1764
Robert Livingston	Drafter of the Declaration of Independence	1765
Gouverneur Morris	Drafter of the Constitution	1768
Alexander Hamilton	First secretary of the treasury	1777

VASSAR'S PULITZER PRIZE WINNERS

	Class	Year of Pulitzer
Margaret Leech	1915	1942, 1960
Edna St. Vincent Millay	1917	1923
Elizabeth Bishop	1934	1956
Lucinda Franks	1968	1971

Edna St. Vincent Millay and Elizabeth Bishop won for poetry, Millay for *The Ballad of the Harp-Weaver*, and Bishop for *Poems, North and South*. Margaret Leech received two Pulitzers for history, *Reveille in Washington* (1942) and *In the Days of McKinley* (1960). Lucinda Franks, a correspondent for United Press International, shared the 1971 award for national reporting with Thomas Powers.

PULITZER PRIZE–WINNING HISTORIANS FROM EMORY

	Class	Year of Pulitzer
Dumas Malone	1910	1975
C. Vann Woodward	1930	1982
David Potter	1932	1977

All three won in the history category: Malone for *Jefferson and His Time*, Woodward for *Mary Chestnut's Civil War*, and Potter for *The Impending Crisis*.

CHICAGO 7

Along with the Mercury astronauts, another group of seven gained fame in the 1960s. A band of political activists, the Chicago 7, made newspaper headlines at the Democratic National Convention in 1968 when they were indicted under the antiriot provisions of the Civil Rights Act. Five of the seven were convicted, but their sentences were overturned on appeal.

	College
Rennie Davis	Oberlin
David Dellinger	Yale

John Froines	U Cal Berkeley
Tom Hayden	Michigan
Abbie Hoffman	Brandeis
Jerry Rubin	Cincinnati
Lee Weiner	Illinois

Tom Hayden was editor of the student newspaper at Michigan. After he graduated in 1961, Hayden helped found Students for a Democratic Society.

David Dellinger graduated magna cum laude from Yale with a degree in economics in 1936.

POSTAGE STAMPS FROM MOUNT HOLYOKE

Mount Holyoke, a small private college in South Hadley, Massachusetts, has the distinction of putting more of its graduates through mail sorting machines than any other women's college. Three Holyoke alumnae have had postage stamps dedicated to them. The first was a 15-cent stamp featuring Frances Perkins, Franklin Roosevelt's secretary of labor; second was poet Emily Dickinson on an 8-cent stamp; and third was the likeness of Mount Holyoke's founder, Mary Lyon, on a 2-cent issue.

Another former Mount Holyoke student is responsible for a stamp of a different kind. Lucy Stone, class of 1842, was an early women's rights advocate who retained her maiden name after marriage. Since that time a woman who chooses not to adopt her husband's name has been labeled a "Lucy Stoner."

ODD SOLDIERS

It is not surprising that West Point lists such famous sons as Robert E. Lee, Ulysses S. Grant, Douglas MacArthur, Dwight D. Eisenhower, and George Patton. Four former cadets who are less well-known for their military accomplishments are Edgar Allan Poe, Abner Doubleday, Carl Sandburg, and Henry Robert, the author of *Robert's Rules of Order*.

MOST ILLUSTRIOUS CLASS

A strong claim to the distinction of being the most famous college class of all time can be made by Hampden-Sydney's class of 1791. Among its eight members were a U.S. senator, a U.S. congressman, a state senator, a state representative, a college president, a cabinet member, and a judge. The eighth class member, who dropped out during his senior year, was William Henry Harrison, the ninth president of the United States.

FIRST CLUBS

The first alumni association was founded at Williams in September 1821.

The first official alumni club on the moon was started when astronauts Dave Scott, Al Worden, and Jim Irwin, all University of Michigan graduates, traveled to the moon aboard Apollo 15 in 1971.

MOST ALUMNI

The colleges with the most living graduates are Ohio State and Michigan, with about 300,000 each. The Ohio State Alumni Association is believed to be the largest in the country, with 87,000 dues-paying members.

ALL PRESENT OR ACCOUNTED FOR

An unusual alumni tradition is Texas A&M's Muster, which is held each year on April 21. On Muster Day, Aggies worldwide (sometimes as many as 70,000 at forty different locations) gather together to pay tribute to their alma mater and honor former students who have died since the last Muster. The ceremony is called "Roll Call for the Absent." Tradition requires a living comrade to answer "Here" when the name of a deceased Aggie is read. Since 1883 Muster has been held in times of both war and peace. It received national attention during World War II when twenty-five Aggies under the leadership of General George Moore, class of 1908, held Muster on a beach on Corregidor in March 1942, only a few days before the U.S. Army was driven from the Philippines by Japanese forces.

INDEX